Lecture Notes in Computer Science 7599

Commenced Publication in 1973
Founding and Former Series Editors:
Gerhard Goos, Juris Hartmanis, and Jan van Leeuwen

T0232339

Joshua A. Levine   Rasmus R. Paulsen
Yongjie Zhang (Eds.)

Mesh Processing in Medical Image Analysis

MICCAI 2012 International Workshop
MeshMed 2012
Nice, France, October 1, 2012
Proceedings

 Springer

Volume Editors

Joshua A. Levine
Clemson University
School of Computing, Visual Computing Division
317 McAdams Hall
Clemson, SC, 29634, USA
E-mail: levine3@clemson.edu

Rasmus R. Paulsen
Technical University of Denmark
DTU Informatics
Richard Petersens Plads
2800 Kgs. Lyngby, Denmark
E-mail: rrp@imm.dtu.dk

Yongjie Zhang
Carnegie Mellon University
Department of Mechanical Engineering
303 Scaife Hall, 5000 Forbes Avenue
Pittsburgh, PA, 15213, USA
E-mail: jessicaz@andrew.cmu.edu

ISSN 0302-9743   e-ISSN 1611-3349
ISBN 978-3-642-33462-7   e-ISBN 978-3-642-33463-4
DOI 10.1007/978-3-642-33463-4
Springer Heidelberg Dordrecht London New York

Library of Congress Control Number: 2012946765

CR Subject Classification (1998): I.4, I.5, I.2.10, I.3.5, J.3, F.2.2

LNCS Sublibrary: SL 6 – Image Processing, Computer Vision, Pattern Recognition,
and Graphics

Typesetting: Camera-ready by author, data conversion by Scientific Publishing Services, Chennai, India

Printed on acid-free paper

Springer is part of Springer Science+Business Media (www.springer.com)

Preface

MICCAI MeshMed 2012, a workshop on mesh processing in medical image analysis, was held at the Acropolis Convention Center in Nice, France on October 1, 2012 in conjunction with the MICCAI 2012 conference. The MeshMed series of workshops was initiated in 2011 with the first event successfully held in conjunction with MICCAI 2011. The primary goal of this event was to bring together the geometry processing, computer graphics, and medical imaging communities to foster joint efforts and specific research. A fundamental theme, the image analysis pipeline and the significant role of geometric computation within it, was a central focus of the submitted works and discussions. Many of the technologies currently being developed by researchers in these communities are done so in an independent and isolated manner. We believe there is significant, fruitful research to be done that requires cross pollination of the geometry and imaging communities. Developing a more sophisticated understanding of the interplay between surface and volume representations (meshes) and clinical analysis and simulation is of utmost importance. Of the nearly twenty submissions, we accepted eight for presentation along with our three plenary talks representative of the meshing, surfacing, geometry processing, and medical imaging communities. Furthermore, eight papers were selected for poster presentations. All papers were reviewed by at least two reviewers from our program committee. The works in these proceedings cover a broad range of topics, including statistical shape analysis and atlas construction, novel meshing approaches, soft tissue simulation, quad dominant meshing and mesh-based shape descriptors. The techniques described were applied to a variety of medical data including cortical bones, ear canals, cerebral aneurysms, and vascular structures.

We would like to thank the program and organizing committees for contributing both their time and ideas. Their efforts pushed this international project forward and enriched both its content and structure. Additionally, we would like to thank all authors who submitted works. The material they provided made this workshop a success, which we hope will initiate a new interest and appreciation of this topic.

Finally, we are exceptionally grateful to the invited speakers Leif Kobbelt, Andrew McCulloch, and Pierre Alliez for contributing their time and attracting external interest for the workshop.

October 2012

Joshua A. Levine
Rasmus R. Paulsen
Yongjie Zhang

Organization

Organizing Committee

Nikos P. Chrisochoides	Old Dominion University, USA
Joshua A. Levine	SCI Institute, University of Utah, USA
Rasmus R. Paulsen	DTU Informatics, Technical University of Denmark
Sylvain Prima	IRISA / INRIA Research Unit, Rennes, France
Ross T. Whitaker	SCI Institute, University of Utah, USA
Yongjie Zhang	Carnegie Mellon University, USA

Program Committee

Michael Bronstein	University of Lugano, Switzerland
Miguel A. Gonzáles Ballester	ALMA IT Systems, Spain
Jakob Andreas Bærentzen	Technical University of Denmark, Denmark
Andrey Chernikov	Old Dominion University, USA
Gary Christensen	University of Iowa, USA
Tim Cootes	University of Manchester, UK
Tron Darvann	Copenhagen University, Denmark
Cindy Grimm	Washington University in St. Louis, USA
Michael Kazhdan	Johns Hopkins University, USA
Sebastian Kurtek	Florida State University, USA
G. Elisabeta (Liz) Marai	University of Pittsburgh, USA
Mads Nielsen	Copenhagen University, Denmark
Wiro Niessen	Erasmus University Rotterdam, The Netherlands
Sebastien Ourselin	University College London, UK
Mauricio Reyes	University of Bern, Switzerland
Daniel Rueckert	Imperial College London, UK
Jonathan Shewchuk	UC Berkeley, USA
Suzanne M. Shontz	Pennsylvania State University, USA
Anuj Srivastava	Florida State University, USA
Martin Styner	University of North Carolina at Chapel Hill, USA
Lilla Zöllei	Harvard Medical School, USA
Lasse Riis Østergaard	Aalborg University, Denmark

Sponsoring Institutions

- NIH/NCRR Center for Integrative Biomedical Computing at the Scientific Computing and Imaging Institute, University of Utah
- Technical University of Denmark

Table of Contents

Poster Session

Robust and Scalable Interactive Freeform Modeling of High Definition Medical Images

Noura Faraj[1], Jean-Marc Thiery[1], Isabelle Bloch[1], Nadège Varsier[2], Joe Wiart[2], and Tamy Boubekeur[1]

[1] Télécom ParisTech, CNRS LTCI
[2] Orange Labs
[3] Whist Lab

Abstract. Whole-body anatomically correct high-resolution 3D medical images are instrumental for physical simulations. Unfortunately, only a limited number of acquired datasets are available and the scope of possible applications is limited by the patient's posture. In this paper, we propose an extension of the interactive cage-based deformation pipeline VoxMorph [1], for labeled voxel grids allowing to efficiently explore the space of plausible poses while preserving the tissues' internal structure. We propose 3 main contributions to overcome the limitations of this pipeline: (i) we improve its robustness by proposing a deformation diffusion scheme, (ii) we improve its accuracy by proposing a new error-metric for the refinement process of the motion adaptive structure, (iii) we improve its scalability by proposing an out-of-core implementation. Our method is easy to use for novice users, robust and scales up to 3D images that do not fit in memory, while offering limited distortion and mass loss. We evaluate our approach on postured whole-body segmented images and present an electro-magnetic wave exposure study for human-waves interaction simulations.

1 Introduction

Despite the increasing number of medical simulations performed on high resolution whole-body 3D images, only a small number of such models are available and their use is limited by the unavoidable upright acquisition position and unwanted links between body parts (e.g. hand and hip). Our goal is to perform deformations of these datasets – possibly made of hundreds of millions of voxels – interactively while providing a suitable input for physical simulations. In this context, we need the deformations to be detail- and volume-preserving. In this paper, we propose an extension the VoxMorph [1] interactive deformation pipeline. We improve the quality of the deformation, we extend the scope of usable datasets by making the pipeline robust and scalable to datasets that do not fit in memory.

1.1 VoxMorph in a Nutshell

In order to preserve the details and the volume, the deformation needs to be quasi-conformal and stretch-minimizing properties when looking at their mathematical

J.A. Levine, R.R. Paulsen, Y. Zhang (Eds.): MeshMed 2012, LNCS 7599, pp. 1–11, 2012.
© Springer-Verlag Berlin Heidelberg 2012

expression. VoxMorph [1] copes with these requirements, while preserving the interactivity constraint, by using a 3-scales deformation algorithm with a suitable deformation method at each scale. VoxMorph offers an intuitive way to control the deformation by the means of a coarse bounding polygonal mesh - a *cage*. At coarse scale, a high-quality non-linear variational method allows to control the cage deformation using a few vertex constraints only while solving for all others in an As-Rigid-As-Possible (ARAP) fashion [2]. At mid-scale, the space inside the cage is deformed using a linear quasi-conformal space deformation method, i.e. the Green Coordinates (GC) [3] which locally preserve angles and distances. The combination of an ARAP cage manipulation and GC space deformations offers high quality volume deformations. Deforming the complete voxel grid using GC is still prohibitive; this problem is solved at the third scale through a linearization scheme of the deformation using a tetrahedral structure which is aware of the grid topology and a defined through a refinement strategy adapting the structure resolution to the deformation. A final rasterization step transfers efficiently the interactively defined cage deformation to the high resolution 3D image.

The VoxMorph system has so far three main limitations: first, the entire model has to **strictly** fit in the controlling cage which makes its construction very difficult either in an automatic and supervised context [3]. Second, when transferring the deformation from the coarse scales to the finer one, the adaptive metric plays a critical role in the deformation quality which can be improved. Last, although VoxMorph is able to deform large images, it remains restricted to incore datasets limiting the scope of usable data since the increasing accuracy of modern 3D acquisition systems generate huge high definition datasets.

1.2   Overview

Consequently, we improve this pipeline, making VoxMorph more robust, accurate and scalable. First, we improve the robustness by proposing a deformation diffusion scheme which allow us to offer a limb separation method and to deform parts of the model that are outside the cage. Second, we improve the accuracy by proposing a new error metric which avoid refining to deeply the transmission structure between mid and high resolution data. Third, we propose an out-of-core implementation in order to scale up to datasets that do not fit in memory. As a result, our new system can handle a larger range of datasets. We validate our pipeline by performing digital dosimetry analysis for radio-wave effects studies on high resolution segmented 3D medical images posed with our approach. All the representations in this pipeline are generated with our system.

2   Background

The deformation of volume datasets are often performed using space deformation methods. The main idea is to control interactively the deformation of a low resolution closed 3D object – the *cage* – and transmit it to the embedded space using some form of generalized barycentric coordinates. The deformation

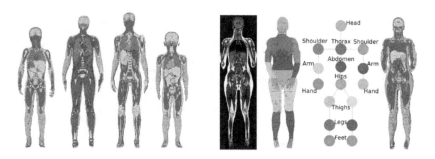

Fig. 1. Typical examples of input whole-body segmented voxel grids

of whole-body medical models for *Specific Absorption Rate* (SAR) analysis is often done using the original free form deformation definition [4], as done by Nagaoka et al. [5]. Recent work in computer graphics improves the quality of such volume deformation. In particular, GC are computed from the integral of the Laplacian Green function on the boundary of the domain which tends to better preserve details. Volume deformations using skeleton-based methods have been proposed by using a dummy model [6] or the interface between the grid and the background [7] to transmit the deformation to the volume. Both methods offer angular control over the joints but need a tedious per model pre-process. Despite the existence of these techniques, most medical image deformations are still performed by cutting and pasting limbs along with a tedious manual adjustment at the junctions [8].

3   Image Data and Segmented Volumes

The input of our system are medical images and the output are images containing interactively deformed models. These images are segmented and the derived models are posed to perform the SAR analysis. Whole-body *magnetic resonance images* (MRI) of children have been acquired thanks to collaborating hospitals. Depending on the patient, around 32 coronal slices are acquired with a slice thickness of $6mm$. The reconstructed voxel size for all images is $1.3 \times 1.3 \times 7.2 \ mm^3$. This strong anisotropy causes the data to exhibit a lot of partial volume effects. Due to the use of multiple coils, the images actually result from the composition of 4 or 5 images (depending on the patient's height), and some artifacts may appear such as missing parts due to field size or lower intensity at the transition between two images. To tackle the problems emerging from the resolution and the position of the patient (e. g. often the patient had his hands leaning on his thigh or the arms stuck to the thorax in the armpit region – Fig. 1 right), a body part segmentation is performed, as described in [9]. Additionally, we use whole-body children models from the Virtual population project [10]. These models, composed of 1mm cubic voxels, are highly detailed with up to 84 represented organs (Fig. 1 left). To demonstrate the scalability of our approach, we also use the Visible Human dataset [11].

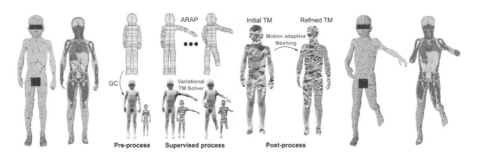

Fig. 2. **Pipeline overview** The input is a segmented voxel grid. We construct a cage and a tetrahedral mesh (TM) with segmentation-aware connectivity from it. The user manipulates the cage – deforming the TM vertices that are inside it using cage coordinates – and the tetrahedral solver computes the position of the outlier vertices interactively. The deformation is transferred from the TM to the grid in real-time. The adaptive resolution of the TM is driven by the deformation.

Segmentations. A segmented medical image is represented by a 3D voxel grid containing the discrete labels assigned to the image. By convention, null values represent the background. In this paper, we note $\mathbb{G}$ the grid representing the organ segmentation and $\mathbb{S}$ the one representing the body part segmentation. If none is available or necessary (i.e. no limb separation needed), we use a binary voxel grid with $\mathbb{S}[v] = 0$ for null voxels and $\mathbb{S}[v] = 1$ otherwise. Note that the user can create a rough segmentation interactively.

4   A Robust and Scalable Deformation Method

The cage can very often cross the model, excluding part of the voxels from the space deformation; we tackle this problem by designing a new variational optimization technique which conveys the inner space deformation to outer voxels. To improve the quality of the deformation, we propose a new error metric to guide the motion adaptive refinement process. Finally, to make the pipeline scalable, we propose an out-of-core deformation process for the high resolution voxel grid. Our general pipeline is illustrated in Fig. 2.

4.1   Robust Cages

To initialize the system, the user supervises a morphological cage creation process acting on $\mathbb{S}$. In the VoxMorph [1] system, a uniform dilation of $\mathbb{S}$ is performed. Then, a high resolution 2D restricted Delaunay triangulation (RDT) is generated, capturing the interface between the resulting grid and the background. To do so, Boissonnat et al. 's refinement process [12] is applied and the result is simplified to a prescribed resolution (typically a few tens or hundreds of vertices) using the *Quadric Error Metric* [13]. This process can create unwanted links between limbs (e.g. armpit, hand and hip) and therefore generate a cage with an incorrect topology. In our system, we propose a limb separation supervision process by offering the possibility to create inset cages: the user selects a region where two limbs need to be separated, then we automatically erode the voxels located at their interface while adaptively dilating elsewhere. Finally, the aforementioned surface creation and simplification process is applied.

4.2   Accurate Motion-Adaptive Structure

GC require the cage to enclose the model to deform, making its creation extremely difficult even for expert users, as well as for automatic methods. Moreover, the full deformation of $\mathbb{G}$ using GC can be prohibitive (e.g., several hours for the models we present in Sec. 5). More precisely, Lipman et al. explained how to extend linearly the coordinates *through* a set of faces of the cage, making the use of partial cages possible. In their setup, the system has to identify the set of coordinates that are *valid*, and the values for the other coordinates are found by inverting a linear system. This approach requires the user to specify manually the faces that need to be extended. More importantly, we need the extension of the deformation to help separating *distinct glued limbs*, and therefore it has to be driven by a *space separation method* similar to the use of a cage. Consequently, the direct use of the extension of the coordinates through facets of the cage [3] is impossible in our context.

In VoxMorph, the scalability issue is solved using a volumetric tetrahedral structure based on $\mathbb{G}$: the *Transfer Mesh* (TM), which is built to enclose the volume to process and has a resolution adapted to the deformation. We propose to apply a deformation diffusion method performed on this structure to solve the robustness problem. We denote $TM = \{V, E, T\}$ with $V = \{v_i\} \subset \mathbb{R}^3$ its vertices, $E = \{e_{ij}\}$ its edges connecting adjacent vertices v_i and v_j, and $T = \{t_k\}$ its tetrahedra.

All TM vertices that are inside the cage are deformed using GC, and all others' positions are recovered by minimizing a *rigidity energy* on TM (Fig. 3). The space deformation is transmitted to the voxel grid using barycentric interpolation, which guarantees *consistent rasterization* of the target voxel grid, and allows real-time deformations of $\mathbb{G}$.

Finally, to cope with the approximations introduced by the linearization scheme, we propose a new error metric for the iterative refinement strategy of the TM, making its structure adaptive to the on-going deformation.

In the following, $T_1(v_i)$ denotes the set of tetrahedra adjacent to a vertex v_i, $T_1(e_{ij})$ the set of tetrahedra adjacent to an edge e_{ij}, and $T_1(t)$ the set of tetrahedra sharing a face with a tetrahedron t. We note B_t the 3×3 transformation matrix of each tetrahedron t, uniquely defined by the transformation of its 4 vertices, $|t|$ its volume before deformation, and $\triangle (B_t)$ the local change of the transformation matrices expressed as:

$$\triangle (B_t) = B_t - \frac{\sum_{t_n \in T_1(t)} |t_n| \cdot B_{t_n}}{\sum_{t_n \in T_1(t)} |t_n|}. \tag{1}$$

Fig. 3. Deformation of the outlier vertices: the green tetrahedra are deformed using GC, the red tetrahedra's geometry – partially located outside the cage – is recovered by minimizing e_{rigid}

We model the energy to minimize as:

$$e_{rigid} = \sum_t |t| \cdot \| \triangle B_t \|^2. \tag{2}$$

using the Frobenius norm.

Set Up. We construct TM as a restricted adaptive Delaunay multi-material *tetrahedrization* generated from $\mathbb{S}$, the limb segmentation associated with $\mathbb{G}$, and constrained by a *sizing field* [14], which allows to control the spatially varying tetrahedron size explicitly. The sizing field is stored in a grid – noted $\mathbb{F}$ – with the same dimension as $\mathbb{G}$ and initialized to a uniform value (5% of the voxel grid's diagonal in our experiments). Depending on the segmentation, the resulting mesh can be composed of several subdomains, therefore a label l_k is associated with each tetrahedron.

Label Separation. We use the limb segmentation to split TM in user-defined regions in order to remove unwanted limb connections. The user draws a selection area and provides a pair of labels to separate. In this area, we duplicate the vertices of TM that belong to a face common to two tetrahedra to separate, i. e. one labeled in the first subdomain and the other in the second. We add the new vertices to the mesh, and re-index the tetrahedra in the second subdomain over them.

Improving Robustness - Tetrahedral Solver. The minimization of e_{rigid} is performed in two steps. We note T_c the tetrahedra of TM whose four vertices are inside the cage (green in Fig. 3), and V_c the vertices of TM that are inside the cage.

In the first step, we compute B_{t_c} for all $t_c \in T_c$ (these are deformed using GC) and set them as constraints, that we note $\tilde{B}_{t_c}$. We then set $\triangle (B_{t_u})$ to be the zero 3×3-matrix for all others (red in Fig. 3). This is done by solving the following linear system in the least squares sense, with B_t its unknowns:

$$\begin{cases} \sqrt{|t_c|} \cdot B_{t_c} = \sqrt{|t_c|} \cdot \tilde{B}_{t_c} \ \forall t_c \in T_c \\ \sqrt{|t_u|} \cdot \triangle (B_{t_u}) = 0_{33} \qquad \forall t_u \in T \setminus T_c \end{cases} \tag{3}$$

The result is a set of transformation matrices B_t for all $t \in T \setminus T_c$.

In the second step, we recover the vertex positions of TM, using the transformation matrices of the tetrahedra. We add the positions of all vertices in V_c as constraints, and set the edges to be the initial ones transformed by B_t. This is done by solving the following linear system in the least squares sense:

$$\begin{cases} \sqrt{\sum_{t \in T_1(v_c)} |t|} \cdot v_c & = \sqrt{\sum_{t \in T_1(v_c)} |t|} \cdot \tilde{v}_c \\ \sqrt{\sum_{t \in T_1(e_{ij})} |t|} \cdot (v_i - v_j) & = \dfrac{\sum_{t \in T_1(e_{ij})} |t| \cdot B_t \cdot (v_i^{init} - v_j^{init})}{\sqrt{\sum_{t \in T_1(e_{ij})} |t|}} \end{cases} \qquad (4)$$

$\forall v_c \in V_c$ and $\forall e_{ij} \in E$. The result is a set of positions for all vertices of TM that were outside the cage during the embedding. The linear systems are factorized at the creation of TM and solved efficiently at each frame using a linear algebra library [15].

Improving the Quality - New Error-Metric. To cope with the piecewise linear approximation introduced by TM, we make the sizing field adaptive to the deformation by refining TM iteratively.

At each step, we define an error e^T for each tetrahedron t as

$$e_t^T = || \triangle B_t ||, \qquad (5)$$

and an error e^V for each vertex v as

$$e_v^V = \frac{1}{\sum_{t \in T_1(v)} |t|} \sum_{t \in T_1(v)} |t| e_t^T \qquad (6)$$

the mean of the errors of its adjacent tetrahedra. We then obtain a smooth *error metric* e^G on the initial grid by rasterizing each tetrahedron, filling up the grid with the barycentric interpolation of its vertices' errors. The sizing field is updated according to the error metric with the following rule:

$$\mathbb{F}[v]* = \sqrt[3]{\frac{e_{mean}}{\max(e^G(v), e_{mean})}}. \qquad (7)$$

with e_{mean} the grid mean error. This process allows to obtain a uniform error on the grid at convergence. This new metric allows to reduce the final resolution by about 40% on average compared to the original VoxMorph system.

4.3 Scalable out-of-core Deformation Upsampling

In the VoxMorph [1] system, the deformation of the grid is performed in-core by computing the barycentric coordinates of the center of all the deformed grid voxels contained in the deformed tetrahedra. Using these coordinates and the initial TM vertex positions, we find their initial positions and project them in the initial grid to get the labels to assign to the final grid. In order to process out-of-core datasets, we propose to perform the entire pipeline on a low resolution version of the grid, which is down-sampled on the fly, and to apply an out-of-core rasterization of the high resolution one. We implemented a streaming process to perform the per-voxel deformation, therefore, both the initial and deformed high resolution voxel grids do not need to be loaded in memory. We use the TM of the low resolution image to assign the label to the high resolution one. To do so, we apply the previously described process to all the voxels of the deformed high resolution grid contained in the deformed tetrahedra and fetch in memory the voxels values where the positions project and directly write the result in a file.

5   Results

Deformation Evaluation. We implemented our system in C++ with OpenGL for rendering. We used CHOLMOD [15] as a Cholesky solver, GSL [16] for the SVD and the CGAL library [14] for tetrahedral mesh generation, surface meshing and simplification. Performances were measured on an Intel Core2 Duo at 2.4 GHz with 8GB of main memory and an nVidia Quadro FX580 device.

Fig. 4 illustrates the results obtained with our method for 5 high-resolution whole-body segmented images. The deformation of the Visible Human is performed out-of-core. The 7 postures of the Thelonious model have been interactively designed using our system and are further used to perform dosimetry analysis. The highest weight variation is -7% for Posture 5, which is still acceptable. For this posture, which is supposedly the worst case, the blue histograms illustrate the quasi-conformal nature of the resulting deformation. For all other postures, the difference is less than 1%. Table 1 summarizes various performance measures of our system on models ranging from 122 to 260 million voxels in core and one out-of-core deformation resulting in a grid of 862 million voxels. Note that, in all cases, the framerate (FPS) is limited by the rendering capabilities and not by our deformation workload.

5.1   Dosimetry Analysis

Materials and Numerical Simulation Conditions. We simulated a far-field exposure of the walking Thelonious, consisting of more than 70 different tissues with a 2 mm resolution, using an incident plane wave polarized vertically,

Table 1. Performance table: with CV (resp. TV) the cage (resp. transfer mesh) vertex count, FPS the framerate during interaction and CT the final full deformation pre- and post-process time. The last row shows the out-of-core processing time to deform the High-Resolution Visible Human model, using the Low-Resolution version for the user interaction process, into a grid of 862 million voxels.

Model	Voxels	CV	FPS	TV	Outliers	CT
Thelonious	122M	303	11.	36 157	393	2m31
Eartha	243M	479	9.	33 308	1890	3m10
Louis	260M	512	7.	27 588	2	4m03
Dizzy	141M	479	10.	29 226	532	2m38
LR Visible Human	108M	152	11.	17 036	1317	1m28
HR Visible Human	*374M*	-	-	-	-	*11m33*

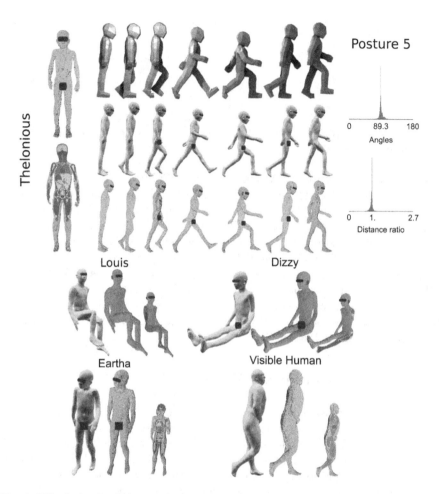

Fig. 4. Whole-body deformations The top part illustrates 7 poses simulating a walk animation on the Thelonious model [10]. The first row shows the cage controlled by the user, the second row the automatic motion adaptive TM and the last row the resulting, full resolution segmented voxel grids after deformation. The deviation from the quasi-conformal deformation is computed for the fifth position which has the highest volume change. The bottom part shows 4 other HD 3D images deformed with our system, the Visible Human deformation was performed out-of-core. Note that all these models contain outliers, and therefore the tetrahedral solver was required to deform them.

with a left side incidence, emitting at the frequency of 2100 MHz. We used the well-known Finite Difference Time-Domain (FDTD) method [17] to evaluate the whole-body exposure of Thelonious while walking for 7 different postures (see Fig. 5) and to calculate the SAR. The SAR, expressed in W/kg, quantifies the exposure to EMFs and represents the power absorbed per mass unit of tissue.

Fig. 5. (left) WBSAR calculated for E = 1 V/m. (right) SAR distribution evolution while Thelonious is walking.

Radiofrequence Exposure Variations of a Walking Child. Fig. 5 shows that the localization of the maximum SAR depends on the posture. We calculated, for each model, the whole-body averaged SAR (WBSAR) in order to analyze the influence of the posture. The whole-body averaged SAR is equal to the whole power absorbed by the numerical model divided by the body weight. This was computed for an incident field E = 1 V/m (which corresponds to a Surface Power Density of 2.65 e-3 W/m2). Fig. 5 plots the variations of the WBSAR with the posture of Thelonious. We can observe, as expected, that the WBSAR is proportional to the cross-section: from Posture 1 to Posture 5 the cross-section increases and so does the WBSAR. Then it decreases from Posture 5 to Posture 6 and increases again at Posture 7.

6 Conclusion and Future Work

We proposed an extension of the cage-based 3D image deformation pipeline Vox-Morph [1], allowing to deform high-resolution whole-body anatomically correct models interactively. We made the pipeline robust by relaxing the constraint of enclosing cages and proposed a separation scheme. We improved the quality of the deformation by proposing a new error-metric for the refinement process of the motion adaptive structure. Finally, we solved the scalability issue by proposing an out-of-core deformation scheme. As a result, our system extended the scope of usable datasets, to deform in-core high resolution voxel grids of over 260 million voxels within less than 4 minutes and to perform out-of-core deformations of the 3D images that do not fit in memory, e.g. 862 million voxels. The resulting deformed images are well suited for physical simulations, as well as variability and uncertainty studies. In particular, we used it to for SAR analysis. Future work includes feed the results of our deformation pipeline to a physically-based deformation system.

Acknowledgment. This work was partially funded by ANR KidPocket, ANR FETUS and EU REVERIE IP projects. Medical images are taken from the *Virtual Population* and *Visible Human* projects.

References

1. Faraj, N., Thiery, J.M., Boubekeur, T.: Voxmorph: 3-scale freeform deformation of large voxel grids. Computers & Graphics 36(5), 562–568 (2012); Shape Modeling International (SMI) Conference (2012)
2. Sorkine, O., Alexa, M.: As-rigid-as-possible surface modeling. In: Proceedings of the Fifth Eurographics Symposium on Geometry Processing, pp. 109–116. Eurographics Association, Aire-la-Ville (2007)
3. Lipman, Y., Levin, D., Cohen-Or, D.: Green coordinates. ACM Trans. Graph. 27, 78:1–78:10 (2008)
4. Sederberg, T.W., Parry, S.R.: Free-form deformation of solid geometric models. SIGGRAPH Comput. Graph. 20, 151–160 (1986)
5. Nagaoka, T., Watanabe, S.: Postured voxel-based human models for electromagnetic dosimetry. Physics in Medicine and Biology 53(24), 7047 (2008)
6. Gao, J., Munteanu, I., Müller, W.F.O., Weiland, T.: Generation of postured voxel-based human models for the study of step voltage excited by lightning current. Advances in Radio Science 9, 99–105 (2011)
7. Nagaoka, T., Watanabe, S.: Voxel-based variable posture models of human anatomy 97(12), 2015–2025 (December 2009)
8. Na, Y.H., Zhang, B., Zhang, J., Caracappa, P.F., Xu, X.G.: Deformable adult human phantoms for radiation protection dosimetry: anthropometric data representing size distributions of adult worker populations and software algorithms. Physics in Medicine and Biology 55(13), 3789 (2010)
9. Fouquier, G., Anquez, J., Bloch, I., Falip, C., Adamsbaum, C.: Subcutaneous Adipose Tissue Segmentation in Whole-Body MRI of Children. In: San Martin, C., Kim, S.-W. (eds.) CIARP 2011. LNCS, vol. 7042, pp. 97–104. Springer, Heidelberg (2011)
10. Christ, A., Kainz, W., Hahn, E.G., Honegger, K., Zefferer, M., Neufeld, E., Rascher, W., Janka, R., Bautz, W., Chen, J., Kiefer, B., Schmitt, P., Hollenbach, H.P., Shen, J., Oberle, M., Szczerba, D., Kam, A., Guag, J.W., Kuster, N.: The virtual family-development of surface-based anatomical models of two adults and two children for dosimetric simulations. Physics in Medicine and Biology 55(2), N23 (2010)
11. Spitzer, V., Ackerman, M.J., Scherzinger, A.L., Whitlock, D.: The visible human male: a technical report. J. Am. Med. Inform. Assoc. 3(2), 118–130 (1996)
12. Boissonnat, J.D., Oudot, S.: Provably good sampling and meshing of surfaces. Graph. Models 67, 405–451 (2005)
13. Garland, M., Heckbert, P.S.: Simplifying surfaces with color and texture using quadric error metrics. In: IEEE Visualization 1998, pp. 263–269 (1998)
14. Cgal, Computational Geometry Algorithms Library, http://www.cgal.org
15. Chen, Y., Davis, T.A., Hager, W.W., Rajamanickam, S.: Algorithm 887: Cholmod, supernodal sparse cholesky factorization and update/downdate. ACM Trans. Math. Softw. 35(3), 1–14 (2008)
16. Contributors, G.P.: GSL - GNU scientific library - GNU project - free software foundation, FSF (2010), http://www.gnu.org/software/gsl/
17. Taflove, A., Hagness, S.C.: Computational Electrodynamics: The Finite-Difference Time-Domain Method, 2nd edn. Artech House, Norwood (2000)

3D Anatomical Shape Atlas Construction Using Mesh Quality Preserved Deformable Models

Xinyi Cui[1], Shaoting Zhang[1,*], Yiqiang Zhan[2],
Mingchen Gao[1], Junzhou Huang[3], and Dimitris N. Metaxas[1]

[1] Dept. of Computer Science, Rutgers Univ., Piscataway, NJ, USA
[2] CAD R&D, Siemens Healthcare, Malvern, PA, USA
[3] Dept. of Computer Science and Engineering, Univ. of Texas at Arlington, TX, USA
`shaoting@cs.rutgers.edu`

Abstract. The construction of 3D anatomical shape atlas has been extensively studied in medical image analysis research for a variety of applications. Among the multiple steps of shape atlas construction, establishing anatomical correspondences across subjects is probably the most critical and challenging one. The adaptive focus deformable model (AFDM) [16] was proposed to tackle this problem by exploiting cross-scale geometry characteristics of 3D anatomy surfaces. Although the effectiveness of AFDM has been proved in various studies, its performance is highly dependent on the quality of 3D surface meshes. In this paper, we propose a new framework for 3D anatomical shape atlas construction. Our method aims to *robustly* establish correspondences across different subjects and simultaneously generate *high-quality* surface meshes without removing shape detail. Mathematically, a new energy term is embedded into the original energy function of AFDM to preserve surface mesh qualities during the deformable surface matching. Shape details and smoothness constraints are encoded into the new energy term using the Laplacian representation An expectation-maximization style algorithm is designed to optimize multiple energy terms alternatively until convergence. We demonstrate the performance of our method via two diverse applications: 3D high resolution CT cardiac images and rat brain MRIs with multiple structures.

Keywords: Shape atlas, one-to-one correspondence, mesh quality, Laplacian surface, deformable models.

1 Introduction

The 3D shape based reconstruction of anatomy has been of particular interest and its importance has been emphasized in a number of recent studies [3,6,10,11,8]. It provides a reference shape and variances for a population of shapes. Such shape information can be useful in numerous applications such as, but not limited to, statistical analysis of populations [5], the segmentation of the structures of interest [22,23], and the detection of disease regions [21]. Besides shape modeling,

---

* Corresponding author.

J.A. Levine, R.R. Paulsen, Y. Zhang (Eds.): MeshMed 2012, LNCS 7599, pp. 12–21, 2012.
© Springer-Verlag Berlin Heidelberg 2012

image atlases have also been extensively investigated [9]. Since an image atlas is not easily adapted to a surface atlas, we will only focus on the methods for the construction of shape models in this paper.

A shape has several different representations. Cootes *et al.* proposed a diffeomorphic statistical shape model which analyzes the parameters of the deformation field [4]. Styner *et al.* used a characteristic 3D shape model dubbed M-Rep to construct the atlas [7,20]. In [3], distance transform was used to create a shape complex atlas. The most widely used 3D shape representation is probably feature point sets or landmarks from a polygon mesh.

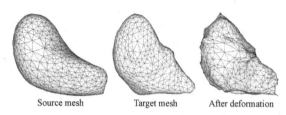

Source mesh   Target mesh   After deformation

Fig. 1. The source mesh is registered to the target one. both of them are already smoothed. The resulting mesh contains many artifacts because of the mesh degeneration during the deformation.

Using this representation, the mean shape and its variances can be easily computed using generalized Procrustes analysis and Principal Component Analysis (PCA). Furthermore, such representations have been used in many segmentation algorithms, e.g., Active Shape Model (ASM) [5]. In this context, the main challenge is to robustly discover geometric correspondences for all vertices among all sample shapes. One widely used approach is to register a reference shape to target ones. The deformed reference shapes are expected to have identical geometric characteristics as the targets shapes and same topology and connectivity of the reference one. Hence, the geometric correspondences between reference shape and target shapes are generated by simply matching the closest vertices between deformed reference shapes and target ones. These shape registration techniques has been widely investigated in biomedical applications [1,13,15,17,18,19]. The adaptive focus deformable model (AFDM) [16] is a very effective approach to do shape registration, since its attribute vectors reflect the geometric structure of the model from a local to global level. Although it has been widely used in many clinical applications, this method is sensitive to mesh qualities because degenerate mesh or skinny triangles can adversely affect the registration performance. Even if preprocessing is applied to smooth the mesh, it may still be degenerate during the deformation (Fig. 1). Furthermore, the resulting mesh is not guaranteed to be smooth, while a high-quality mesh is usually preferred since it benefits the performance of many applications, such as statistical analysis and segmentation.

In this paper, we propose a unified framework to compute geometry correspondence for all vertices among sample shapes, and generate high quality meshes without significantly sacrificing shape details. A new type of energy term is incorporated into the AFDM framework to preserve mesh quality during deformation. Combining this quality energy with the model energy in the original AFDM, our method is able to robustly discover one-to-one correspondence even for very complex or degenerate shapes. The whole energy function is optimized using an Expectation-maximization type of algorithm. Three energy terms are minimized alternately until converge.

Our algorithm is evaluated in two diverse applications: 1) high resolution cardiac shape model in CT images, and 2) multiple structure shape model of rat brains in dense brain MRI. For cardiac application, our method can find the anatomical point correspondence both among multiple instances of the same phase of a cardiac cycle and sequential phases of one cycle. The ability to fit the atlas to all temporal phases of a dynamic study can benefit the automatic functional analysis. For the rat brain application, our approach can discover the spatial relationship among multiple structures and construct a shape atlas for all structures.

The major contributions are: 1) propose a unified framework to improve the traditional AFDM by incorporating an energy term to preserve mesh quality during runtime. The resulting meshes are generally smooth without significantly sacrificing shape details. It can also robustly discover the one-to-one correspondence for very complex data (e.g., the shapes from high resolution cardiac CT images); 2) this approach enables us to solve two diverse and challenging tasks. Specifically, we create a high resolution cardiac shape atlas with many complex shape features such as papillary muscles and the trabeculae. We also effectively construct the atlas of multiple rat brain structures using a small set of samples.

2   Methodology

2.1   Algorithm Framework

As we discussed, the performance of the AFDM relies on the mesh quality. Though pre-processing techniques using mesh smoothing methods such as [2,24,25] can alleviate the problem to some degree, it is still highly possible that the mesh is degenerate during shape deformation. Thus it is desirable to design a unified framework to consider shape deformation and mesh quality simultaneously.

We define this shape modeling problem as an energy minimization procedure. Three energy functions are introduced to control the model deformation and preserve the mesh quality: *model energy*, *external energy* and *quality energy*. Here we use M_o, M_t and M_d to denote the original mesh, the target mesh and the deformed mesh. Our goal is to deform an original mesh M_o to a target mesh. M_d is the deformed mesh we want to compute. It needs to be close to the target mesh M_t on the boundaries and keep the geometric characteristics and mesh quality similar to the original mesh M_o. M_d is initialized as M_o. The energy function is defined as:

$$E = E_{model}\,(M_d, M_o) + E_{ext}\,(M_d, M_t) + E_{quality}(M_d, M_o) \tag{1}$$

The *model energy* $E_{model}\,(M_d, M_o)$ reflects the geometric differences between M_o and M_d. The *external energy* $E_{ext}(M_d, M_t)$ drives the model deforming towards the boundaries of the target model M_t. By jointly minimizing these two terms, the model will deform to the boundaries of the target and still preserve its geometric characteristics. In our study, an additional term *Quality energy* $M_{quality}(M_d, M_o)$ is designed to ensure that vertices are evenly distributed and shape details are roughly preserved. Using only E_{model} and E_{ext} produces similar results as the AFDM, which makes it sensitive to mesh quality. The quality energy $M_{quality}$ we introduce here ensures that the mesh quality is improved during deformation procedure, making the whole model more robust to handle diverse input.

The minimization of *external energy* E_{ext} is fairly standard. First, a distance transform is applied to M_t to obtain a binary distance 3D image I_t, which is the implicit embedding space of the target mesh. Then the deformed mesh M_d is placed in the embedding space I_t. The standard gradient on M_d vertices is computed from I_t. The gradient force drives M_d to be close to M_t on the boundaries. The details of E_{model} and $E_{quality}$ are introduced in the next two subsections.

2.2   Model Energy

The *model energy* measures the geometric differences between the original model and its deformed version. It is defined by the differences of geometric attribute vectors. An attribute vector is attached to each vertex of the model, which reflects the geometric structure of the model from a local to global level. For a particular vertex V_i in 3D, each attribute is defined as the volume of a tetrahedron on that vertex. The other three vertices form the tetrahedron are randomly chosen from the lth level neighborhood of V_i. Smaller tetrahedrons reflect the local structure near a vertex while larger tetrahedrons reflect a more global information around a vertex. The attribute vector, if sufficient enough, uniquely characterizes the different parts of a boundary surface. The volume of a tetrahedron is defined as $f_l(V_i)$. The attribute vector on a vertex is defined as $F(V_i) = [f_1(V_i), f_2(V_i), ..., f_{R(V_i)}(V_i)]$, where $R(V_i)$ is the neighborhood layers we want to use around V_i.

The model energy term is defined by the difference of the attribute vectors between the original model and the deformed model:

$$E_{model}(M_d, M_o) = \sum_{i=1}^{N} \sum_{l=1}^{R(V_i)} \delta_l (f_{d,l}(V_i) - f_{o,l}(V_i))^2, \qquad (2)$$

where $f_{d,l}(V_i)$ and $f_{o,l}(V_i)$ are components of attribute vectors of the deformed model and the model at vertex V_i, respectively. δ_l here denotes the importance of the lth neighborhood layers. $R(V_i)$ is the number of neighborhood layers around vertex V_i.

E_{model} is optimized by exploiting the affine invariant property of the geometric attribute vector $f_l(V_i)$. According to the proof provided by [16], $\delta_l(f_{d,l}(V_i) - f_{o,l}(V_i)) \equiv 0$ under affine transformation. Therefore, during registration process, we divide a surface into a set of segments and deform them using a local affine transformation. In this way, the geometric properties of the original surface is preserved while it still deforms to the target one.

2.3   Quality Energy

The *Quality Energy* is introduced to ensure that vertices are evenly distributed and shape details are roughly preserved during the deformation procedure. In many cases, there is a tradeoff between smoothing and keeping shape details. The energy term we use here is able to smooth the shape without losing important details. We extend the Laplacian coordinate [12] to achieve this. The mesh $\mathbb{M}$ of the shape is denoted by a pair $(\mathbb{V}, \mathbb{E})$, where $\mathbb{V} = \{v_1, ..., v_n\}$ denotes the geometric positions of the vertices in $\mathbb{R}^3$ and $\mathbb{E}$ describes the connectivity. The neighborhood ring of a vertex i is the set of adjacent vertices $\mathbb{N}_i = \{j | (i, j) \in \mathbb{E}\}$. The degree d_i of this vertex is the number of elements in $\mathbb{N}_i$. Instead of using absolute coordinates $\mathbb{V}$, the mesh geometry is described as a set of differentials $\Delta = \{\delta_i\}$. Specifically, coordinate i is represented by the difference between v_i and the weighted average of its neighbors using $\delta_i = v_i - \sum_{j \in \mathbb{N}_i} w_{ij} v_j$. This δ_i can approximate the normal vector of v_i, if we use the cotangent weight as w_{ij} [14]. Assume V is the matrix representation of $\mathbb{V}$. Using a small subset $\mathbb{A} \subset \mathbb{V}$ of m anchor points, a mesh can be reconstructed from connectivity information alone. The x, y and z positions of the reconstructed object $(V'_p = [v'_{1p}, ..., v'_{np}]^T, p \in \{x, y, z\})$ can be solved separately by minimizing the quadratic energy:

$$E_{quality}(M_d, M_o) = \|M_d - L(M_o)\| = \|L_u V'_p - \Delta\|^2 + \Sigma_{a \in \mathbb{A}} \|v'_{ap} - v_{ap}\|^2, \quad (3)$$

where L denotes the Laplacian representation of the original shape. L_u is the Laplacian matrix computed by using uniform weights (i.e., $w_{ij} = \frac{1}{d_i}$), and the v_{ap} are anchor (landmark) points. $\|LV'_p - \Delta\|^2$ tries to smooth the mesh when keeping it similar to the original shape, and $\sum_{a \in \mathbb{A}} \|v'_{ap} - v_{ap}\|^2$ keeps the anchor points unchanged. Since the cotangent weights approximate the normal direction, and the uniform weights point to the centroid, minimizing the difference of these two (i.e., $L_u V'$ and Δ) means to move the vertices along the *tangential direction*. Since this scheme prevents the movement along the vertices' normal directions, the shape is smoothed without significantly losing the detail. With m anchors, (3) can be rewritten as a $(n + m) \times n$ overdetermined linear system $AV'_p = b$ as $[L \ \ I_{ap}]^T \cdot V'_p = [\Delta \ \ V_{ap}]^T$. m can be chosen as 4 to n ($\frac{n}{10}$ in our applications). Since $AV'_p = b$ is overdetermined, this can be always solved in the least squares sense using the method of normal equations $V'_p = (A^T A)^{-1} A^T b$ [12]. The conjugate gradient method is used in our system to solve it efficiently. The first n rows of $AV'_p = b$ are the Laplacian constraints, corresponding to $\|LV'_p - \Delta\|^2$, while the last m rows are the positional constraints, corresponding to $\sum_{a \in A} \|v'_{ap} - v_{ap}\|^2$. I_{ap} is the index matrix of V_{ap}, which maps each V'_{ap} to V_{ap}. The reconstructed shape is generally smooth, while shape details are still preserved.

2.4   Optimization Framework

To optimize this energy function, we use an expectation-maximization (EM) type of algorithm. During the "E" step, the model energy and external energy are minimized using similar approach as the AFDM. Thus the reference shape is deformed to fit the target one, although this deformation may not be accurate due to the mesh quality. In the "M" step, the mesh quality is improved by minimizing the quality energy. This step is formulated as a least square problem and solved efficiently. Two procedures are alternately employed to robustly register the reference model to the target model. Note that theocratically this EM algorithm may lead to local minima since this is not a convex problem. However, in our extensive experiments in Sec. 3 , we did not observe this situation yet.

3   Experiments

We validate our method using two applications: 1) high resolution shape model in CT images, and 2) multiple structure shape model of rat brains in MR Microscopy.

3.1   High Resolution Cardiac Model

Recent developments on the CT technologies are able to produce 4D high resolution cardiac images in a single heart beat of humans. The reconstruction of the endocardial surface of the ventricles with incorporation of finer details can greatly assist doctors in diagnosis and functional assessment. In this experiment, we applied our framework to create the shape atlas from 4D cardiac reconstructions, which captures a whole cycle of cardiac contraction from high resolution CT images. The CT data were acquired on a 320-MDCT scanner using a conventional ECG-gated contrast-enhanced CT angiography protocol. The imaging protocol parameters include: prospectively triggered, single-beat, volumetric acquisition; detector width 0.5 mm, voltage 120 KV, current $200 - 550$ mA. Reconstructions were done at 10 equally distributed time frames in a cardiac cycle. The resolution of each time frame is 512 by 512 by 320.

Fig. 2 shows the reconstruction results of high resolution cardiac CT images at different time frames. The three-dimensional structures, their relationship and their movement during the cardiac cycle are much more readily appreciated from the shape model than from the original volumetric image data. Since these shapes are independently reconstructed, there is no one-to-one correspondence for vertices, and they may have different topologies for some small details, which prevent the statistical analysis. Shape registration can be applied to establish the one-to-one correspondence relations. However, this task is very challenging because of the complex shape details and the presence of degenerate skinny triangles. Our proposed model successfully and robustly registers these meshes together, by starting from the the middle frame and propagating in two directions. Once one-to-one correspondence is obtained, PCA can be applied straightforwardly to obtain shape statistics. Fig. 3 visualizes the shape variation along the first and second principal directions. The first mode represents the changing of the volume magnitude, and the second mode captures the changing of shape details such as the papillary muscles and the trabeculae. Such information can be used in clinical applications to categorize the cardiac properties.

Fig. 2. The cardiac shapes extracted from high resolution CT images. The complex shape details are captured, such as the papillary muscles and the trabeculae.

Fig. 3. Modes with largest variances, from -3σ to 3σ. The first mode represents the changing of the volume size. The second mode is the changing of shape details such as papillary muscles. For better visualization, please refer to the video sequence in the supplementary materials.

Table 1 shows the quantitative comparisons of two methods, by evaluating the mesh quality, registration accuracy, and running time. To evaluate the mesh quality, radius ratio is computed: $t_i = 2\frac{r}{R}, t_i \in [0,1]$, where R and r are the radii of the circumscribed and inscribed circles respectively. $t_i = 1$ indicates a well shaped triangle, while small values mean degenerate meshes. The min and mean values of radius ratio are reported, which are two important measurements for robust modeling and simulation. To evaluate the accuracy, we compute the mean and standard deviation of voxel distances between two shapes. In general, the proposed method achieves better mesh quality and accuracy than the traditional AFDM, showing that our method improves the mesh quality with detail preserved and without sacrificing the accuracy. Furthermore, its computational cost is also comparable to the AFDM, even with an extra mesh quality energy term. It is a C++ implementation on a Quad CPU 2.4GHZ PC. The reason is that mesh quality constraint aims to produce evenly distributed vertices, which also speeds up the convergence of the AFDM.

Table 1. Quantitative comparisons of the proposed method and the AFDM, including the mesh quality measured by the min and mean values of radius ratio (Q_{mean}, Q_{min}), the accuracy of registration measured by the mean and standard deviation of voxel distances between the target and deformed shapes (*Distance*), and the running time (*Time*). #V denotes the number of vertices of one shape.

	High Resolution Cardiac				Rat Brain Structures				
	#V	Q_{min}	Q_{mean}	*Distance*	*Time*	#V	Q_{min}	Q_{mean}	*Distance*	*Time*
AFMD	20K	0.00	0.73	2.03 ± 0.72	$8'37''$	2.5K	0.05	0.81	0.58 ± 0.15	$17''$
Ours	20K	0.02	0.97	0.47 ± 0.13	$7'56''$	2.5K	0.10	0.93	0.21 ± 0.08	$19''$

3.2   Multiple Structures of Rat Brains

Reconstruction of brain images is important to understand the relationship between anatomy and mental diseases in brains. Volumetric analysis of various brain structures such as the cerebellum plays a critical role in studying the structural changes in brain regions. Rat brains images are often used as models for human disease since they exhibit key features of abnormal neurological conditions and are served as a convenient starting point for novel studies. In this study, we use the proposed method to create a 3D shape atlas of multiple brain structures based on MR images of the rat brain. In our experiments, 11 adult male Sprague-Dawley rats were transcardially perfused with 4% paraformaldehyde. Heads were stored in paraformaldehyde and scanned for MRI. Brains remain in skulls during scanning in order to avoid tissue and shape distortions during brain extraction. The heads were scanned on a 21.1T Bruker Biospin Avance scanner (Bruker Biospin Corporation, Massachusetts, USA). The protocol consisted of a 3D T2-weighted scan with echo-time (TE) $7.5ms$, repetition time (TR) $150ms$, 27.7 kHz bandwidth, field of view (FOV) of $3.4 \times 3.2 \times 3.0mm$, and voxel size $0.08mm$, isotropic. Because of this high resolution, real 3D annotation is performed manually by multiple clinical experts. We focus on three complex structures of the rat brain: a) the cerebellum, b) the left and right striatum, and c) the left and right hippocampus.

Fig. 4 shows the shape variation along the first and second principal directions. Our method is able to capture the spatial relationships among different

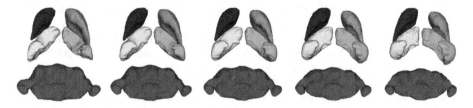

Fig. 4. Modes with largest variances, from -3σ to 3σ. The first mode represents the changing of the size. For better visualization, please refer to the video sequence in the supplementary materials.

neighboring structures. The first mode is the changing of the volume size. The second mode is the changing of the local details, such as two protruding parts of the cerebellum. Table 1 shows the quantitative comparisons of our method and the AFDM, which follows the same pattern as the previous experiment.

4   Conclusions

In this paper we presented an algorithm to robustly discover geometric correspondence and effectively model 3D shapes. This method improves the traditional adaptive focus deformable model by incorporating a quality energy, which ensures the mesh quality during the deformation. Thus the shape registration is robust and the defomed mesh is generally smooth without sacrificing shape details. After registration, one-to-one correspondence can be obtained for all vertices among sample shapes. Such correspondences can be used to generate PDM for many segmentation methods, and can also be used to obtain high temporal resolution using interpolations. We extensively validated this method in two applications. In the future, we plan to use these generated shape models to facilitate the segmentation algorithms by using it as the shape prior information.

References

1. Baldwin, M., Langenderfer, J., Rullkoetter, P., Laz, P.: Development of subject-specific and statistical shape models of the knee using an efficient segmentation and mesh-morphing approach. Computer Methods and Programs in Biomedicine 97(3), 232–240 (2010)
2. Busaryev, O., Dey, T.K., Levine, J.A.: Repairing and meshing imperfect shapes with delaunay refinement. In: 2009 SIAM/ACM Joint Conference on Geometric and Physical Modeling, SPM 2009, pp. 25–33. ACM (2009)
3. Chen, T., Rangarajan, A., Eisenschenk, S.J., Vemuri, B.C.: Construction of Neuroanatomical Shape Complex Atlas from 3D Brain MRI. In: Jiang, T., Navab, N., Pluim, J.P.W., Viergever, M.A. (eds.) MICCAI 2010, Part III. LNCS, vol. 6363, pp. 65–72. Springer, Heidelberg (2010)
4. Cootes, T.F., Twining, C.J., Babalola, K.O., Taylor, C.J.: Diffeomorphic statistical shape models. IVC 26, 326–332 (2008)
5. Cootes, T., Taylor, C., Cooper, D., Graham, J.: Active shape model - their training and application. Computer Vision and Image Understanding 61, 38–59 (1995)
6. Durrleman, S., Pennec, X., Trouvé, A., Gerig, G., Ayache, N.: Spatiotemporal Atlas Estimation for Developmental Delay Detection in Longitudinal Datasets. In: Yang, G.-Z., Hawkes, D., Rueckert, D., Noble, A., Taylor, C. (eds.) MICCAI 2009, Part I. LNCS, vol. 5761, pp. 297–304. Springer, Heidelberg (2009)
7. Fletcher, P.T., Lu, C., Pizer, S.M., Joshi, S.: Principal geodesic analysis for the study of nonlinear statistics of shape. TMI 23, 995–1005 (2004)
8. Gao, M., Huang, J., Zhang, S., Qian, Z., Voros, S., Metaxas, D., Axel, L.: 4D Cardiac Reconstruction Using High Resolution CT Images. In: Metaxas, D.N., Axel, L. (eds.) FIMH 2011. LNCS, vol. 6666, pp. 153–160. Springer, Heidelberg (2011)

9. Gerber, S., Tasdizen, T., Joshi, S., Whitaker, R.: On the Manifold Structure of the Space of Brain Images. In: Yang, G.-Z., Hawkes, D., Rueckert, D., Noble, A., Taylor, C. (eds.) MICCAI 2009, Part I. LNCS, vol. 5761, pp. 305–312. Springer, Heidelberg (2009)

10. Langs, G., Lashkari, D., Sweet, A., Tie, Y., Rigolo, L., Golby, A.J., Golland, P.: Learning an Atlas of a Cognitive Process in Its Functional Geometry. In: Székely, G., Hahn, H.K. (eds.) IPMI 2011. LNCS, vol. 6801, pp. 135–146. Springer, Heidelberg (2011)

11. Lorenzo-Valdes, M., Sanchez-Ortiz, G.I., Elkington, A.G., Mohiaddin, R.H., Rueckert, D.: Segmentation of 4D cardiac MR images using a probabilistic atlas and the em algorithm. Medical Image Analysis 8(3), 255–265 (2004)

12. Nealen, A., Igarashi, T., Sorkine, O., Alexa, M.: Laplacian mesh optimization. In: International Conference on Computer Graphics and Interactive Techniques in Australasia and Southeast Asia, pp. 381–389 (2006)

13. Park, J., Shontz, S., Drapaca, C.: A combined level set/mesh warping algorithm for tracking brain and cerebrospinal fluid evolution in hydrocephalic patients. In: Image-Based Geometric Modeling and Mesh Generation, pp. 107–141 (2012)

14. Pinkall, U., Polthier, K.: Computing discrete minimal surfaces and their conjugates. Experimental Mathematics 2, 15–36 (1993)

15. Sastry, S., Kim, J., Shontz, S., Craven, B., Lynch, F., Manning, K., Panitanarak, T.: Patient-specific model generation and simulation for pre-operative surgical guidance for pulmonary embolism treatment. Image-Based Geometric Modeling and Mesh Generation pp. 223–249

16. Shen, D., Davatzikos, C.: An adaptive-focus deformable model using statistical and geometric information. PAMI 22(8), 906–913 (2000)

17. Sigal, I., Hardisty, M., Whyne, C.: Mesh-morphing algorithms for specimen-specific finite element modeling. Journal of Biomechanics 41(7), 1381–1389 (2008)

18. Sigal, I., Whyne, C.: Mesh morphing and response surface analysis: quantifying sensitivity of vertebral mechanical behavior. Annals of Biomedical Engineering 38(1), 41–56 (2010)

19. Sigal, I., Yang, H., Roberts, M., Downs, J.: Morphing methods to parameterize specimen-specific finite element model geometries. Journal of Biomechanics 43(2), 254–262 (2010)

20. Styner, M., Gerig, G., Lieberman, J., Jones, D., Weinberger, D.: Statistical shape analysis of neuroanatomical structures based on medial models. Medical Image Analysis 7, 207–220 (2003)

21. Thompson, P.M., Toga, A.W.: Detection, visualization and animation of abnormal anatomic structure with a deformable probabilistic brain atlas based on random vector field transformations. Medical Image Analysis 1(4), 271–294 (1997)

22. Zhan, Y., Shen, D.: Deformable segmentation of 3D ultrasound prostate images using statistical texture matching method. TMI 25(3), 256–272 (2006)

23. Zhang, S., Zhan, Y., Dewan, M., Huang, J., Metaxas, D., Zhou, X.: Towards robust and effective shape modeling: Sparse shape composition. Medical Image Analysis, 265–277 (2012)

24. Zhang, Y., Xu, G., Bajaj, C.: Quality meshing of implicit solvation models of biomolecular structures. Computer Aided Geometric Design 23(6), 510–530 (2006)

25. Zhang, Y., Bajaj, R., Xu, G.: Surface smoothing and quality improvement of quadrilateral/hexahedral meshes with geometric flow. In: Proceedings, 14th International Meshing Roundtable, pp. 449–468. John Wiley and Sons (2005)

Automatic Fracture Reduction

Thomas Albrecht and Thomas Vetter

University of Basel

Abstract. We present a method to automatically reposition the fragments of a broken bone based on surface meshes segmented from CT scans. The result of this virtual fracture reduction is intended to be used as an operation plan for a medical procedure. Particularly in minimally invasive surgery like intramedullary nailing, the correct repositioning of bone fragments is not always apparent or visible without an operation plan. We propose to achieve automatic fracture reduction by fitting the bone fragments to an intact reference bone mesh with a modified Iterative Closest Point (ICP) algorithm. A suitable reference could be the same patient's contra-lateral bone. In the absence of a CT scan of this bone, we propose to use a statistical shape model as a reference. The shape model is automatically adapted to match the anatomy of the broken bone, apart from the bone's length, which has to be correctly initialized. Our experiments show that we can limit the rotational alignment error to below 5 degrees, compared to 15 degrees in current medical practice.

1   Introduction

Fracture reduction, i.e. the task of repositioning the fragments of a broken bone into their original position is a common task in everyday medical practice. For many fractures, the correct repositioning is apparent and straight-forward to carry out in practice. For some fractures however, an accurate reduction is difficult to achieve, because the desired position of the fragments is difficult to deduce from the available medical images. The most widely researched fracture in this area, which has become somewhat of a model problem, is the femoral shaft fracture. Figure 1 shows an example, along with its minimally invasive treatment by intramedullary nailing. In this procedure, a long nail is inserted into the bone via a small incision at the hip or knee. The fracture site is not directly visible, and the surgeon has to rely on radiographs to align the fragments. This allows a fairly accurate repositioning in the image planes of the radiographs. The rotational alignment around the longitudinal axis of the bone poses a much greater challenge, as it cannot be observed in these radiographs. A recent retrospective clinical study has found a rotational malalignment of over 15 degrees in 28% of patients [5]. In our experiments we were able to limit the malalignment to 5 degrees. While we focus on this model problem in this paper, our method has the advantage that it can be applied to virtually any bone and fracture.

J.A. Levine, R.R. Paulsen, Y. Zhang (Eds.): MeshMed 2012, LNCS 7599, pp. 22–29, 2012.
© Springer-Verlag Berlin Heidelberg 2012

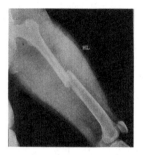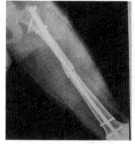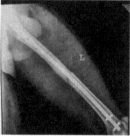

Fig. 1. A broken femur (left) treated with an intramedullary nail (right). Even in views from two perspectives, it is hard to judge the rotational alignment of the fragments.

1.1   Reduction Method

In our reduction method, the fragments of the broken bone are represented as surface meshes generated from segmented CT scans. The main idea is to align the main and functionally important fragments to an intact reference bone. This ensures an anatomically correct repositioning of the main fragments, independent of the geometry of the fracture surfaces and possible small additional fragments. Figure 2 shows an example of our proposed reduction method. The repositioning of the smaller fragments seen in Figure 2(d) will be postponed until Section 2.4.

In order to apply our method we need a mesh representation of a reference bone that is as similar to the broken bone as possible. If a CT scan of the broken bone from before the fracture, or a scan of the contra-lateral bone are available, these can be used to generate a reference mesh. In many cases however, such scans will not be available and for these we propose to use a statistical shape model [2] as reference. The mesh of the statistical shape model is automatically adapted to the characteristics of the fragments during the reduction in order to reflect the shape of the specific broken bone as accurately as possible. We performed experiments on real and simulated fractures. They show the importance of correctly adapting the shape model. We achieve to limit the rotational alignment error to 5 degrees when using a statistical shape model and to 0 degrees when using the ground truth bone as reference.

Prior Work. A few groups have worked on automatic bone fracture reduction. In [7], Moghari and Abolmaesumi align fragments of the proximal femur to the mean of a statistical shape model built from only 5 bones. However, they do not adapt the shape model to the individual anatomy of the broken bone. In [4], Gong et al. perform a reduction of distal radius fractures that uses a 3D statistical shape model to help align the fragments in calibrated 2D x-ray images. In [9] Westphal, Winkelbach et al. address femoral shaft fractures in terms of a "3D puzzle problem". The individual fragments are aligned based on the fracture surfaces, i.e. the surfaces of the fracture site which should be rejoined by the fracture reduction. We argue however that such a method may depend heavily

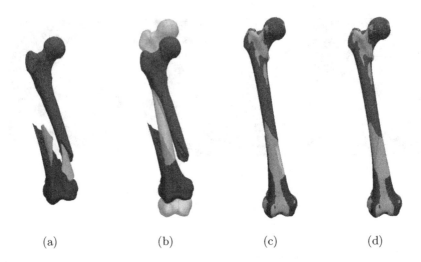

(a)   (b)   (c)   (d)

Fig. 2. Our proposed reduction algorithm. Instead of directly trying to puzzle the fragments of a broken bone (a) together, we align the main fragments to a reference bone (b), ensuring their functionally correct placement (c). If desired, the remaining fragments can later be fitted to the remaining parts of the reference (d).

on the accurate scanning, segmentation, and alignment of these fracture surfaces. A very small error in any of these steps, a shattering or compression of the bone structure could cause a large malalignment at the functionally important ends of the bones.

Any reduction plan, will have to be used in conjunction with a navigation or robot system to provide the surgeon with visual and/or haptic feedback about the current and desired position of the fragments. For such systems, we refer to [9] and references therein.

2   The Reduction Algorithm

Our method consists of two steps: 1. A rigid alignment of the fragments to the reference (Section 2.1). 2. The adaption of the statistical shape model to the given bone fragments' individual anatomy (Section 2.2). The adaption is only possible if the fragments are already aligned to the model. The rigid alignment in turn depends on a good model adaption. We propose to solve these two steps simultaneously in an iteration scheme, alternating step 1 and 2. If the ground truth or contra-lateral bone is used as reference, step 2 is omitted.

2.1   Rigid Alignment

For the rigid alignment of each of the fragments, we use the well known Iterative Closest Point (ICP) mesh alignment algorithm as implemented in VTK [1]. For each "source point", i.e. a point on the fragment, the ICP algorithm identifies a "target point", which is the closest points on the reference bone. Then, it computes the unique rigid transformation that minimizes the distance between the source and target points. This method is only guaranteed to give a correct alignment if the source and target points are *corresponding* points, which is in general not the case initially. But if the method is reasonably initialized, i.e. the shapes are roughly pre-aligned, and is iterated several times, the ICP algorithm has shown to provide a fast and accurate alignment of the shapes.

2.2 Model Mesh Adaption

If a statistical shape model is used as the reference bone, we adapt its shape to agree as well as possible with the fractured bone. After the rigid alignment, the individual fragments are already approximately aligned with the current model instance. Therefore, we can assume that source-target point pairs from the last ICP iteration, are not only pairs of *closest* points but also pairs of *corresponding* points, at least approximately. With a set of aligned and corresponding points, it is straight-forward to adapt the model shape to the fragments:

A (linear) statistical shape model represents instances of an object class (e.g. the human femur bone), as a sum $\mathbf{T}(\boldsymbol{\alpha}) = \boldsymbol{\mu} + \mathbf{U}\boldsymbol{\alpha}$ of a mean mesh $\boldsymbol{\mu}$ and a linear combination of shape deformations, expressed as the product of a model matrix $\mathbf{U}$ and coefficients $\boldsymbol{\alpha}$. For more information see [2,6].

Now let us denote the source points on fragment i as $\mathbf{S}_i$, and the corresponding target points on the reference model as $\mathbf{T}_i$. Being points of a model instance, the latter can be represented as $\mathbf{T}_i(\boldsymbol{\alpha}) = \boldsymbol{\mu}_i + \mathbf{U}_i\boldsymbol{\alpha}$, where $\boldsymbol{\mu}_i$ and $\mathbf{U}_i$ are the appropriate sub-vector and sub-matrix of $\boldsymbol{\mu}$ and $\mathbf{U}$. Then, to adapt the model mesh, we wish to find a set of shape model coefficients $\boldsymbol{\alpha}$ such that the mean square difference between all point pairs given by $(\mathbf{S}_i, \mathbf{T}_i(\boldsymbol{\alpha}))$ is minimized:

$$\boldsymbol{\alpha} = \operatorname*{argmin}_{\boldsymbol{\alpha}} \sum_i \|\mathbf{T}_i(\boldsymbol{\alpha}) - \mathbf{S}_i\|^2 = \operatorname*{argmin}_{\boldsymbol{\alpha}} \sum_i \|\boldsymbol{\mu}_i + \mathbf{U}_i\boldsymbol{\alpha} - \mathbf{S}_i\|^2. \qquad (1)$$

By $\|\cdot\|^2$ we denote the sum of squared distance norm for point sets, i.e. $\|\mathbf{P}\|^2 := \sum_{p\in\mathbf{P}}\|p\|_2^2$ for $\mathbf{P} \subset \mathbb{R}^3$. Equation (1) is a convex optimization problem which admits a unique minimum $\boldsymbol{\alpha}$. It can furthermore be regularized in order to permit only parameters $\boldsymbol{\alpha}$ that represent plausible instances from the shape model. [2,6]

The model adaption depends on the accuracy of finding corresponding points by the rigid alignment and vice versa. Iterating both steps alternatively improves them in turn and is repeated until a given number of iterations or a convergence criterion is attained.

2.3 Initialization

As most iterative algorithms, our reduction method relies on a reasonable initialization. Regarding the rigid alignment, our experiments have shown that it suffices to place the reference and the fractured bone roughly in the same area and orientation. This amounts to placing the reference in the center of the CT scan.

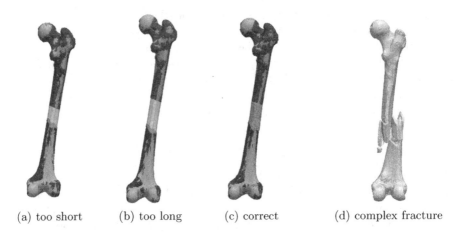

(a) too short   (b) too long   (c) correct   (d) complex fracture

Fig. 3. Difficulty in bone length estimation. The main fragments can be fitted equally well to a reference model with incorrect length (a) (b), because bone length and shape are relatively independent. Only with the middle fragment do we realize the correct length (c). This seems less feasible in a complex fracture like (d).

Regarding the shape adaption, the experiments have shown that for long bones it suffices to start the algorithm with the shape model's mean bone, with one important exception: The length of the bone should be initialized as accurately as possible.

The main principle of our algorithm is that only a correctly adapted shape will minimize the model adaption, which in turn causes a correct alignment. However, Figure 3 illustrates how this can fail if the length is not correctly initialized. In long bones like femur, tibia, humerus, etc., the length of the shaft is relatively independent of the shape and size of the joint regions. Therefore, the joint regions do not carry enough information for determining the length during model adaption. The shaft is rather featureless and can be fitted equally well to bones of almost any length.

We therefore define the length as a mandatory user parameter. It can be estimated by the user/physician for instance by measuring the length of the patient's contra-lateral bone or summing up the length of the fragments. Relying on the length of the individual fragments to determine the bone length automatically seems unfeasible for complicated fractures like Figure 3(d).

2.4   Implementational Details

We have improved the accuracy of the basic algorithm with a few enhancements.

Finding Closest Points. Both the ICP algorithm and the model adaption rely on finding closest points as an approximation to *corresponding* points in the source and target meshes. Typically, this approximation gets better with each iteration and in a perfect fit the two meshes and the corresponding points should almost coincide with each other. In reality however, the ICP can converge to a local minimum where the matched closest points are not necessarily corresponding points. This is a well-known shortcoming of the ICP algorithm and has been discussed in the literature. We use a method proposed by Feldmar and Ayache in [3] to take the curvature and the normal vectors of the two meshes into account when searching for closest points, in order to have a higher chance of finding corresponding points. This is relatively straight-forward to include into the ICP algorithm [8] by re-implementing the sub-routine that searches for the closest point on the target mesh for a given source point. Even though this method still is not guaranteed to find corresponding points, it improves the results significantly.

Fitting Remaining Fragments. Finally, as we stated above, our main goal is to align the main fragments of a broken bone to their anatomically correct position. We do not aim at solving the "3D puzzle problem" [9], nor do we wish to rely on the shape of the fracture surfaces for bone alignment. Nevertheless, it is unsatisfactory to leave small fragments that were left out of the original fitting unaligned. Therefore, for easy cases, we propose an ad-hoc way to align the remaining fragments after the main fragments have already been aligned and the reference model has been adapted to their shape. At this stage, the aligned fragments and the reference model almost coincide, except in those parts where the remaining fragments have been left out, see Figure 2(c) for an example. We can therefore align the remaining fragments to these remaining parts of the model mesh with an additional ICP alignment. We do not claim that complex fractures like that in Figure 3(d) can be reduced in this way.

3   Evaluation

Figures 2 and 3 show successful reductions of real femur fractures. Because no ground truth data is available for these real fractures, we have additionally evaluated our method on artificial fractures. For this purpose, we separated a database of 145 human femora into a training set of 120 bones, from which we built our statistical model, and a test set of 25 bones. In order to test the reduction method on these intact bones, we cut the bone meshes in two parts and randomly displaced these two fragments. Figure 4(a) shows a few of these simulated fractures. The fracture site, angle, rotation, and translation were drawn from a uniform distribution on varying intervals. We used an interval of $[-100, 100]$mm for the offset of the fracture from the middle of the bone, $[-20, 20]°$ for each component of the rotation represented by Euler angles, and $[-30, 30]$mm for the translation. The algorithm was initialized with the correct bone length.

Ideally, the reduction algorithm should compute the inverse of the random transforms, putting the fragments back into place. The composition of the random transforms with the reduction results should be the identity map. By measuring the deviation from the identity, we can evaluate the accuracy of the reduction. Figure 4(b), visualizes the results of our experiment. We measured the

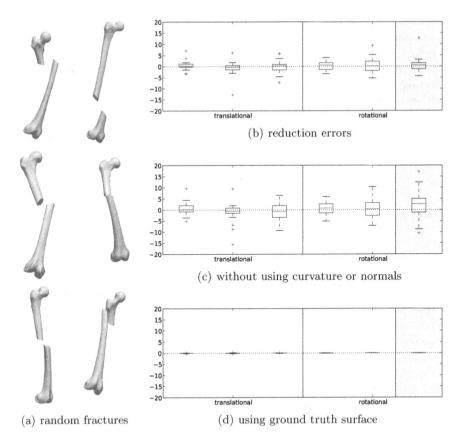

(b) reduction errors

(c) without using curvature or normals

(a) random fractures

(d) using ground truth surface

Fig. 4. Evaluation: Box plots of the alignment errors of the reduction algorithm

translation error along and the rotation error around the left-right (x), anterior-posterior (y) and superior-inferior (z) axis of the bone, in that order. The errors from the two bone fragments were added to get a measure of the overall reduction accuracy. The most important plot for our application scenario is therefore the very rightmost plot. It represents the rotational malalignemnt of the two fragments along the long axis of the bone and corresponds to the value measured in [5]. We see that, besides one outlier, we have successfully limited the amount of malrotation to within ±5°, with a mean of 0.44° and a standard deviation of $\sigma = 3.13°$. If these results can be carried through in the operating room, this will mean a massive improvement over the results reported in [5].

A closer look at the single outlier revealed that it exhibits a bone deformity known as *coxa retrotorta*, in which the relative rotation of the distal and proximal joint area, known as the *antetorsion* of the femur, is close to 0°. The statistical shape model on the other hand favors more common bone shapes with normal antetorsion angles. Extreme cases as this outlier will always have to be individually evaluated by a medical professional.

Figure 4(c) reveals that without using the curvature and surface normals in the fitting, the error is higher $(1.54 \pm 6.26°)$, because the model mesh is not as well adapted to the individual anatomy. If the original ground truth bone is used as reference, Figure 4(d), the reduction error is almost zero, $(-0.002 \pm 0.03°)$.

4 Conclusion

We have presented a method for automatic fracture reduction by aligning bone fragments to an intact reference bone. In the absence of a ground truth or contralateral bone as reference, we use a statistical shape model which is adapted to the broken bone's individual anatomy. While automatic bone length estimation remains a challenge, we have shown visually plausible reductions of real bone fractures and experimental errors that are far smaller than the current target error of 15 degrees rotational malalignment in medical practice. Future work will need to address the implementation of these reduction plans in the operating room using a navigation system.

References

1. Besl, P., McKay, H.: A method for registration of 3-D shapes. IEEE Transactions on Pattern Analysis and Machine Intelligence 14(2), 239–256 (1992)
2. Blanz, V., Vetter, T.: Reconstructing the complete 3d shape of faces from partial information. Informationstechnik und Technische Informatik 44(6), 1–8 (2002)
3. Feldmar, J., Ayache, N.: Rigid, affine and locally affine registration of free-form surfaces. International Journal of Computer Vision 18(2), 99–119 (1996)
4. Gong, R., Stewart, J., Abolmaesumi, P.: Reduction of multi-fragment fractures of the distal radius using atlas-based 2d/3d registration. In: Proceedings of the SPIE, Medical Imaging, p. 726137–1 (2009)
5. Jaarsma, R., Pakvis, D., Verdonschot, N., Biert, J., van Kampen, A.: Rotational malalignment after intramedullary nailing of femoral fractures. Journal of Orthopaedic Trauma 18(7), 403 (2004)
6. Lüthi, M., Albrecht, T., Vetter, T.: Probabilistic Modeling and Visualization of the Flexibility in Morphable Models. In: Hancock, E.R., Martin, R.R., Sabin, M.A. (eds.) Mathematics of Surfaces. LNCS, vol. 5654, pp. 251–264. Springer, Heidelberg (2009)
7. Moghari, M.H., Abolmaesumi, P.: Global registration of multiple bone fragments using statistical atlas models: feasibility experiments. In: 30th Annual International Conference of the IEEE Engineering in Medicine and Biology Society, EMBS 2008, pp. 5374–5377. IEEE (2008)
8. Schroeder, W., Martin, K., Lorensen, B.: The visualization toolkit. Prentice Hall PTR (1998)
9. Westphal, R., Winkelbach, S., Gösling, T., Oszwald, M., Hüfner, T., Krettek, C., Wahl, F.: Automated robot assisted fracture reduction. In: Advances in Robotics Research, pp. 251–262 (2009)

Age-Related Changes in Vertebral Morphometry by Statistical Shape Analysis

Tristan Whitmarsh[1,2], Luis M. Del Río Barquero[3], Silvana Di Gregorio[3], Jorge Malouf Sierra[4], Ludovic Humbert[1], and Alejandro F. Frangi[1,2]

[1] Center for Computational Imaging & Simulation Technologies in Biomedicine, Universitat Pompeu Fabra and CIBER-BBN, Barcelona, Spain
[2] Department of Mechanical Engineering, University of Sheffield, Sheffield, UK
[3] CETIR Centre Mèdic, Barcelona, Spain
[4] Department of Internal Medicine, Hospital Santa Creu i Sant Pau, Barcelona, Spain

Abstract. The morphological changes of the vertebrae associated with normal aging are still subject of debate, whereas this knowledge is important in detecting vertebral fractures and degenerative shape changes. The aim of this study is to present a method to statistically analyze the vertebral shape and determining the morphometric changes related to normal aging. The analysis is performed on the L2 lumbar vertebrae from a large dataset of Computed Tomography scans. The surface meshes of all vertebrae, with a groupwise vertex correspondence between them, are first acquired by an intensity based registration process onto a segmented reference. Principal component analysis then reduces the dimensionality to the main modes of variation which were subsequently analyzed by multiple linear regression to acquire the global shape variations with respect to the age of the subjects. In addition, the correlation with age of the deformation at each mesh vertex is analyzed, giving a significance map of the age related changes. This analysis shows several shape changes which are in agreement with previous studies while also giving a more detailed global shape analysis. Understanding the normal shape changes allows for a better diagnosis of vertebral fractures and spinal pathologies.

1 Introduction

The spine is subject to years of repetitive motion and large compressive forces and the vertebra are therefore at high risk of degenerative changes. Each vertebra has a cylindrical anterior vertebral body which supports the weight and allows for an upright position of the trunk. The associated compressive forces can cause a reduced height or wedging of the vertebral body. Posteriorly from the vertebral body are the pedicles and laminae which form the spinal column that houses the spinal cord. A narrowing of the spinal column can cause pressure on the spinal cord known as spinal stenosis. Reaching upwards and downwards are the superior and inferior articular processes. These form the intervertebral joints which allow for the spinal motion. Intervertebral disk degeneration, commonly associated

J.A. Levine, R.R. Paulsen, Y. Zhang (Eds.): MeshMed 2012, LNCS 7599, pp. 30–39, 2012.

with normal aging, may precipitate a forward displacement of the vertebra which causes more strain and can result in an enlargement of the pedicles, laminae and articular processes.

Even though these degenerative changes are often asymptomatic, they can result in great pain and discomfort from nerve impingement. The detection of this abnormal bone morphometry, however, is often difficult. In addition, the shape changes associated with normal aging are still under debate. In particular, there is no consensus on whether a mild wedging of the vertebral body is the result of a continuous remodeling with the advancing age or due to micro fractures. To be able to diagnose osteoporotic vertebral fractures and other pathological morphological changes, these should be distinguishable from normality.

Various models of growth and evolution of shape have already been investigated in the field of computational anatomy [1] and in particular in neuroimaging, where abnormal shape change is related to neurological conditions such as dementia [2].

The vertebral shape is commonly analyzed by geometric measurements from planar radio graphs. Common measures for vertebral fracture detection are the anterior, middle and posterior heights of the vertebral body and the ratios between them [3]. More complete measurements and dimensions of various anatomical parts of the selected vertebrae can be acquired from Computed Tomography (CT) [4][5] or Magnetic Resonance Imaging (MRI) [6] which allow for three dimensional measurements. These measurements, however, are still limited descriptors of the complex vertebral shape.

Some previous work applies statistical shape models to the segmentation of the bone contours from X-ray images [7] and the analysis of the shapes with respect to vertebral fractures [8]. This analysis, however, is limited by its two-dimensionality, and focuses only on the vertebral body shape with respect to fractures.

In this work we therefore present a method to statistically analyze the global 3D shape from a large dataset of CT scans and determine the morphometric changes related to normal aging. The surface mesh of the L2 vertebrae with a groupwise vertex correspondence is first acquired by an intensity based registration process onto a segmented reference scan. Principal Component Analysis (PCA) then reduces the dimensionality to the main modes of variation which were subsequently analyzed by a multiple linear regression to acquire the global shape variations related to aging. In addition to the global shape change, the displacement of the individual vertices was correlated with the age, giving an associated r^2 and p-value for each vertex.

2   Methods

2.1   Data

A cross-sectional dataset of 82 CT scans of the lumbar spine was collected at the CETIR Medical Center (Barcelona, Spain). The set consists of only female subjects with an average age of 58 ± 8 years and ranging between 45 and 77 years. The patients consisted of volunteers who required densitometry scans for body composition analysis. Subjects were rejected in case of the presence of spinal pathologies or vertebral fractures. Ethical approval was granted for all data acquisitions by the Institutional Review Board and written informed consent was provided by all the subjects included in this study. The CT scans were performed using the Philips Gemini GXL 16 system (Philips Healthcare, Best, The Netherlands). The CT scans had a pixel spacing ranging between 0.47 and $1.04mm$ and a slice thickness of $0.5mm$. A thresholding on 60 hounsfield units was applied to the volumes to remove the soft tissue structures. For all the scans 24 anatomical landmark locations (Fig. 1(a)) are required to initialize the registration process as explained below, which were identified in the volumes by a graphical user interface.

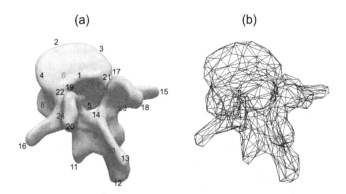

Fig. 1. The 24 landmarks locations for initializing the registration process (a) and the decimated reference mesh whereby the vertices define the control points for the TPS registration and the edges define a regularization term in the similarity measure (b).

2.2   Automatic Shape Extraction

The shapes of the L2 vertebrae were extracted from the CT volumes by an intensity based registration process of which the pipeline is depicted in Fig. 2. First a reference subject was selected based on its regular shape. The vertebral bone in this reference volume was subsequently segmented using ITK-SNAP [9], which provides a semi-automatic segmentation using active contour methods. A surface mesh was subsequently extracted from the segmentation onto which some additional processing was done, resulting in a smooth regular triangle mesh consisting of 28,586 vertices.

All CT volumes are first registered onto this reference by a rigid transformation defined by the landmark locations. The rigid transformation is computed according to [10], which gives the optimal mapping of the landmarks in a least squares sense. This is followed by an intensity based Thin Plate Spline (TPS) registration using the vertices from the decimated reference mesh (Fig. 1(b)) as the control points. The mesh decimation algorithm incorporates the quadric error metric outlined in Hoppe [11] and results in a mesh with 300 vertices. Here,

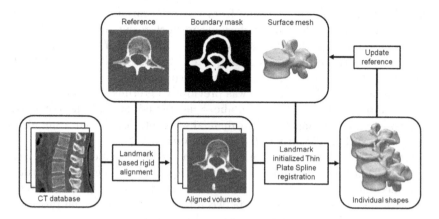

Fig. 2. The statistical model construction pipeline. A reference is first chosen and segmented to acquire the surface mesh and boundary mask of the vertebra. Each vertebra in the CT database is then registered onto this reference by a landmark based rigid alignment followed by a landmark initialized TPS registration resulting in the patient specific individual shapes. The reference is subsequently updated by the mean shape and the registration process is performed once more.

the 24 manually defined landmarks define a TPS transformation which is used to initialize the TPS registration process.

For the intensity based TPS registrations the L-BFGS-B optimizer [12] was used in conjunction with Mattes Mutual Information similarity metric [13]. The similarity measure was extended by a regularization term to prevent the control points from drifting and to maintain a smooth regular mesh. The regularization term is derived from the displacements $\mathbf{d}$ of the vertices in the decimated reference mesh M whereby the magnitude of the stretching or compression of all edges $e \in M$ defines an energy E as such:

$$E(\mathbf{d}) = \sum_{e \in M} \lambda \left(\frac{\|e(\mathbf{d})\| - \|e\|}{\|e\|} \right)^2 \qquad (1)$$

Here, $\|e\|$ denotes the length of edge e, $\|e(\mathbf{d})\|$ the length of the edge resulting from the displacements $\mathbf{d}$ and λ a weight factor. This energy is subsequently added to the Mutual Information measure MI as a penalty value. The optimization problem to find the point displacements $\mathbf{d}$, which defines the TPS transformation T that maximizes the similarity between the reference volume V_{ref} and the target volume V_{target}, can now be formulated as:

$$\arg \min_{\mathbf{d}} (-MI(V_{ref}, V_{target} \circ T(\mathbf{d})) + E(\mathbf{d})) \qquad (2)$$

To constrain the similarity measure to the region of interest and to reduce the computation time, a mask is defined of the bone boundary (Fig. 2) by dilating the segmentation and subtracting an image mask of the erosion.

The TPS transformation resulting from the registration process was finally applied to the detailed references surface mesh which results in the detailed surface mesh for the L2 vertebra of each subject. The addition of the regularization term in the registration process not only preserves the mesh quality, but also prevents self intersections in the resulting surface mesh.

The accuracy of meshing process was previously determined by acquiring the surface mesh of 20 subjects using the above mentioned method and computing the point-to-surface distances to their manual segmentation, which resulted in a mean point-to-surface distance of $0.34 \pm 0.33mm$.

To remove the reference selection bias and to improve the individual registrations, the reference is deformed to the mean shape and the registration process is performed once more. This results in the aligned subject specific vertebral shapes with a point correspondence between them, which, in a final processing step were smoothed by a volume preserving Laplacian smoothing.

2.3 Statistical Analysis

The shape deformation is examined by applying PCA to the shapes and relating the modes of variation to the age differences using a multiple linear regression analysis. For each i-th subject the shape $\mathbf{s}_i$ can be described by the vertex coordinates as such: $\mathbf{s}_i = (x_1, y_1, z_1, ..., x_n, y_n, z_n)^T$. The average shape $\bar{\mathbf{s}}$ is subsequently computed and subtracted from all k shapes to form the data matrix $D = [(\mathbf{s}_1 - \bar{\mathbf{s}})|(\mathbf{s}_2 - \bar{\mathbf{s}})| \cdots |(\mathbf{s}_k - \bar{\mathbf{s}})]$. Singular value decomposition then computes the eigenvectors of the covariance matrix of D, which describes the modes of variation of the shape. Each shape $\mathbf{s}_i$ can now be expressed by the average shape $\bar{\mathbf{s}}$ and a linear combination of the eigenvectors. By using the eigenvectors corresponding to the m largest eigenvalues, the dimensionality can be reduced to the main modes of variation:

$$\mathbf{s}_i = \bar{\mathbf{s}} + \mathbf{Pb}_i \approx \bar{\mathbf{s}} + \sum_{i=1}^{m} \mathbf{p}_i \lambda_i. \tag{3}$$

Here $\mathbf{p}_i$ is the i-th eigenvector from the matrix of ordered eigenvectors $\mathbf{P}$ and $\mathbf{b}_i$ the vector of coefficients λ_i associated with the corresponding eigenvectors. The number of modes of variation m to retain is determined by Horn's parallel analysis.

A multiple linear regression was performed with the patient age as the dependent variable and the eigenvector coefficients as independent variables. This determines the global linear change in shape related to the age. Model instances can now be generated for specific ages relative to the average shape to examine in what way the global shape changes with respect to aging.

In addition to the global shape change, also the local shape change is analyzed at the vertex level. For each vertex, a multiple linear regression is performed with

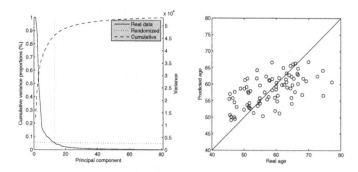

Fig. 3. Left: A plot of the eigenvalues set against the modes of variation together with a randomized version of the data. The lines cross at approximately the 13th mode of variation which corresponds to 87% of the total variance as determined by the graph of the cumulative variance. Right: The predicted age resulting from the multiple linear regression on the eigenvector coefficients plotted against the real age.

the x-, y- and z-axis deviations from the mean shape, given by matrix D, as the independent variables, and the age again as the dependent variables. This results in a coefficient of determination and corresponding significance for every vertex which are then visualized as color coded surface maps on the mean shape.

3   Results

Horn's parallel analysis resulted in 13 modes of variation which together describe 87% of the shape variance (Fig. 3). The multiple linear regression on the corresponding eigenvector coefficients of the input population resulted in a coefficient of determination of 0.34 ($p < 0.05$). In Fig. 3 the predicted age resulting from the multiple regression is plotted against the real age. A leave-one-out cross validation yielded a mean absolute error of 6.19 ± 4.29 years.

Visual inspection of the deformation patterns from Fig. 4 show an apparent age related increase in vertebral body width and decrease in vertebral body height (compression). In particular the lower end plate increasingly protrudes from the vertebral body. Also the pedicles increase in both the horizontal and vertical diameter throughout aging.

In Fig. 5 the magnitude of the deformation (mm/year) is presented as a color coded surface map on the mean shape. In addition, the mappings of the r^2 and p-values resulting from the multiple linear regression on the vertex coordinates with the age are presented. These indicate that the regions with significant correlations (Bonferroni correction, $p < 0.05/3$)) are in the vertebral body region. Large deformations can also be seen in the articular processes although these show weak correlations with age and low significances.

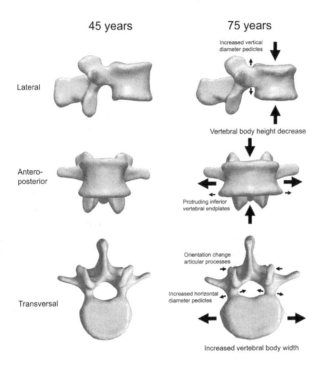

Fig. 4. The mean shape deformed to correspond to the age of 45 and 75 according to the direction in the eigenvector space resulting from the multiple linear regression on the eigenvector coefficients. The most prominent changes are indicated by arrows with corresponding descriptions.

4   Discussion and Conclusions

Our analysis shows a prominent increase in the vertebral width related to aging. The vertebral body size has previously been shown to increase with aging, which has been explained by a physiological reaction to compensate for a decrease in stiffness due to bone degradation [14]. The increase in endplate size can also be explained by the growth of bone spurs at the vertebral rim, known as osteophytes [15]. The vertebral body endplates have been shown to became more concave with age [16] which is believed to be the result of a decreased structural integrity of the mid vertebral body. This, however, does not become apparent from our analysis.

A general decrease in height of the lumbar vertebrae has been widely reported [17][18] and is also reflected in our findings. In the case of a wedge deformity, the anterior height of the vertebra decreases comparatively more than the posterior height. This is measured as a decrease in vertebral body height ratios and is reported to be related to aging [19][20][17]. In Fig. 4, however, the anterior and posterior heights appear to change in a similar manner. This is consistent with recently reported height ratio measurements from MRI [6].

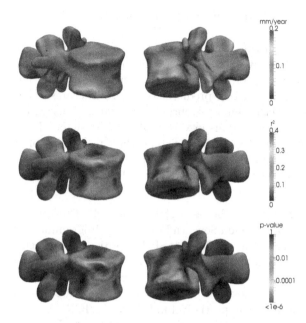

Fig. 5. Color coded mappings of the vertex displacement per year and the r^2 and p-values of the vertex wise multiple linear correlation with the age.

The female horizontal and vertical diameters of the pedicles have shown a tendency to increase throughout normal aging [21][14]. Also this is reflected in our analysis. Understanding this effect is of particular importance with respect to spinal stenosis whereby a narrowing of the spinal canal causes the impingement of the spinal nerve.

Due to normal aging, the intervertebral disc height decreases and consequently causes the facet joints to place an increased pressure on each other. This type of overloading is the most common causes of facet hypertrophy (an enlargement of the facet joint) and is also thought to increase the growth of osteophytes in the facet joints. Although some shape change in the articular processes are visible, they do not appear to be enlargements due to facet hypertrophy or osteophytes. Moreover, the changes in these regions are not shown to be significantly correlated with the age and thus structural changes of the articular processes remain absent in our analysis.

Morphometrical changes in vertebral shape differ greatly between the thoratic and lumbar vertebrae due to different loading conditions. For the thoracic spine the forces are primarily exerted on the anterior margins, which makes these more susceptible to wedge deformations, whereas this wedging remains absent for the lumbar vertebrae [22]. In addition, the stiffer thoracic spine remains rigid while the lumbar segments are more mobile and are subject to greater compressive forces. It is therefore important to analyze each of the thoracic and lumbar vertebrae separately. Furthermore, the geometric changes are greatly dependent on the gender [23] and thus a separate analysis should be performed on males as well.

To conclude, in this work a method was presented for deriving the morphometric changes related to normal aging from a large population. Diagnosing vertebral fractures is of particular importance considering the presence of a vertebral fracture is a strong predictor of future fractures. There is, however, no consensus on whether mild vertebral body compressions are considered fractures or simply normal variations in vertebral size and shape. The method presented in this work determines to what extend the compression of the vertebral body is related to a normal aging which can potentially be used to diagnose fractures as well as other pathological morphological deviations from normality.

Acknowledgements. The research leading to these results has received funding from: the European Union Seventh Framework Programme (FP7/2007-2013) under grant agreement nr 269909, MySPINE project; the ERDF Operational Programme of Catalonia 2007-2013, through the 3D-FemOs project (exp. VALTEC 09-02-0012) and the VERTEX project (exp. RD10-1-0034); the Spanish Ministry Science and Innovation (ref. TIN2009-14536-C02-01), Plan E and ERDF funds. A.F. Frangi was partially funded by the ICREA-Academia programme and T. Whitmarsh was financially supported by the Instituto de Salud Carlos III (FI09/00757).

References

1. Durrleman, S., Pennec, X., Trouvé, A., Gerig, G., Ayache, N.: Spatiotemporal Atlas Estimation for Developmental Delay Detection in Longitudinal Datasets. In: Yang, G.-Z., Hawkes, D., Rueckert, D., Noble, A., Taylor, C. (eds.) MICCAI 2009, Part I. LNCS, vol. 5761, pp. 297–304. Springer, Heidelberg (2009)
2. Qiu, A., Younes, L., Miller, M.I., Csernansky, J.G.: Parallel transport in diffeomorphisms distinguishes the time-dependent pattern of hippocampal surface deformation due to healthy aging and the dementia of the Alzheimer's type.. Neuroimage 40(1), 68–76 (2008)
3. Guglielmi, G., Diacinti, D., van Kuijk, C., Aparisi, F., Krestan, C., Adams, J., Link, T.: Vertebral morphometry: current methods and recent advances. European Radiology 18, 1484–1496 (2008)
4. Zhou, S.H., McCarthy, I.D., McGregor, A.H., Coombs, R.R.H., Hughes, S.P.F.: Geometrical dimensions of the lower lumbar vertebrae–analysis of data from digitised CT images. European Spine Journal 9, 242–248 (2000)
5. Urrutia Vega, E., Elizondo Omaña, R.E., De la Garza Castro, O., Guzmán López, S.: Morphometry of Pedicle and Vertebral Body in a Mexican Population by CT and Fluroscopy. International Journal of Morphology 27, 1299–1303 (2009)
6. Sevinc, O., Barut, C., Is, M., Eryoruk, N., Safak, A.A.: Influence of age and sex on lumbar vertebral morphometry determined using sagittal magnetic resonance imaging. Annals of Anatomy - Anatomischer Anzeiger 190(3), 277–283 (2008)
7. Roberts, M., Oh, T., Pacheco, E., Mohankumar, R., Cootes, T., Adams, J.: Semiautomatic determination of detailed vertebral shape from lumbar radiographs using active appearance models. Osteoporosis International 23, 655–664 (2012)

8. de Bruijne, M., Lund, M.T., Tankó, L.B., Pettersen, P.C., Nielsen, M.: Quantitative vertebral morphometry using neighbor-conditional shape models. Medical Image Analysis 11(5), 503–512 (2007)

9. Yushkevich, P.A., Piven, J., Hazlett, H.C., Smith, R.G., Ho, S., Gee, J.C., Gerig, G.: User-guided 3D active contour segmentation of anatomical structures: Significantly improved efficiency and reliability. NeuroImage 31(3), 1116–1128 (2006)

10. Horn, B.K.P.: Closed-form solution of absolute orientation using unit quaternions. Journal of the Optical Society of America A 4(4), 629–642 (1987)

11. Hoppe, H.: New quadric metric for simplifying meshes with appearance attributes. In: Proceedings of the 10th IEEE Visualization Conference (1999)

12. Zhu, C., Byrd, R.H., Lu, P., Nocedal, J.: Algorithm 778: L-BFGS-B: Fortran subroutines for large-scale bound-constrained optimization. ACM Transactions on Mathematical Software 23(4), 550–560 (1997)

13. Mattes, D., Haynor, D., Vesselle, H., Lewellen, T., Eubank, W.: PET-CT image registration in the chest using free-form deformations. IEEE Transactions on Medical Imaging 22(1), 120–128 (2003)

14. Rühli, F.J., Müntener, M., Henneberg, M.: Age-dependent changes of the normal human spine during adulthood. American Journal of Human Biology 17(4), 460–469 (2005)

15. Klaassen, Z., Tubbs, R., Apaydin, N., Hage, R., Jordan, R., Loukas, M.: Vertebral spinal osteophytes. Anatomical Science International 86, 1–9 (2011)

16. Shao, Z., Rompe, G., Schiltenwolf, M.: Radiographic Changes in the Lumbar Intervertebral Discs and Lumbar Vertebrae With Age. Spine 27(3), 263–268 (2002)

17. Ito, M., Hayashi, K., Yamada, M., Nakamura, T.: Vertebral measurements for assessment of osteoporosis. British Journal of Radiology 67(800), 759–763 (1994)

18. Diacinti, D., Acca, M., D'Erasmo, E., Tomei, E., Mazzuoli, G.F.: Aging changes in vertebral morphometry. Calcified Tissue International 57, 426–429 (1995)

19. Sone, T., Tomomitsu, T., Miyake, M., Takeda, N., Fukunaga, M.: Age-related changes in vertebral height ratios and vertebral fracture. Osteoporosis International 7, 113–118 (1997)

20. Amonoo-Kuofi, H.: Morphometric changes in the heights and anteroposterior diameters of the lumbar intervertebral discs with age. Journal of Anatomy 175, 159–168 (1991)

21. Amonoo-Kuofi, H.: Age-related variations in the horizontal and vertical diameters of the pedicles of the lumbar spine. Journal of Anatomy 186, 321–328 (1995)

22. Eastell, R., Cedel, S.L., Wahner, H.W., Riggs, B.L., Melton, L.J.: Classification of vertebral fractures. Journal of Bone and Mineral Research 6(3), 207–215 (1991)

23. Cheng, X.G., Sun, Y., Boonen, S., Nicholson, P.H.F., Brys, P., Dequeker, J., Felsenberg, D.: Measurements of vertebral shape by radiographic morphometry: sex differences and relationships with vertebral level and lumbar lordosis. Skeletal Radiology 27, 380–384 (1998)

Automatic Meshing of Femur Cortical Surfaces from Clinical CT Images

Ju Zhang[1], Duane Malcolm[1], Jacqui Hislop-Jambrich[2],
C. David L. Thomas[3], and Poul Nielsen[1,4]

[1] Auckland Bioengineering Institute, The University of Auckland, New Zealand
{ju.zhang,d.malcolm,p.nielsen}@auckland.ac.nz
[2] Clinical Applications Research Center, Toshiba Medical, Sydney, Australia
JHislop@Toshiba-TAP.com
[3] The Melbourne Dental School, The University of Melbourne, Victoria, Australia
cdthomas@unimelb.edu.au
[4] Department of Engineering Science, The University of Auckland, New Zealand

Abstract. We present an automated image-to-mesh workflow that meshes the cortical surfaces of the human femur, from clinical CT images. A piecewise parametric mesh of the femoral surface is customized to the in-image femoral surface by an active shape model. Then, by using this mesh as a first approximation, we segment cortical surfaces via a model of cortical morphology and imaging characteristics. The mesh is then customized further to represent the segmented inner and outer cortical surfaces. We validate the accuracy of the resulting meshes against an established semi-automated method. Root mean square error for the inner and outer cortical meshes were 0.74 mm and 0.89 mm, respectively. Mean mesh thickness absolute error was 0.03 mm with a standard deviation of 0.60 mm. The proposed method produces meshes that are correspondent across subjects, making it suitable for automatic collection of cortical geometry for statistical shape analysis.

1 Introduction

The femoral cortex is a vital consideration in nearly all femur-related analysis. From an anthropological and forensic perspective, cortical morphology varies with respect to factors such as age [1], stature [9], and ethnicity [11]. In terms of predicting hip fracture risk, cortical geometry and thickness distribution have been shown to be important factors [7,12,10]. Cortical geometry and thickness are also important for the accuracy of finite-element models of femur mechanics [15].

The prevalence of x-ray computed tomography (CT) means that a wealth of 3-D femoral cortex data exist in clinical CT images. However, segmenting the images manually is prone to subjective error, and, when large datasets are required, the task becomes prohibitively laborious. It is thus beneficial to automate the accurate segmentation and modelling of femoral cortex from clinical CT images.

Active Shape Modelling (ASM) [3], and other similar methods, have been used for the automatic segmentation of a wide range of anatomic structures [6].

J.A. Levine, R.R. Paulsen, Y. Zhang (Eds.): MeshMed 2012, LNCS 7599, pp. 40–48, 2012.

ASM uses a statistical model of object shape, and object appearance normal to its surface, to robustly segment the object's surface from images. At the same time, the segmented surface is parametrised in a way that is correspondent across subject. This is beneficial for any subsequent statistical analysis across subjects. While the accuracy of ASM is limited by that of its training set, in the case of bones, it provides a starting point for analysing the cortex in greater detail.

In clinical CT images, the accuracy of cortical surface estimation is limited by the image resolution. Simple methods such as thresholding become inaccurate, or fail altogether when thin cortex is blurred by partial volume effects [4]. Treece et al. [14] proposed modelling the appearance of the cortex using a function that accounts for imaging characteristics. The model is able to predict the positions of the inner and outer cortical surfaces, taking into account blurring. They were able to achieve significantly more accurate thickness estimates than previous methods. In this paper, we will refer to this model-based method as Cortical Profile Modelling (CPM).

Both ASM and CPM require an underlying surface description. High-order parametric surfaces offer a number of advantages over commonly used bilinear triangle meshes. High-order polynomial parametric surfaces typically require fewer degrees of freedom to represent complex surfaces. A triangle mesh has a fixed number of vertices on which image analysis can be performed. In contrast, parametric surfaces can be discretised to any desired resolution. Also, the smooth nature of parametric surfaces makes them more robust when representing noisy data.

In this paper, we propose using a high-order piecewise-polynomial parametric surface model of the femur, with ASM segmentation and CPM to segment and model the inner and outer cortical surfaces. We will describe the methods in the next section. Validation experiments are described in Sect. 3, and their results are presented in Sect. 4.

2   Methods

Our method begins with a generic piecewise-polynomial parametric mesh of the femoral surface (Fig. 1(a)). This generic mesh is customized to represent the inner and outer cortical surfaces in a CT image in three main steps (Fig. 1(b)). First, an active shape model customizes the generic mesh to approximate the femoral surface. Second, cortical profile modelling is performed normal to the ASM mesh to estimate cortical thickness, and segment the inner and outer cortical surfaces. Third, data from cortical profile modelling is used to further customize the ASM mesh to represent the inner and outer cortical surfaces.

In the following subsection, we describe the femur mesh. Then ASM training and segmentation using the mesh is explained in Sect. 2.2. In Sect. 2.3, we describe how CPM is implemented on the femur mesh. Finally, the placement of the cortical surface meshes is detailed in Sect. 2.4.

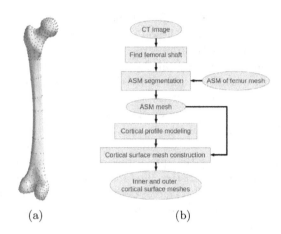

(a)   (b)

Fig. 1. Overview of the proposed method. The generic piecewise-polynomial parametric femur mesh is shown in (a) with node locations in red. The key steps in the meshing process are illustrated in (b).

2.1 Femoral Surface Mesh

We model femoral surfaces using a piecewise-polynomial parametric mesh. The mesh is composed of rectangular and triangular patches, in which the surface is given by

$$s(\xi_1, \xi_2) = \sum_{i=1}^{K} \mathbf{x}_i \phi_i(\xi_1, \xi_2) \tag{1}$$

where ξ_1 and ξ_2 are the 2-D patch coordinates, K is the number of nodes in the patch, $\mathbf{x} = (x_x, x_y, x_z)$ are the 3-D coordinates of a patch node, and ϕ is the quartic Lagrange polynomial basis function associated with a node. The generic mesh, containing 634 nodes and 63 patches, is shown in Fig. 1(a).

Given a patch number and patch coordinates, we can define a unique point on the mesh. We will refer to such points as material points. Since we will represent, or parametrize, all femoral surfaces using the same generic mesh, a material point corresponds to the same anatomic position on all surfaces. In other words, a material point is a landmark on which statistical shape analysis, image segmentation, and CPM can be performed.

2.2 Active Shape Model Segmentation

Active shape models combine a statistical shape model with models of local image texture to iteratively segment a surface from an image. Our shape model is trained by fitting the generic mesh to a training set of manually segmented femoral surfaces. First, a coarse free-form deformation [13] minimises ϵ_d - the sum of squared distances between each segmented data point $\mathbf{d}$ and its closest point on the mesh $\mathbf{d}_s$:

$$\epsilon_{\mathrm{d}} = \sum_{i=1}^{D} \|\mathbf{d}_i - \mathbf{d}_{\mathrm{s}_i}\|^2 \tag{2}$$

A finer least-squares mesh fit follows that adjusts mesh node coordinates $\mathbf{u}$ to minimize

$$\epsilon_{\mathrm{LS}} = \epsilon_{\mathrm{d}}(\mathbf{u}) + w_{\mathrm{s}}\epsilon_{\mathrm{s}}(\mathbf{u}) + w_{\mathrm{b}}\epsilon_{\mathrm{b}}(\mathbf{u}) \tag{3}$$

Smoothness within patches is enforced by a Sobolev penalty ϵ_{s} [2]. Smoothness across patches is enforced by ϵ_{b}, which penalises the mismatch of surface normal vectors across patch boundaries. The influence of ϵ_{s} and ϵ_{b} are weighted by constants w_{s} and w_{b}.

The training set of fitted meshes is aligned using Procrustes analysis [5], and principal component analysis [8] is performed on their nodal coordinates to create the shape model. Statistical models of image texture normal to the mesh surface are trained at a fixed set of material points. The material points are spaced evenly in patch coordinates, in a ten by ten grid per patch, giving a total of 4230 points. For more details on ASM training and segmentation, please see [3].

Segmentation is initiated by aligning the position and orientation of the mean mesh to the femoral shaft. The shaft is identified by locating cubic image volumes of the appropriate size that possess moments of inertia similar to that of a cylinder. Iterative ASM segmentation follows. During each iteration, image samples normal to the mesh at each material point are compared to the material point's image texture model. Specifically, we follow [3] in calculating the Mahalanobis distance between sample and model. The coordinates of the best matching sample for each and every material point generates a cloud of points to which the mesh is fitted, minimising (2). The fit optimises rigid transformations, scaling, and the parameters of the shape model. Mesh correspondence across femurs is established in this step by the shape model. In all subsequent modifications of the mesh, the deformations are small, and normal to the surface, so correspondence is preserved.

Once the segmentation converges, the mesh is fitted to the final data cloud, adjusting all node coordinates to minimise (3). This is so the resulting mesh s_{ASM} is close enough to the femoral cortex for cortical profile modelling to reliably locate the inner and outer cortical surfaces.

2.3   Cortical Profile Modelling

Cortical profile modelling is performed at material points to find the inner and outer cortical surfaces. We sample the image normal to the mesh at the same set of material points as for the ASM, and follow the methods of [14] in fitting cortical profile models to the sampled profiles.

As shown in Fig. 2(b), the model is a 1-D function y_{blur}: a piecewise constant function y convolved by two point spread functions simulating in-plane and out-of-plane blurring. y is composed of three sections representing cancellous bone, cortical bone, and external tissue. The inner and outer cortical boundaries, c_0 and c_1, are determined when y_{blur} is fitted.

Cortical thickness $t = c_1 - c_0$ is calculated at each material point. In addition, c_0 and c_1 are converted into the 3-D coordinates of points, $\mathbf{c}_{in}$ and $\mathbf{c}_{out}$, on the inner and outer cortical surfaces, respectively. Data points $\mathbf{C}_{in} = \{\mathbf{c}_{in_1}, ..., \mathbf{c}_{in_M}\}$, $\mathbf{C}_{out} = \{\mathbf{c}_{out_1}, ..., \mathbf{c}_{out_M}\}$ and corresponding thickness estimates $\mathbf{t} = \{t_1, ..., t_M, \}$, where M is the number of material points, are then used to customize s_{ASM} to represent the inner and outer cortical surfaces.

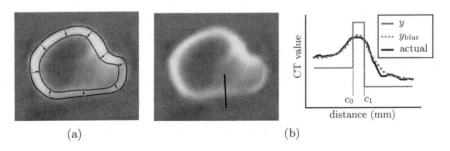

(a)   (b)

Fig. 2. Cortical profile modelling and cortical mesh construction. (a) shows how parts of the inner cortical mesh is created by projecting the outer mesh inwards according to estimated cortical thickness. (b) illustrates cortical profile modelling. An image sample across the cortex (actual) is approximated by y_{blur}, which is derived from function y with cortical surface positions c_0 and c_1.

2.4   Inner and Outer Cortical Surfaces

The inner and outer cortical surface meshes, s_{in} and s_{out} respectively, are both produced by customizing s_{ASM} according to $\mathbf{C}_{in}$, $\mathbf{C}_{out}$ and $\mathbf{t}$. s_{out} is created by fitting s_{ASM} to $\mathbf{C}_{out}$. However, due to noise and fitting errors, simply fitting s_{ASM} to $\mathbf{C}_{in}$ for the inner cortical mesh may result in the thickness between s_{in} and s_{out} not accurately reflecting CPM thickness estimates.

Over the proximal and distal regions of the femur, the cortex is thin enough to assume that the inner and outer cortical surfaces have coincident surface normals. Because of this, and the fact that s_{out} and s_{in} share the same mesh topology, the proximal and distal regions of s_{in} are created by offsetting its nodes inwards from their positions in s_{out} (Fig. 2(a)). The direction of the offset is along the surface normal evaluated at the nodes.

The offset for each node is determined by the thickness field τ, a piecewise parametric scalar field

$$\tau(\xi_1, \xi_2) = \sum_{i=1}^{K} u_i \phi_i(\xi_1, \xi_2) \tag{4}$$

that shares the mesh topology and interpolants of the surface meshes. We fit τ by minimising the sum of squared differences between the values of τ and $\mathbf{t}$ at each material point CPM was performed. Because τ shares the same mesh topology with s_{in} and s_{out}, the fitted thickness value at a node is equivalent to the inward offset of that node in s_{in} (in the proximal and distal regions).

In the femoral shaft, the thick cortex and prominent ridges mean that s_{in} and s_{out} normals are not coincident at many places. Displacing nodes in the same manner as for the proximal and distal regions results in self-intersecting meshes. Instead, we set the shaft region of s_{in} to be cylindrical in geometry. Then, shaft patches are fitted to data points in the shaft region of $\mathbf{C}_{\text{in}}$.

3   Method Evaluation and Validation

We evaluated the proposed cortical surface meshing procedure using 48 post-mortem femur CT images. The image were collected at the Victorian Institute of Forensic Medicine (VIFM), with ethical approval from the VIFM and the University of Melbourne. Image voxel resolution was approximately 1 mm in-plane, and 1.6 mm out of plane. The left femur from 31 images were manually segmented and used to train the ASM. The remaining 17 images were used for validating meshing accuracy, by comparing our method to Stradwin[1]. Stradwin applies the CPM methods of [14] to manually segmented surfaces, and has been validated on the proximal femur to have a mean thickness error of 0.01 mm $\pm$ 0.58 mm, against measurements made on high-resolution peripheral CT images.

For each femur, the inner and outer cortical meshes, s_{in} and s_{out}, were compared against the equivalent surfaces given by Stradwin, $s_{\text{in}}^{\star}$ and $s_{\text{out}}^{\star}$, respectively. The surfaces extracted from Stradwin were clouds of points. Therefore, error for each mesh was calculated as the Root Mean Square (RMS), and standard deviation, of the closest distance between the mesh surface and each data point.

Mesh thickness was compared against Stradwin thickness estimates made at points in $s_{\text{out}}^{\star}$. Mesh thickness was calculated as the euclidean distance between s_{in} and s_{out} at a common material point. For each point in $s_{\text{out}}^{\star}$, the difference between its thickness value and the mesh thickness of its closest point on s_{out} was calculated. The closest point on s_{out} was not restricted to the CPM material points. The RMS and standard deviation of this thickness difference was calculated for each femur, along with the absolute mean.

4   Results and Discussion

The 17 validation images were processed on a laptop computer with a quad-core 2.4 GHz CPU. Runtime for each image was about 15 minutes. ASM segmentation failed to converge for two images, so they were excluded from further analysis. Results for the remaining 15 images are summarised in Tab. 1.

The outer cortical surface mesh (s_{out}) was, on average, less than 0.75 mm RMS from the corresponding Stradwin surface ($s_{\text{out}}^{\star}$). The accuracy of s_{in} was slightly worse than that of s_{out}. This was due to s_{in}'s dependency on s_{out} and the thickness field τ, so that error in s_{out} and τ were compounded. Despite this,

---

[1] Machine Intelligence Laboratory, University of Cambridge.
http://mi.eng.cam.ac.uk/~rwp/stradwin/

Table 1. Mean error statistics from the validation experiment comparing automatically extract cortical meshes to those produced by Stradwin

Meshes	Errors (mm)		
	RMS	S.D.	Abs. Mean
Outer Mesh (s_{out})	0.74	0.53	-
Inner Mesh (s_{in})	0.89	0.67	-
Mesh Thickness	0.61	0.60	0.03

the average thickness between s_{in} and s_{out} differed from Stradwin estimates by only 0.03 mm, with a standard deviation only marginally higher than that of Stradwin (0.58 mm). This shows that cortical thickness modelled by the meshes preserved the accuracy of CPM well.

Figures 3(a) and 3(b) show mean errors over the average outer and inner cortical surface meshes, respectively. Error was below voxel resolution over most of the surfaces. The highest error was found on the femoral head. This was due to two factors. Firstly, the femoral head possessed very thin cortical bone, and in some cases, was undetectable in the images (Fig. 4(a)). Secondly, the nearby pelvis appeared much brighter in the images due to its higher density. In some cases, these two factors resulted in CPM mistaking the pelvic surface for the femoral head surface. The same problems were present in the condyles, with thin femoral cortex close to the patella and tibia (Fig. 4(c)). Since the CPM methods implemented in Stradwin are similar to our own, similar inaccuracies were present in the ground-truth data. The thinnest cortex in the femoral head

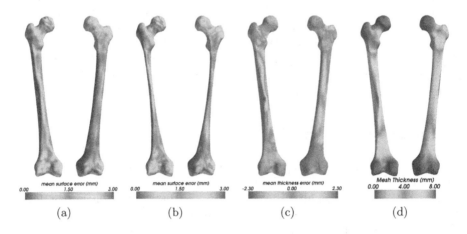

(a)   (b)   (c)   (d)

Fig. 3. Average cortical surface meshes. The posterior and anterior views of the mean outer and inner cortical surface meshes are shown in (a) and (b), respectively. Average closest distance between ground-truth surface and mesh are shown as heat maps over the surfaces. The average difference between ground-truth thickness and mesh thickness is shown in (c). (d) shows mean mesh thickness of the validation set, mapped over the mean outer cortical surface mesh.

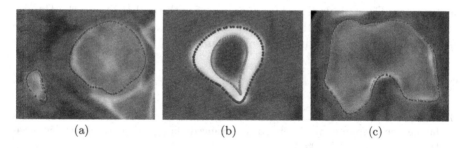

(a)   (b)   (c)

Fig. 4. Mesh outlines at selected image slices for one of the validation images. The slices are from the femoral head (a), femoral shaft (b), and condyles (c). Red and green dots are sampled from the outer and inner cortical meshes, respectively.

and condyles are far below the resolution of our images. Therefore, without higher resolution images, we cannot reliably quantify the errors in these regions.

Figure 3(c) shows average absolute error in mesh thickness. Errors were below measurement accuracy over most of the surface, even over the femoral head and condyle regions. So cortical thickness accuracy was not compromised by factors that lowered geometric accuracy. Indeed, high thickness (and geometric) absolute error was seen on the linea aspera of the femoral shaft. However, these values are again dubious due to unreliable CPM by both our method, and Stradwin. This was caused by the sharp, ridge-like morphology of the linea aspera, which can be seen in Fig. 4(b). A profile sampled normal to the outer surface may pass tangentially through the cortex, leading to an unreliable estimate of the inner cortical surface, and thickness. Smoothing penalties applied during inner mesh fitting mitigated this problem to a degree, giving the thick average linea aspera shown in Fig. 3(d), as expected. However, better ground-truth data, and a better definition of cortical thickness where external ridges are present, will be needed to validate the true accuracy.

5   Conclusions and Future Work

We have presented a fully automated method for segmenting and modelling femur cortical surfaces from clinical CT images. Given a generic piecewise-polynomial parametric mesh of the femoral surface, active shape modelling and cortical profile modelling were adapted to customize the mesh to inner and outer cortical surface geometries. The method produced meshes with accuracy of better than 0.9 mm RMS, when compared to an established semi-automated technique. Improvements can be made to increase accuracy in small parts of the femoral head and shaft. Also, validation against other forms of ground truth data is planned. Our method will be used to collect femoral geometry from a large set of clinical CT images, for statistical analysis of femoral morphology.

Acknowledgements. The authors are grateful to the Director and staff at the VIFM for supporting J. Hislop-Jambrich in accessing and collecting the post-mortem CT data under ethics approval of both the VIFM and the University of Melbourne. The authors are also grateful to G.M. Treece and A.H. Gee for their help in implementing their algorithm.

References

1. Bertelsen, P., Clement, J., Thomas, C.: A morphometric study of the cortex of the human femur from early childhood to advanced old age. Forensic Science international 74(1-2), 63–77 (1995)
2. Bradley, C., Pullan, A., Hunter, P.: Geometric Modeling of the Human Torso Using Cubic Hermite Elements. Biomedical Engineering Society 25, 96–111 (1997)
3. Cootes, T., Taylor, C., Cooper, D., Graham, J., et al.: Active shape models-their training and application. Computer Vision and Image Understanding 61(1), 38–59 (1995)
4. Dougherty, G., Newman, D.: Measurement of thickness and density of thin structures by computed tomography: a simulation study. Medical Physics 26, 1341 (1999)
5. Goodall, C.: Procrustes methods in the statistical analysis of shape. Journal of the Royal Statistical Society. Series B (Methodological) 53(2), 285–339 (1991)
6. Heimann, T., Meinzer, H.P.: Statistical shape models for 3D medical image segmentation: a review. Med. Image Anal. 13(4), 543–563 (2009)
7. Holzer, G., Von Skrbensky, G., Holzer, L., Pichl, W.: Hip fractures and the contribution of cortical versus trabecular bone to femoral neck strength. Journal of Bone and Mineral Research 24(3), 468–474 (2009)
8. Jolliffe, I.: Principal component analysis, vol. 2. Wiley Online Library (2002)
9. Looker, A.C., Beck, T.J., Orwoll, E.S.: Does body size account for gender differences in femur bone density and geometry? J. Bone Miner. Res. 16(7), 1291–1299 (2001)
10. Mayhew, P., Thomas, C., Clement, J., Loveridge, N., Beck, T., Bonfield, W., Burgoyne, C., Reeve, J.: Relation between age, femoral neck cortical stability, and hip fracture risk. The Lancet 366(9480), 129–135 (2005)
11. Peacock, M., Buckwalter, K.A., Persohn, S., Hangartner, T.N., Econs, M.J., Hui, S.: Race and sex differences in bone mineral density and geometry at the femur. Bone 45(2), 218–225 (2009)
12. Pulkkinen, P., Partanen, J., Jalovaara, P., Jamsa, T.: Combination of bone mineral density and upper femur geometry improves the prediction of hip fracture. Osteoporos Int. 15(4), 274–280 (2004)
13. Sederberg, T., Parry, S.: Free-form deformation of solid geometric models. ACM Siggraph Computer Graphics 20(4), 151–160 (1986)
14. Treece, G.M., Gee, A.H., Mayhew, P.M., Poole, K.E.: High resolution cortical bone thickness measurement from clinical CT data. Med. Image Anal. 14(3), 276–290 (2010)
15. Zdero, R., Bougherara, H., Dubov, A., Shah, S., Zalzal, P., Mahfud, A., Schemitsch, E.: The effect of cortex thickness on intact femur biomechanics: a comparison of finite element analysis with synthetic femurs. Proceedings of the Institution of Mechanical Engineers, Part H: Journal of Engineering in Medicine 224(7), 831–840 (2010)

Statistical Surface Recovery:
A Study on Ear Canals

Rasmus R. Jensen[1], Oline V. Olesen[1], Rasmus R. Paulsen[1],
Mike van der Poel[2], and Rasmus Larsen[1]

[1] Informatics and Mathematical Modelling, Technical University of Denmark,
Richard Petersens Plads, Building 321, DK-2800 Kgs. Lyngby, Denmark
{raje,ovol,rrp,rl}@imm.dtu.dk
http://www.imm.dtu.dk
[2] 3Shape A/S
mike.poel@3shape.com
http://www.3Shape.com

Abstract. We present a method for surface recovery in partial surface scans based on a statistical model. The framework is based on multivariate point prediction, where the distribution of the points are learned from an annotated data set. The training set consist of surfaces with dense correspondence that are Procrustes aligned. The average shape and point covariances can be estimated from this set. It is shown how missing data in a new given shape can be predicted using the learned statistics. The method is evaluated on a data set of 29 scans of ear canal impressions. By using a leave-one-out approach we reconstruct every scan and compute the point-wise prediction error. The evaluation is done for every point on the surface and for varying hole sizes. Compared to state-of-the art surface reconstruction algorithm, the presented methods gives very good prediction results.

Keywords: surface recovery, hole closing, multivariate statistics, shape modeling, in ear scanning.

1   Introduction

Direct surface scanning of humans is an increasingly used modality where the applications range from model creation in the entertainment industry, plastic surgery planning and evaluation, craniofacial syndrome evaluation [12,8], and in particular hearing aid production [15]. In this paper, we are concerned with a particular surface shape namely that of the ear canal. Ear canal surface scans are used in custom hearing aid fitting. This is a very large industry that probably makes the ear the most scanned part of the human anatomy. A standard hearing aid producer generates more than a thousand scans per week. When producing custom in-the-ear devices like hearing aids and monitors, the standard routine is to inject silicone rubber in the patients ear and then laser scan this impression, thereby creating a model of the ear canal. While this technique normally creates

J.A. Levine, R.R. Paulsen, Y. Zhang (Eds.): MeshMed 2012, LNCS 7599, pp. 49–58, 2012.
© Springer-Verlag Berlin Heidelberg 2012

complete surfaces, direct ear scanners are emerging and it is expected that scans with these devices will require handling of missing data due to the complex anatomy of the human ear and the limited space for the scanner probe.

In this paper we are presenting a method for predicting missing data based on the information in the partial scan. Hole filling and missing data recovery is a well studied problem, in particular for 2D images. In 3D, data recovery is sometimes considered a by-product of the surface reconstruction algorithm. The algorithms used to generate triangulated surfaces from a point clouds will usually try to cover missing areas using some mathematical or physical assumptions. One series of approaches uses Delaunay triangulation of border points [11]. Such methods are obviously susceptible to noise in the border points and will typically require some form of smoothing. An alternative strategy is to interpolate implicit (signed distance) functions locally or globally under various forms of regularization [10,16]. Other methods, inspired from 2D inpainting approaches have also been investigated [20,4,3]. These are typically based on a variational definition of the behavior of the surface where the holes are. In [3] it is the mean curvature of the surface that is being regularized and in [4] it is the Willmore energy over the surface. The reported results of these techniques seem similar to the results from the Markov Random Field surface reconstruction algorithm [16] that we are using as reference.

In our method, we aim at predicting the missing points based on the existing points in the scan. Instead of using a variational formulations or physical assumptions on the behaviour of the surface, we utilize a population statistics of the given class of surfaces learnt from an annotated and co-registered training set. In the chosen example, we base our population statistics of the ear canal on a statistical shape model of the ear canal originally presented in [14]. However, the method is general and can be applied to all types of surface scans.

2   Data

The data consists of 29 scanned ear impressions. For further processing, point correspondence over the set was created using the method initially described in [14]. Here a template mesh is thin plate spline warped to fit each shape using a sparse set of landmarks. This is followed by a propagation of template mesh vertices to each shape based on a nearest neighbor search. Since the ears are topologically equivalent to open cylinders special care must be taken in the non-overlap regions and the template is pruned accordingly. Furthermore, the Markov Random Field regularization of the correspondence field described in [13] was used to further optimize the dense correspondence. The 29 scans with dense correspondence was then aligned using the Generalized Procrustes Alignment [7] and the shapes scaled to the scale of the mean shape. The result of this is a set of aligned shapes (triangulated surfaces), with dense point correspondence (3000 vertices per scan) as seen in Fig. 1(a). This type of data is normally used to build statistical shape models as for example described in [5,14].

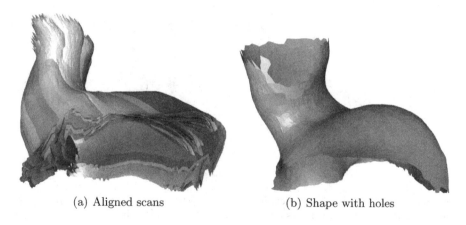

(a) Aligned scans   (b) Shape with holes

Fig. 1. a) shows the Procrustes aligned scans. Each scan has a different color. b) shows a surface scan with three holes with identical center but different radii, $r = [2\text{mm}, 3\text{mm}, 5\text{mm}]$.

In Fig. 1(b) an example of a partial scan is seen. It is synthetically created by cutting a hole in a complete ear canal surface scan. In the example, holes with radii of 2, 3, and 5 mm are shown.

3   Statistical Surface Recovery

The aim of the method is to predict the unknown data from the known data. The unknown data is in this case the vertices placed in the missing parts of the scanned surface. The known data is the vertices in the partial scan. Since the method predicts one vertex at a time, we can define three sets of vertices:

$\mathbf{x}_1^T = (u_{11}, v_{11}, w_{11})$: the unknown vertex we want to predict.

$\mathbf{x}_2^T = (u_{21}, v_{21}, w_{21}, u_{22}, v_{22}, w_{22}, \ldots)$: remaining unknown vertices

$\mathbf{x}_3^T = (u_{31}, v_{31}, w_{31}, u_{32}, v_{32}, w_{32}, \ldots)$: known vertices.

In Fig. 2 the situation is exemplified, with $\mathbf{x}_1$ shown as a gray sphere and the known vertices, $\mathbf{x}_3$, shown as vertices in the blue mesh. The remaining unknown vertices, $\mathbf{x}_2$, are obviously not used to predict $\mathbf{x}_1$. However, any point in $\mathbf{x}_2$ can be estimated by setting it to be $\mathbf{x}_1$. In the following we assume that a point correspondence has been established between the partial scan and the training set described in Sec. 2. The correspondence allows for differentiation between known vertices and missing vertices in the partial scan. We will elaborate on this later.

In conclusion, we will determine how the unknown vertex $\mathbf{x}_1$ is predicted from known vertices in $\mathbf{x}_3$. Without any prior knowledge of the distribution of data, we consider $\mathbf{x}_1$ and $\mathbf{x}_3$ as belonging to the normal distribution:

$$\begin{bmatrix} \mathbf{x}_1 \\ \mathbf{x}_3 \end{bmatrix} \in N \left(\begin{bmatrix} \mu_1 \\ \mu_3 \end{bmatrix}, \begin{bmatrix} \mathbf{\Sigma}_{11} & \mathbf{\Sigma}_{13} \\ \mathbf{\Sigma}_{31} & \mathbf{\Sigma}_{33} \end{bmatrix} \right) , \ \mathbf{\Sigma}_{13}^T = \mathbf{\Sigma}_{31}$$

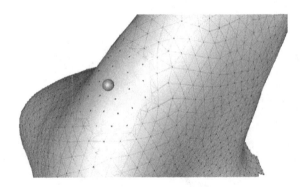

Fig. 2. A hole in a mesh. To predict the unknown vertex shown $\mathbf{x}_1$ as a gray sphere, the known vertices $\mathbf{x}_3$ shown vertices on the blue mesh are used. The remaining unknown vertices $\mathbf{x}_2$ are shown as black dots in the hole.

The expected value of $\mathbf{x}_1$ given $\mathbf{x}_3$ is:

$$E\{\mathbf{x}_1|\mathbf{x}_3\} = \mu_1 + \Sigma_{13}\Sigma_{33}^{-1}(\mathbf{x}_3 - \mu_3)$$

With the variance:

$$V\{\mathbf{x}_1|\mathbf{x}_3\} = \Sigma_{11} - \Sigma_{13}\Sigma_{33}^{-1}\Sigma_{31}$$

The vertex distributions are determined using the Procrustes aligned training shapes with point correspondence. So for example Σ_{11} is the covariance of the vertex $\mathbf{x}_1$ as learned from the training set. The covariance Σ_{13} between $\mathbf{x}_1$ and $\mathbf{x}_2$ is also estimated from the training set along with (μ_1, μ_3) that are the average vertex positions from the Procrustes average estimation. As there are far less shapes (28 leaving one out) than points (3000), Σ_{33} will be singular. Let $\Sigma_{33} = \mathbf{P}\Lambda\mathbf{P}^T$ be the Eigenvalue decomposition. We restrict Σ_{33} to its affine support, i.e. the dimensions spanned by the Eigenvectors corresponding to the k positive Eigenvalues, such that:

$$\Lambda^* = \text{diag}(\lambda_1, \lambda_2, \ldots, \lambda_k) \text{ and } \mathbf{P}^* = [\mathbf{p}_1\ \mathbf{p}_2\ \cdots\ \mathbf{p}_k]$$

The projection of $\mathbf{x}_3$ using the k selected Eigenvectors $\mathbf{P}^*$: $\mathbf{y}_3 = \mathbf{P}^{*T}\mathbf{x}_3$ has affine support for $\mathbf{x}_3$ and the variance:

$$V\{\mathbf{y}_3\} = V\{\mathbf{P}^*\mathbf{x}_3\} = \mathbf{P}^{*T}\Sigma_{33}\mathbf{P}^* = \Lambda^*$$

The covariance of $\mathbf{x}_1$ and $\mathbf{y}_3$ is:

$$C\{\mathbf{x}_1, \mathbf{y}_3\} = C\{\mathbf{x}_1, \mathbf{P}^{*T}\mathbf{x}_3\} = C\{\mathbf{x}_1, \mathbf{x}_3\}\mathbf{P}^* = \Sigma_{13}\mathbf{P}^*$$

Finally, the prediction of the unknown vertex $\mathbf{x}_1$ can be done using the projection $\mathbf{y}_3$:

$$E\{\mathbf{x}_1|\mathbf{y}_3\} = \mu_1 + \Sigma_{13}\mathbf{P}^*\Lambda^{*-1}\mathbf{P}^{*T}(\mathbf{x}_3 - \mu_3)$$

This expectancy can be used for any unknown vertex $\mathbf{x}_1$ given a known set of vertices $\mathbf{x}_3$. While the Eigenvalue decomposition only has to be done once for the known vertices $\mathbf{x}_3$, the Σ_{13} has to be calculated for each vertex to be predicted.

If every unknown vertex is predicted according to the described method the known triangulation from the training set can be propagated to the predicted point and will then constitute a full surface reconstruction.

The described point prediction method requires point correspondence to the training set. This means that given a new surface scan of an ear canal with missing data, the first step is to create point correspondence. This is a non-trivial matter with a variety of existing approaches [9] and not the main topic of this paper. A usable approach could be to use a variant of the iterative closest point algorithm that handles non-overlapping regions [19].

4   A Standardized Test

To compare the performance of the statistical prediction to a state-of-the art sur-face reconstruction algorithm, we do the following standardized test. We define:

$\mathbf{x}_1$: the vertex in the center of a hole.
$\mathbf{x}_2$: vertices within radius r of $\mathbf{x}_1$ defines a hole.
$\mathbf{x}_3$: known vertices.

We predict every vertex in a shape with the vertex being the center of a hole. We repeat this experiment for holes with different radii. It seems intuitive that in the prediction of a given hole, the center is generally the hardest to accurately reconstruct as it is furthest from any known vertices. This is also seen in Fig. 2, where the predicted vertex is the unknown vertex furthest away from known data. Therefore, the prediction of the center points is considered a soft upper bound on how well a given hole can be closed. Figure 1(b) shows an ear scan where holes with the same center but varying radii have been cut out.

The MRFSurface reconstruction described in the following will be used for comparison against our proposed method.

5   Markov Random Field Surface Reconstruction

Markov Random Field surface reconstruction (MRFSurface) as described in [16] is based on an implicit reconstruction and regularization of the true surface represented by the available, noise filled, and potentially hole infested data. A signed distance field on a regular voxel grid is used to maintain the implicit surface as the zero-level iso-surface. Obviously, the distance field is not properly defined in regions with missing data or holes and the novelty in [16] is the Markov Random Field based regularization of the distance field leading to good hole filling and noise handling properties. In the Bayesian setting, a prior voxel energy is used that implicitly defines how the surface behaves in areas with missing data. While several models are possible, we focus on two. The first is based on penalizing nearest neighbour voxel value differences leading to membrane like behavior of the surface. The second is using the difference of the Laplacian of the neighbouring voxel values leading to a higher-order, spline like behavior of the surface. In order to maintain distance field values in high-confidence areas a quadratic observation term is used that punishes distance values different from the original estimates. The balance between the prior and the observation term is governed by a confidence factor based on local point cloud sampling densities. The goal is now to optimize the values of the entire distance field and thereby creating an implicit zero-level that behaves well in both dense sampled areas and areas with holes. Since the problem can basically be cast into a massive set of linear equations several approaches can be used. In [16] sparse Cholesky factorization, conjugate gradients and multi-scale, banded iterated conditional modes (MS-ICM) were evaluated. In this work, we use the MS-ICM solver. The result is a well regulated zero-level iso-surface that is then polygonised using a standard iso-surface extractor [1]. Furthermore, an iterative triangle-optimiser is used in the post-processing to create near-equilateral triangles [16].

6   Experiments and Results

To test the performance of our method, we use the Procrustes aligned data set of 29 scans with point correspondence and use 28 to build a statistical model and reconstruct the last one. To simulate that the scan is a new and previously unseen scan we start by removing the point correspondence to the training set. This is done by re-triangulating the surface, such that it contains two thirds the number of vertices being 2000 relative to 3000 in the original mesh. The re-triangulation is done using the method described in [2] and results in a mesh with vertices evenly distributed and with near equilateral triangles.

As described in Sec. 3 point correspondence to the training set is needed. For the sake of testing the point prediction algorithm, we have adopted a rather simple approach. We find the scan of the 28 that produces the best point correspondence. A point $x_{original}$ is said to have correspondence if the nearest point $x_{remeshed}$ in the re-meshed surface also has the also has $x_{original}$ as its nearest point. This produces a unique point correspondence. We use the correspondence from the scan that creates the minimum average distance between correspondence points. This approach produces around 1500 unique correspondences.

One note about the alignment and point correspondence: We use the original Procrustes alignment for our re-meshed scan, this alignment is fair but not optimal as it is an alignment to the mean shape. Our point correspondence is also very crude, though speaking of correspondence is somewhat vague as good landmarks are hard to accurately determine on a shape such as an ear.

Using our statistical approach we reconstruct every shape. The reconstruction is done vertex by vertex, each time the vertex defines the center of a hole. This is repeated for holes with radii $r = [2\text{mm}, 3\text{mm}, 5\text{mm}]$. Figure 3 shows two statistically reconstructed scans with reconstruction error as color. The measure of the error is the distance from the reconstructed hole center to the original hole center, this error constitutes a upper bound (meaning worst) for the reconstruction error, whereas a point to surface distance should produce the lower bound (most optimistic). It is worth noticing that we get good reconstructions even though the holes are big relative to the size of the scans. The reconstruction

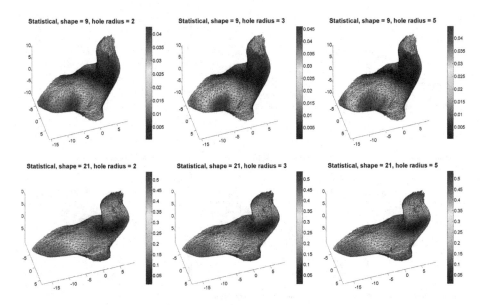

Fig. 3. The reconstruction of two ears ranging from very good to reasonable, the reconstruction is done for holes with radius $r = [2\text{mm}, 3\text{mm}, 5\text{mm}]$. The reconstruction error is shown in color. Notice the difference in color scale for the to reconstructions.

error is very similar for different hole sizes which leads to assume that there is a strong correlation between points across the shape of the ear canal. To compare the proposed reconstruction with a recent surface reconstruction algorithm, the experiments are repeated using MRFSurface to again reconstruct all points in all shapes for varying hole sizes. It has been used with two different hole closing priors: Laplacian and Membrane. While the reconstruction using these two priors is fair for small holes the reconstruction collapses as the holes get bigger. Figure 4 shows the standard deviation from zero of the reconstruction of the 29 scans using all three methods for holes with varying radius, $r = [2\text{mm}, 3\text{mm}, 5\text{mm}]$. As with the statistical method the upper bound error is used, again being the distance from the original hole center to the closest point in the reconstructed surface. Comparing the results of the three different reconstructions it can be seen that all reconstructions are good for hole sizes with $r = 2\text{mm}$, with the statistical reconstruction outperforming the other to. As the hole sizes increases to $r = 3\text{mm}$ the Membrane prior reconstruction begins to fail while the Laplacian prior reconstruction is still good. The statistical method stays almost unchanged. Finally the holes are increases to $r = 5\text{mm}$ and the Laplacian prior reconstruction also begins to fail. The statistical reconstruction stays very constant (the three top figures are very close to but not identical). This again suggest a very strong correlation between the surface points in ear scans, even though the shapes of the ear impressions vary a lot, as can be seen in Fig. 1(a). Using a statistical model also allows for surface reconstruction of large areas near borders. The distribution of reconstruction of error is right skewed. A less

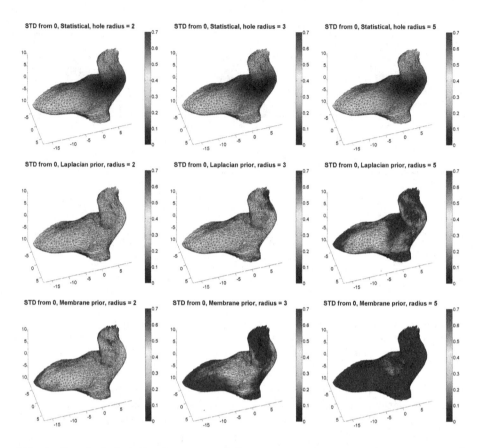

Fig. 4. Standard deviation from zero of the reconstruction error using our proposed Statistical reconstruction and MRFSurface reconstruction with both Laplacian and Membrane prior energy for holes with radius $r = [2\text{mm}, 3\text{mm}, 5\text{mm}]$. Notice that the three top figures are not identical, the reconstruction results are just very close to being identical.

skew biased measure of the reconstruction is the median and the interquartile range for the three reconstructions. Table 1 shows the median and interquartile range over all shapes and vertices. The table clearly shows that our proposed method performs better in the reconstruction. The interquartile range is also quite narrow making the overall reconstruction error consistently small.

It is well known that the ear canal deforms when people are chewing or doing other facial movements. This is partly due to the movement of the mandibular bone [6]. Furthermore, the impression taking and scanning is also influenced by several factors, including viscosity [18] of the impression material and the subsurface scattering encountered during laser scanning. The use of wax alone also adds to the error during today's impression taking [17]. The article suggest a tolerance of 0.3mm, which puts our surface recovery results within tolerance.

Table 1. Total median error and interquartile range for the three reconstructions (in mm)

Reconstruction	$r = 2$mm		$r = 3$mm		$r = 5$mm	
	med	iqr	med	iqr	med	iqr
Statistical	0.1111	0.2003	0.1115	0.2004	0.1124	0.2011
Laplacian	0.3387	0.1573	0.3798	0.1713	0.5666	0.4947
Membrane	0.3745	0.1758	0.5515	0.4130	1.4683	1.3314

7   Conclusions and Discussion

We have shown that we can predict the missing parts of partial scans using a statistical model. Especially when the holes become big relative to the size of the shape, our method outperforms surface reconstructions that only use the immediate vicinity in the reconstruction.

We have focussed mainly on the statistical method given an alignment and then creating some point correspondences. Future work should focus on getting a better alignment and point correspondence. Different variations of the ICP algorithm [19] are know to produce good alignment. Also, it is possible that non-rigid alignment will improve on the point correspondence and thus the final result. We have also made the assumption that a partial scan can be aligned as well as a full scan, this assumption holds true for holes up to a certain size. As the holes grow and scans become more partial, at some point alignment will no longer be functional and the method can not be applied or it might need to be manually assisted.

The performance of the proposed method is very good, the only really time consuming operation (a matter of seconds for our data set) of the statistical hole closing method is the singular value decomposition used for the variance matrix of *known* points in the statistical model. For a real world application once an alignment and a point correspondence has been established, the singular value decomposition is only done once and can be used to reconstruction all the missing parts. The proposed method is not restricted to the used data, but can be applied to data, where point correspondence throughout the data set can be obtained.

Acknowledgements. This work was (in part) financed by the *Danish National Advanced Technology Foundation* (project no 019-2009-3).

References

1. Bloomenthal, J.: An implicit surface polygonizer. In: Graphics Gems IV, pp. 324–349 (1994)
2. Botsch, M., Kobbelt, L.: A remeshing approach to multiresolution modeling. In: Proceedings of the 2004 Eurographics/ACM SIGGRAPH Symposium on Geometry Processing, pp. 185–192 (2004)
3. Caselles, V., Haro, G., Sapiro, G., Verdera, J.: On geometric variational models for inpainting surface holes. Computer Vision and Image Understanding 111(3), 351–373 (2008)

4. Clarenz, U., Diewald, U., Dziuk, G., Rumpf, M., Rusu, R.: A finite element method for surface restoration with smooth boundary conditions. Computer Aided Geometric Design 21(5), 427–446 (2004)
5. Cootes, T., Taylor, C., Cooper, D., Graham, J., et al.: Active shape models-their training and application. Computer Vision and Image Understanding 61(1), 38–59 (1995)
6. Darkner, S., Larsen, R., Paulsen, R.R.: Analysis of Deformation of the Human Ear and Canal Caused by Mandibular Movement. In: Ayache, N., Ourselin, S., Maeder, A. (eds.) MICCAI 2007, Part II. LNCS, vol. 4792, pp. 801–808. Springer, Heidelberg (2007)
7. Gower, J.C.: Generalized procrustes analysis. Psychometrika 40(1), 33–51 (1975)
8. Hammond, P., Hutton, T., Allanson, J., Campbell, L., Hennekam, R., Holden, S., Patton, M., Shaw, A., Temple, I., Trotter, M., et al.: 3d analysis of facial morphology. American Journal of Medical Genetics Part A 126(4), 339–348 (2004)
9. Kaick, O., Zhang, H., Hamarneh, G., Cohen-Or, D.: A survey on shape correspondence. In: Computer Graphics Forum, vol. 20, pp. 1–23 (2010)
10. Kazhdan, M., Bolitho, M., Hoppe, H.: Poisson surface reconstruction. In: Proceedings of the Fourth Eurographics Symposium on Geometry Processing. pp. 61–70. Eurographics Association (2006)
11. Kolluri, R., Shewchuk, J., O'Brien, J.: Spectral surface reconstruction from noisy point clouds. In: Proceedings of the 2004 Eurographics/ACM SIGGRAPH Symposium on Geometry Processing, pp. 11–21. ACM (2004)
12. Lanche, S., Darvann, T.A., Ólafsdóttir, H., Hermann, N.V., Van Pelt, A.E., Govier, D., Tenenbaum, M.J., Naidoo, S., Larsen, P., Kreiborg, S., Larsen, R., Kane, A.A.: A Statistical Model of Head Asymmetry in Infants with Deformational Plagiocephaly. In: Ersbøll, B.K., Pedersen, K.S. (eds.) SCIA 2007. LNCS, vol. 4522, pp. 898–907. Springer, Heidelberg (2007)
13. Paulsen, R.R., Hilger, K.B.: Shape Modelling Using Markov Random Field Restoration of Point Correspondences. In: Taylor, C., Noble, J.A. (eds.) IPMI 2003. LNCS, vol. 2732, pp. 1–12. Springer, Heidelberg (2003)
14. Paulsen, R.R., Larsen, R., Nielsen, C., Laugesen, S., Ersbøll, B.: Building and Testing a Statistical Shape Model of the Human Ear Canal. In: Dohi, T., Kikinis, R. (eds.) MICCAI 2002, Part II. LNCS, vol. 2489, pp. 373–380. Springer, Heidelberg (2002)
15. Paulsen, R.R.: Statistical shape analysis of the human ear canal with application to in-the-ear hearing aid design. IMM, Informatik og Matematisk Modellering, Danmarks Tekniske Universitet (2004)
16. Paulsen, R.R., Bærentzen, J., Larsen, R.: Markov random field surface reconstruction. IEEE Transactions on Visualization and Computer Graphics 16(4), 636–646 (2010)
17. Pirzanski, C.: Despite new digital technologies, shell modelers shoot in the dark. The Hearing Journal 59(10), 28 (2006)
18. Pirzanski, C., Berge, B.: Earmold impressions: Does it matter how they are taken. Hear. Rev. 10(4), 18–20 (2003)
19. Rusinkiewicz, S., Levoy, M.: Efficient variants of the ICP algorithm. In: 3dim, p. 145. IEEE Computer Society (2001)
20. Verdera, J., Caselles, V., Bertalmio, M., Sapiro, G.: Inpainting surface holes. In: Proceedings. 2003 International Conference on Image Processing, ICIP 2003, vol. 2 (2003)

Automated Segmentation of Cerebral Aneurysms Based on Conditional Random Field and Gentle Adaboost

Hong Zhang[1], Yuanfeng Jiao[2], Yongjie Zhang[1,2], and Kenji Shimada[1,2]

[1] Department of Mechanical Engineering, Carnegie Mellon University, USA
[2] Department of Biomedical Engineering, Carnegie Mellon University, USA
{hongzh,yuanfeng,jessicaz,shimada}@andrew.cmu.edu

Abstract. Quantified geometric characteristics of cerebral aneurysms such as volume, height, maximum diameter, surface area and aspect ratio are useful for predicting the rupture risk. Moreover, a newly developed fluid structure interaction system requires healthy models generated from the aneurysms to calculate anisotropic material directions for more accurate wall stress estimation. Thus the isolation of aneurysms is a critical step which currently depends primarily on manual segmentation. We propose an automated solution to this problem based on conditional random field and gentle adaboost. The proposed method was validated with eight datasets and four-fold cross-validation, an accuracy of 89.63%±3.09% is obtained.

Keywords: Cerebral Aneurysm, Segmentation, Isolation, Conditional Random Field, Gentle Adaboost.

1 Introduction

Cerebral aneurysms (CAs) [1] are one kind of major disease inside the brain due to blood-vessel dilations at spots with weakened walls and the formation of bulges as shown in Fig. 1. They usually happen near a bifurcation and grow gradually in size and weaken the wall strength, which may lead to rupture finally. Though ruptures are not always fatal and complications are not observed in all cases, there is a 40% chance of mortality within 24 hours and an additional 25% chance of death due to complications within the next six months [2]. In order to prevent or reduce the rupture risk, an accurate prediction system based on computational simulation would be valuable.

While simple geometric characteristics, such as maximum diameter, neck diameter, height, aspect ratio and convexity ratio, could be used to predict the rupture risk [3], identifying and isolating an aneurysmal dome is the first critical step toward the computational simulation of aneurysms. Wall stress estimation is an important application of such computational simulation, and a recently proposed framework [4] utilizes healthy models generated from aneurysms after isolating aneurysmal domes. Currently it is performed primarily by manual segmentation. Some research has been conducted in segmenting aneurysms.

J.A. Levine, R.R. Paulsen, Y. Zhang (Eds.): MeshMed 2012, LNCS 7599, pp. 59–69, 2012.

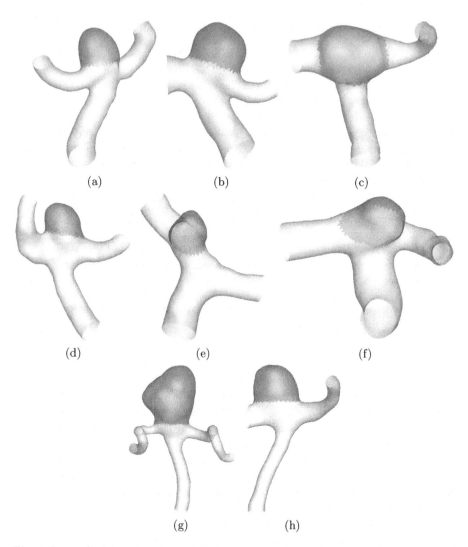

(a)   (b)   (c)

(d)   (e)   (f)

(g)   (h)

Fig. 1. Manually labeled surface of eight aneurysms. Magenta represents a aneurysmal dome and grey represents a healthy vessel.

McLaughlin et al. [5] applied region-splitting to isolate the aneurysms while may fail on wide-neck cases. Sgouritsa et al. [6] employed a graph-cut algorithm based on curvature to separate aneurysms, but since curvature is very sensitive to noise relying solely on this feature is not reliable. Baloch et al. [7] used conditional random field (CRF) to label aneurysms. All the above methods require a user to pick seeds as input and cannot provide a fully automated solution. A general automated solution similar to [7] was presented in [8], but it is based on triangles. This may decrease the discrimination ability of features since nearly all features are based on vertices.

In this paper, we propose an automated method to identify an aneurysm, based on CRF and gentle adaboost classifiers using unary features and pairwise features, respectively. The unary classifier measures the probability of a vertex belonging to an aneurysm, and the pairwise classifier measures the probability of two connected vertices belonging to different parts to smooth the segmentation boundary and penalize the inconsistent labels. The conditional probability of CRF is optimized through graph-cuts. This framework utilizes gentle adaboost techniques based on vertices, therefore no user input is required, and the discrimination ability of features is improved. We validate the proposed method with eight datasets, and four-fold cross-validation is applied to estimate the accuracy. The experimental results demonstrate that the automated system can obtain an accuracy of 89.63%±3.09%.

The paper is organized as follows: CRF is defined in Section 2, and the unary energy and the pairwise energy are described in Sections 3 and 4, respectively. The classifier is formulated in Section 5. We present and discuss the results in Section 6. Finally, Section 7 draws conclusions.

2   Conditional Random Field

A three dimensional embedded surface generated from cerebral aneurysm computed tomography angiography (CTA) images is mapped isomorphically onto a graph $G = \{V, E\}$, where V represents vertices of a surface mesh, and E represents the connectivity between these vertices. For each vertex, a group of observation $\mathbf{x}$ called *unary features* and a binary random variable c are associated, and another group of observations $\mathbf{y}$ called *pairwise features* is associated with each edge. $\mathbf{x}$ describes the local and global geometric characteristics, the label c is "-1" when the vertex belongs to the healthy vessel and "1" when it belongs to the aneurysm. $\mathbf{y}$ defines the similarity between two adjacent vertices and provides clues on whether or not they should share the same label. To isolate the aneurysm, we need to assign a correct label to each vertex based on the underlying geometric feature properties.

The task is described as a partition process that minimizes an objective energy function:

$$E(\mathbf{c}, \theta) = \sum_i a_i E_1(c_i; x_i, \theta_1) + \sum_{i,j} l_{i,j} E_2(c_i, c_j; y_{i,j}, \theta_2), \tag{1}$$

where the unary energy E_1 represents consistency between the feature x_i of Vertex i and its associated label c_i; the pairwise energy E_2 represents consistency between adjacent Vertex i and Vertex j, given the labels c_i, c_j and $y_{i,j}$; and $\theta = \{\theta_1, \theta_2\}$ are model parameters. The two energy terms are weighted by the normalized average area, a_i, of triangles connecting to Vertex i and the normalized edge length $l_{i,j}$ between Vertices i and j. The normalization factors are the median of all average areas and edge lengths.

The above undirected graphical model is referred as CRF [9], where the joint conditional probability of labeling on a given mesh is

$$P(\mathbf{c}|\mathbf{x}, \mathbf{y}, \theta) = exp(-E(\mathbf{c}, \theta))/Z(\mathbf{x}, \mathbf{y}, \theta), \tag{2}$$

where $Z(\mathbf{x}, \mathbf{y}, \theta)$ is a normalization factor. The probability can be optimized using the alpha-expansion graph-cuts [10].

3   Unary Energy

The unary energy is derived from the output of a binary classifier gentle adaboost [11], which returns a probability distribution $P(c|x, \theta_1)$ defined in Section 5. Thus the unary energy of Vertex i with label c_i is defined as the negative log-probability of the vertex:

$$E_1(c_i; x_i, \theta_1) = -\log P(c_i|x_i, \theta_1). \tag{3}$$

From the definition, we can find that a high probability decreases the energy.

For Vertex i on the surface, a group of features x_i are extracted to predict the label for the vertex. The features can be roughly divided into three categories: local, regional and global descriptors. The local descriptors mainly represent the local geometric characters (usually 1-ring to 5-ring neighbors). The regional descriptors describe the regional geometric characteristics by casting rays from a certain point and stopping at the surface. The global descriptors depend on the position of other vertices relative to Vertex i.

3.1   Local Descriptors

Curvature [12] is a general tool to measure the "bending" degree in every direction at a vertex on a surface. Among these directions, the maximum curvature κ_1 and the minimum curvature κ_2 are known as the principal curvatures. Around the vertex, we select 1-ring through 5-ring neighbors to form various-size patches and estimate the principal curvatures. At each ring neighbor, we include nine local descriptors as features: $\kappa_1, |\kappa_1|, \kappa_2, |\kappa_2|, \kappa_1\kappa_2, |\kappa_1\kappa_2|, (\kappa_1+\kappa_2)/2, |(\kappa_1+\kappa_2)/2|, \kappa_1-\kappa_2$. Then we obtain a total of $5 \times 9 = 45$ features. One of the features, $|\kappa_1\kappa_2|$, is shown in Fig. 2(a), in which the high curvatures are located around the neck and bifurcation.

Principal Component Analysis (PCA) provides the linear pattern of a group of data. The singular value s_1, s_2, s_3 of the covariance of coordinates of each ring neighbor are used to generate 15 features: $s_1, s_2, s_3, s_1/(s_1 + s_2 + s_3), s_2/(s_1 + s_2 + s_3), s_3/(s_1 + s_2 + s_3), (s_1 + s_2)/(s_1 + s_2 + s_3), (s_1 + s_3)/(s_1 + s_2 + s_3), (s_2 + s_3)/(s_1 + s_2 + s_3), s_1/s_2, s_1/s_3, s_2/s_3, s_1/s_2 + s_1/s_3, s_1/s_2 + s_2/s_3, s_1/s_3 + s_2/s_3$. We obtain a total of $5 \times 15 = 75$ features. One of the features, $s_1/(s_1 + s_2 + s_3)$, is shown in Fig. 2(b) and, it mainly follows the shape directions.

3.2   Regional Descriptors

Cerebral aneurysms are deformed from hyperelastic vessels. Though most aneurysmal surface shapes are close to a sphere, they are still irregular as shown in Fig. 1. As a result, local feature variance such as the curvature is high on aneurysmal dome, and this character decreases the discrimination ability of local features.

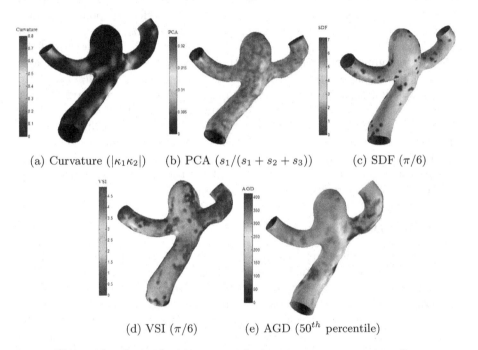

(a) Curvature ($|\kappa_1\kappa_2|$)   (b) PCA ($s_1/(s_1 + s_2 + s_3)$)   (c) SDF ($\pi/6$)

(d) VSI ($\pi/6$)   (e) AGD (50th percentile)

Fig. 2. The obtained various unary features over an aneurysm surface

To address this issue, Shape Diameter Function (SDF) [13] provides a solution for improving the robustness. SDF starts from calculating the inward-normal direction on a vertex. A cone using the vertex as the apex and the inward-normal as the axis is placed on the surfaces, and several rays starting from the vertex inside the cone are cast to the other side of the surface until an intersection is found or the length of the ray is beyond a preset threshold. SDF is the weighted average, and the weights are the inverse of the angle between the ray to the cone axis. SDF is invariant to rigid transformations and robust to deformations. Four kinds of cones with angles $\pi/6, \pi/3, \pi/2, 2\pi/3$ are used, and for each cone the SDF and the logarithmized SDF are used to define the normalized SDF:

$$nsdf(i) = \log(\frac{sdf(i) - \min(sdf(1:n))}{\max(sdf(1:n)) - \min(sdf(1:n))} * \alpha + 1)/\log(\alpha + 1), \quad (4)$$

where α is the normalizing parameter ($\alpha = 1, 2, 4, 8$), and n is the number of vertices on the surface. In this way, $5 \times 4 = 20$ shape diameter features are included. The SDF with angles $\pi/6$ is shown in Fig. 2(c), and the values are larger around the dome.

As an extension to the idea of SDF, a group of features called Volumetric Shape Image (VSI) is proposed to aim at part-discrimination problem [14]. VSI simulates the navigation along the medial centerline of the surface. Given a vertex on the surface, the corresponding medial center called the reference point is the center of the maximal sphere which is inside the surface and tangent to the surface at the vertex. The process of locating the reference point is similar to the process of calculating SDF. The rays are defined as l_j, and the estimated sphere diameter is $d_i = \max_{j=1:m}(||l_j||/\cos\beta_j)$, where $||l_j||$ is the length of the ray, m is the number of rays, and β_j is the angle between l_j and the cone axis n_i. In this term, the position of the reference point r_i is $v_i + 0.5 \cdot d_i \cdot n_i$, where v_i is the position of the vertex. Starting from the reference points, rays are cast uniformly sampled from a Gaussian sphere, and the length of rays is processed in the same way as SDF to generate 20 features. VSI changes smoothly inside the same part (such as the aneurysm dome), while it alters sharply when crossing the junction between parts (such as the aneurysm neck). Thus VSI performs high discrimination between parts. The VSI with angles $\pi/6$ is shown in Fig. 2(d), and the values are larger along the main branch.

3.3   Global Descriptors

As shown in Fig. 1, all aneurysms have the same topology with one inlet and two outlets. This provides a strong prior knowledge, and global descriptors utilize the relative position of a vertex to the rest of the vertices to store the topology.

Average Geodesic Distance (AGD)[15] is one of global descriptors that measure the separation degree of a vertex on the surface S, e.g., a vertex on the boundary usually has a large AGD. AGD can be defined as average, squared mean, the $10^{th}, 20^{th}, ..., 90^{th}$ percentile of the geodesic distances of Vertex i to the rest of the vertices, yielding 11 features after normalized by dividing the minimum over the surface. Under this definition, the AGD is large at the inlet and outlets and small at the aneurysm. The 50th percentile AGD is shown in Fig. 2(e), and the values are smaller around the middle of the mesh.

Shape contexts [16] are originally 2D shape descriptors for measuring shape similarity and are later extended to 3D [17]. The basic idea is to place a 3D sphere centered at the vertex, and spatial bins are created by logarithmic geodesic distance bins and uniform angle bins via spherical coordinates. The features are generated by a histogram that counts the number of vertices falling in each bin. 180 features are built from 36 angle bins and 5 distance bins ($36 \times 5 = 180$). Since it is a high-dimensional feature, we cannot visualize it easily.

A global descriptor named spin image [18] is invariant to rotation. The normal of a vertex on the surface is estimated, and a plane containing the normal is spun 2π degrees using this normal as the rotation axis. A coordinate system using the vertex as the origin, the perpendicular distance to the normal as γ axis, and the normal as ω axis is placed. The plane is divided into rectangle bins based on the coordinate. During the spin, the vertices are cast to the plane and the number of cast vertices in each bin is calculated as a feature, and 55 features (5 bins along γ axis and 11 bins along ω axis, $5 \times 11 = 55$) are obtained. Again, we cannot visualize it easily since it is a high-dimensional feature.

4   Pairwise Energy

The main role of the pairwise energy is to smooth the boundary between the segmentations. It is defined as:

$$E_2(c_i, c_j; y_{i,j}, \theta_2) = L(c_i, c_j)G(y_{i,j}, \theta_2), \tag{5}$$

where $L(c_i, c_j)$ is zero when $c_i = c_j$ and a preset constant when $c_i \neq c_j$; and $G(y_{i,j}, \theta_2) = -\rho \log P(c_i \neq c_j | y_{i,j}, \theta_2)$. ρ is a parameter balancing the effects of the unary energy and the pairwise energy. The pairwise energy is zero when Vertex i and j are not connected. The pairwise features $y_{i,j}$ are based on unary features of Vertex i and j, and are represented as the difference of curvature, SDF and VSI between these two vertices.

5   Gentle Adaboost

Gentle Adaboost [11] is one type of binary adaboost classifiers which can automatically pick up groups of significant features to output the probability that can be used in CRF. In the unary term, the input is a feature vector x_i and the output is the likelihood of Vertex i belonging to a label. In the pairwise term, the input is a feature vector $y_{i,j}$, and the output is the likelihood of a pair of neighboring Vertices i and j with different labels.

The classifier is a linear combination of weak classifiers called *stumps* which are one-layer decision tree [19]. During the training step, all training data are assigned weights equally, and at each iteration a weak classifier f_m is applied on the training data. The weights on false prediction data are increased and passed to the next iteration, and a weight of current weak classifier w_m is calculated according to the accuracy. The iterative process stops at a preset number M, and the weak classifiers and corresponding weights are recorded. During the testing step, the softmax transformation of the weighted linear sum of weak classifiers is used as output. We take the unary probability as an example and the pairwise probability follows the same scheme as

$$P(c_i|x_i, \theta_1) = \frac{\exp(\sum\limits_{m} w_m f_m(x_i))}{\exp(\sum\limits_{m} w_m f_m(x_i)) + \exp(\sum\limits_{m} -w_m f_m(x_i))}. \tag{6}$$

6   Results and Discussion

Eight cases shown in Fig. 1 are used in the experiment and a four-fold cross-validation process is performed to estimate the accuracy of the system. Here, we divide the eight cases into four groups evenly and run the classification four times. At each time, three groups are selected as the training data, and the other one group is selected as the testing data. As shown in Fig. 4, the obtained average accuracy is 89.63%±3.09%. The accuracy is defined as the percentage of error-labeled vertices among the segmentation results according to the manually labeled results. The errors are mainly around the neck due to the arbitrary definition on the boundary and the large range of vessel sizes. The gentle adaboost induces intrinsic errors too. A close form classifier combining CRF and gentle adaboost may potentially improve the results.

In each classifier, 400 weak classifiers are contained, and the significance of the unary feature is proportional to the weight of the corresponding weak classifier. The most significant feature is the SDF with $\pi/2$-degree angle cone with a weight of 0.3801, and the splitting point is 4.5192. The result is very reasonable; it can be clearly observed from Fig. 2 that SDFs around the apex of the dome are higher than other spots. Therefore, SDF is a very good discriminating feature in the cerebral aneurysm isolation application.

It is usually believed that more training data can produce more accurate results. The relationship between the number of training meshes and the accuracy is shown in Fig. 3 and we can observe that we can achieve the accuracy of 89.41% with seven training meshes.

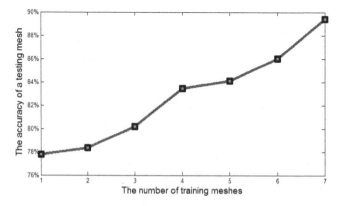

Fig. 3. The relationship between the number of training meshes and the accuracy of a testing mesh

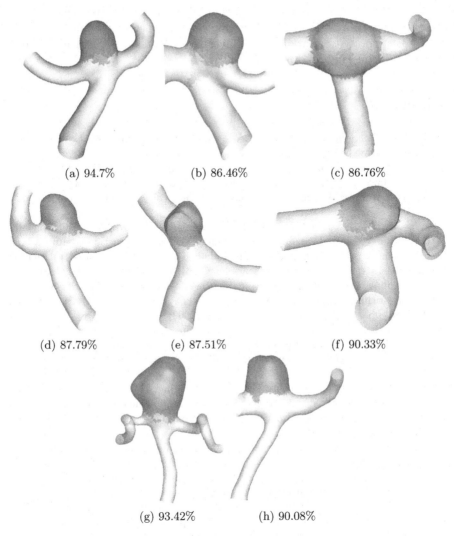

(a) 94.7%   (b) 86.46%   (c) 86.76%

(d) 87.79%   (e) 87.51%   (f) 90.33%

(g) 93.42%   (h) 90.08%

Fig. 4. Segmentation results with accuracy percentage. Magenta represents the aneurysm and grey represents the healthy vessel.

7   Conclusion

We have proposed a CRF and gentle adaboost based method for segmenting cerebral aneurysms from healthy vessel regions. This method utilizes various mesh features ranging from local features to global features to strengthen the robustness of the classifier. The final results are polished with CRF by minimizing the energy function with graph-cuts. In the future, more models need to be included in the project, and more unary features will be tested.

Acknowledgments. We would like to thank University of Pittsburgh Medical Center for providing us the patient-specific cerebral aneurysm models. This research was supported in part by the University of Pittsburgh Medical Center's Healthcare Technology Innovation Grant.

References

1. Brisman, J.L., Song, J.K., Newell, D.W.: Cerebral aneurysms. New England Journal of Medicine 355(9), 928–939 (2006)
2. NINDS. Cerebral aneurysm fact sheet. NIH Publication (08-5505) (2008)
3. Ma, B., Harbaugh, R.E., Raghavan, M.L.: Three-dimensional geometrical characterization of cerebral aneurysms. Annals of Biomedical Engineering 32(2), 264–273 (2004)
4. Zhang, H., Jiao, Y., Johnson, E., Zhang, Y., Shimada, K.: Modeling anisotropic material property of cerebral aneurysms for fluid-structure interaction computational simulation. In: Third Computational Modeling of Objects Presented in Images: Fundamentals, Methods and Applications, COMPIMAGE 2012, p. 6 (2012)
5. McLaughlin, R.A., Noble, J.A.: Demarcation of Aneurysms Using the Seed and Cull Algorithm. In: Dohi, T., Kikinis, R. (eds.) MICCAI 2002, Part I. LNCS, vol. 2488, pp. 419–426. Springer, Heidelberg (2002)
6. Sgouritsa, E., Mohamed, A., Morsi, H., Shaltoni, H., Mawad, M.E., Kakadiaris, I.A.: Neck localization and geometry quantification of intracranial aneurysms. In: IEEE International Symposium on Biomedical Imaging: From Nano to Macro, pp. 1057–1060 (2010)
7. Baloch, S., Cheng, E., Zhu, Y., Mohamed, A., Ling, H., Fang, T.: Shape based conditional random fields for segmenting intracranial aneurysms. In: Workshop on Mesh Processing in Medical Image Analysis in Conjunction with MICCAI, 12 pages (2011)
8. Kalogerakis, E., Hertzmann, A., Singh, K.: Learning 3D mesh segmentation and labeling. ACM Transactions on Graphics (TOG) 29(3), 102 (2010)
9. Lafferty, J., McCallum, A., Pereira, F.C.N.: Conditional random fields: Probabilistic models for segmenting and labeling sequence data. In: Proceedings of the Eighteenth International Conference on Machine Learning, pp. 282–289 (2001)
10. Boykov, Y., Veksler, O., Zabih, R.: Fast approximate energy minimization via graph cuts. IEEE Transactions on Pattern Analysis and Machine Intelligence 23(11), 1222–1239 (2001)
11. Friedman, J., Hastie, T., Tibshirani, R.: Additive logistic regression: a statistical view of boosting. The Annals of Statistics 28(2), 337–407 (2000)
12. Garimella, R.V., Swartz, B.K.: Curvature estimation for unstructured triangulations of surfaces. Tech. Rep. LA-UR-03-8240, Los Alamos National Laboratory (2003)
13. Shapira, L., Shamir, A., Cohen-Or, D.: Consistent mesh partitioning and skeletonisation using the shape diameter function. The Visual Computer 24(4), 249–259 (2008)
14. Liu, R., Zhang, H., Shamir, A., Cohen-Or, D.: A part-aware surface metric for shape analysis. Computer Graphics Forum 28(2), 397–406 (2009)
15. Zhang, E., Mischaikow, K., Turk, G.: Feature-based surface parameterization and texture mapping. ACM Transactions on Graphics (TOG) 24(1), 1–27 (2005)

16. Belongie, S., Malik, J., Puzicha, J.: Shape matching and object recognition using shape contexts. IEEE Transactions on Pattern Analysis and Machine Intelligence 24(4), 509–522 (2002)
17. Körtgen, M., Park, G.J., Novotni, M., Klein, R.: 3D shape matching with 3D shape contexts. In: The 7th Central European Seminar on Computer Graphics, vol. 3, pp. 5–17 (2003)
18. Johnson, A.E., Hebert, M.: Using spin images for efficient object recognition in cluttered 3D scenes. IEEE Transactions on Pattern Analysis and Machine Intelligence 21(5), 433–449 (1999)
19. Safavian, S.R., Landgrebe, D.: A survey of decision tree classifier methodology. IEEE Transactions on Systems, Man and Cybernetics 21(3), 660–674 (1991)

Carving Mesh with Deformation
for Soft Tissue Removal Simulation

Youngjun Kim, Seungbin Lee, Frédérick Roy,
Deukhee Lee, Laehyun Kim, and Sehyung Park

Center for Bionics, Korea Institute of Science and Technology,
39-1, KIST, Hawolgok-dong, Seongbuk-gu, Seoul 136-791, South Korea
junekim@kist.re.kr

Abstract. We present a novel method of volume removal for deformable mesh
data. The proposed method has the advantages of both volumetric mesh removal technique and hexahedral mesh deformation. Barycentric mapping combines
the volumetric mesh for carving and the hexahedral mesh for deformation. The
proposed algorithm for carving the deformable mesh is applied to a laparoscopic surgery training virtual simulation of gallbladder removal. In order to simulate the procedure of identifying the cystic duct and cystic artery by fat tissue
removal, carving mesh with deformation is applied. This paper introduces
mesh-processing algorithms to implement volume removal of soft tissue in
detail.

Keywords: mesh carving, mesh deformation, volume removal, laparoscopic
surgical training, gallbladder removal simulation.

1   Introduction

In virtual medical training simulation, real-time mesh deformation is essential.
Because many internal human organs are deformable, the virtual simulation of the
organs entails many mesh deformation problems. In this paper, we report a new deformable mesh carving technique for medical simulation. The proposed method can
simulate soft tissue removal using the carving mesh model while calculating deformations of the model at the same time.

The purpose of this study derives from implementation of a laparoscopic surgical
simulation. Laparoscopic surgery is a minimally invasive surgery, which minimizes
incisions using long laparoscopic surgical instruments. In laparoscopic surgery, several laparoscopic instruments are inserted through tiny incisions in the abdomen and a
laparoscope through the umbilicus is used to view inside the abdomen [1, 2]. Laparoscopic surgery is beneficial to patients in terms of short recovery time and less pain,
compared to conventional open laparotomic surgery. However, it is difficult to acquire laparoscopic surgical skills. To this end, recently, virtual laparoscopic surgical
training systems have been developed, which can provide a safe and convenient
environment to medical students or novice surgeons. Several laparoscopic surgical

J.A. Levine, R.R. Paulsen, Y. Zhang (Eds.): MeshMed 2012, LNCS 7599, pp. 70–79, 2012.
© Springer-Verlag Berlin Heidelberg 2012

training systems have been introduced in the market, such as SEP (SimSurgery, Norway) [3], LapSim (Surgical-Science, Sweden) [4], LAP Mentor (Simbionix, USA) [5], and LapVR (Immersion, USA) [6]. Studies on liver simulation for laparoscopic surgical training have been reported in the literature [7, 8]. Fig. 1 shows the laparoscopic surgical training system that we have developed [9]. We implemented the simulation software using Simulation Open Framework Architecture (SOFA) [10, 11]. SOFA provides robust simulation functions such as various force fields, including finite element method (FEM), collision detection, numerical integration, data loading and modelling. We further added a new library and functions regarding the proposed method that SOFA does not support as plug-ins for our purpose.

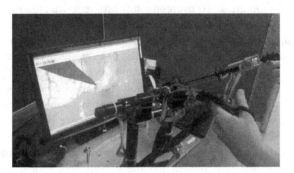

Fig. 1. Developed laparoscopic simulation system [9]

Cholecystectomy (gallbladder removal) is one of the major procedures conducted using laparoscopic surgeries. The cholecystectomy procedure is as follows: (1) identifying cystic duct and cystic artery, (2) ligation of cystic duct and artery using clips, (3) cutting the cystic duct and artery, (4) dissection of gallbladder from liver by removing connective tissues, (5) gallbladder removal through umbilicus [12]. In this paper, we focus on procedure step (1), i.e. identifying cystic duct and cystic artery by removing fat tissues. The proposed method of mesh carving with deformation is applied to simulate the burning of the fat tissues covering the cystic duct and artery by electrical cautery. Mesh processing algorithms and results of volume removal for the soft tissue are described in detail in the following sections.

2   Methods

2.1   Mesh Carving by Tetrahedral Model (Approach #1)

As the first approach for carving mesh with deformation, we tested a tetrahedral mesh-based method. First, a tetrahedral mesh was generated from the original triangular mesh by isosurface stuffing [13]. During simulation, when collisions were detected between the tetrahedrons of the soft tissue model and the cautery's geometrical mesh model, the colliding tetrahedrons were erased in each time step. We employed Mapping Tetrahedron to Triangle in SOFA [10] for removing such tetrahedrons. We visualized the tetrahedrons of the carved region to have smooth edges by applying transparency. Deformation of the tetrahedral mesh was computed by the tetrahedral FEM. Because we used the same mesh for removal and deformation, no additional algorithm was required for carving with deformation.

2.2   Mesh Carving by Volume Model (Approach #2)

For deformable mesh removal using the tetrahedral model in the previous section (Approach #1), too many tetrahedrons are needed in order to obtain realistic visual results. For the size of the tetrahedron to be sufficiently small for realistic simulation, the number of tetrahedrons required exceeds 100,000. Thus, the computational costs of this approach are too great. To overcome this problem, we present a new approach of volumetric model-based mesh carving. Although other mesh morphing methods can be found in the literatures [14–16], they are not suitable for our simulation.

In a previous study, the volume-based approach to mesh carving was proposed and successfully applied to a dental training simulation system [17]. Mauch's closest point transform (CPT) [18] and Velho's adaptive polygonization techniques [19] were used for tooth drilling simulation. However, soft tissue carving simulation is different from dental simulation, whose models are rigid bodies. Thus, we present a new method to deal with the deformation calculation of a mesh model during carving operation. We calculate deformation of the model using the bounding grid model from the object's volume model. Both the grid model and the carved geometrical mesh model are linked together by mapping. Relevant algorithms are described in detail in the next subsections.

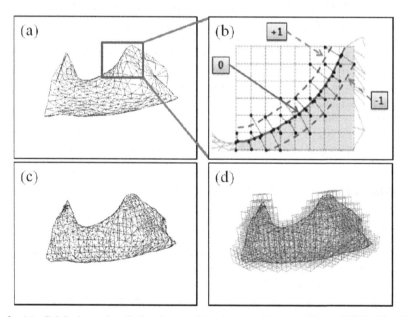

Fig. 2. (a) Original mesh of fat tissue, (b) closest point transform (CPT) algorithm, (c) mesh after adaptive polygonization and (d) bounding grid model for deformation

Volumetric Implicit Surface Representation

A volumetric implicit surface is used for shape modification during carving operations. First, the potential field is prepared from the input geometrical mesh by the CPT algorithm. The potential values around the mesh surface range from −1 to +1 according to the proximity to the surface. The potential values are negative inside the surface, and positive outside. The potential value of 0 represents the surface itself. Only this narrow band close to the surface is involved during the shape modification process. We employ Mauch's fast CPT algorithm [18] for the volumetric implicit surface representation. The algorithm first creates regular grids subdividing the bounding volume of the input mesh model. Then, it calculates the closest point and distance to the mesh at each grid point. (Refer to Fig.2(a) and (b))

Mesh Regeneration for Carving

After creating the potential fields for the volumetric implicit surface, triangular mesh on the surface (zero-potential surface) is generated by the method suggested by Velho et al. [19]. The adaptive polygonization method comprises two steps. At the initial polygonization step, uniform space decomposition is used to create the initial mesh as a base model for adaptive refinement. In the second step, the triangular mesh is refined adaptively at midpoints of non-flat edges according to the surface curvature. Mesh refinement is performed until the desired accuracy is achieved, and the midpoints are projected onto the implicit surface because they may not be on the surface. During carving simulation, the potential fields of the soft tissue model are updated while detecting collisions with the cautery's mesh model. The model for the cautery's tip is represented as a cylinder in our system. Only the neighbouring grids to the collisions are involved in the update of potential fields. After updating the potential fields in each step, the mesh is regenerated according to the new potential values in realtime. The adaptive polygonization algorithm efficiently regenerates the mesh using fewer polygons in simple-shaped surfaces and more polygons in complex surfaces. (Refer to Fig.2(c))

Mesh Deformation

As the carving process involves a grid, we use that structure to apply the forces according to a hexahedral corotational FEM [20], suitable for deforming soft tissue like fat or organs. We may use a finer hexahedral model to achieve more realistic deformations or a coarse hexahedral model in order to accelerate the simulation. (Refer to Fig.2(d) and Fig.3)

 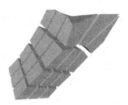

Fig. 3. Deformation of a 3 × 4 × 3 grid using a hexahedral corotational force field

Because the mesh for carving is triangular and the mesh for deformation is hexahedral, they need to be concatenated. We decided to use barycentric mapping implemented in SOFA [10]. This mechanism efficiently maps the simulated model (the carving model) and the mechanical model (on which the forces are computed), as illustrated in Fig. 4. The barycentric mapping computes forces on the mapped model according to its barycentric coefficients from the hexahedral grid model. Finally, the combination of these two mechanisms allows us to efficiently perform a realistic free-form deformation on a complex model.

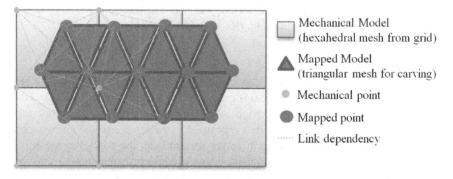

Fig. 4. Barycentric mapping between grid (hexahedral) model and triangular mesh model

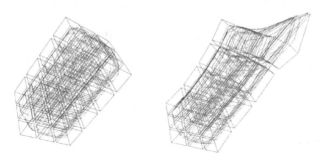

Fig. 5. Hexahedral mesh deformation: the inside cylindrical mesh is mapped onto the hexahedral mesh (the cylindrical mesh's bounding grid model) by barycentric mapping

2.3   Soft Tissue Removal Simulation for Cholecystectomy

Fat Tissue Removal for Cholecystectomy Simulation

Fig. 6 shows the necessary organs for cholecystectomy simulation. We modelled the liver, gallbladder, cystic duct, cystic artery, fat tissue, and bile duct. The geometrical mesh models of the organs were obtained by segmentation from Visible Korean Human data [21], and they were appropriately modified for simulation manually by an illustrator.

An initial step of the cholecystectomy procedure is identifying the cystic duct and cystic artery through removal of fat tissues by cautery. This step involves dissection of the fat tissues covering the cystic duct and artery. The two important tube-like organs of the cystic duct and artery should not be damaged by cautery during the identification step. After identifying the cystic duct and artery, they are to be clamped and cut before the gallbladder removal. The methods of carving mesh with deformation that we described in the previous sections are used for this fat tissue removal step.

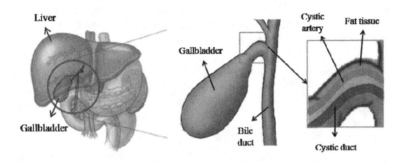

Fig. 6. Modelling for gallbladder removal simulation

Visualization for Cholecystectomy Simulation
One problem in the carving process is that the resulting mesh is constantly changing. Consequently, traditional texture mapping cannot be applied because the newly generated points will not have texture coordinates. To overcome this problem, we use a tri-planar texture technique on the visual model, as described in [22]. This permits us to avoid the need for texture coordinates, even during the deformation and carving process. Tri-planar texturing is convenient for objects with repetitive patterns, which is the case of fat tissue in our application.

Fig. 7. Tri-planar texturing applied with a chessboard-like texture on a carved cylinder

3   Results and Discussion

Fig. 8 shows the results of mesh carving using a tetrahedral mesh described in Section 2.1. The simulation results of fat tissue removal and identifying the cystic duct and artery by Approach #1 are shown in the snapshots. In the figure, the tetrahedrons of the fat tissue colliding with the cautery's tip are being removed. The number of tetrahedrons for the simulation is 5,083 in order to have a visual update rate of about 25 fps. However, the size of the tetrahedron is so large that the boundary edges of the removed part can be seen during the carving operation. Increasing the number of tetrahedrons to make them considerably smaller can solve the boundary edge problem, but real-time computation cannot be achieved in this case.

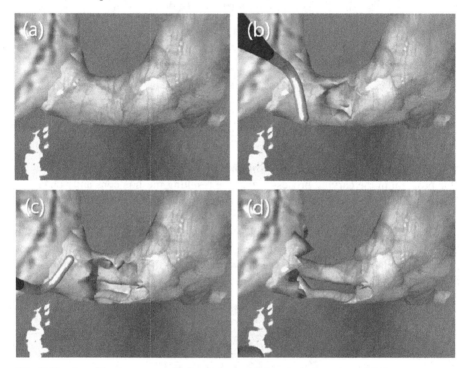

Fig. 8. Results of fat tissue removal simulation using tetrahedral mesh model (Approach #1)

The simulation results of the carving mesh using the volume model in Section 2.2 are shown in Fig. 9. In the snapshots, we can see that the fat tissue removal can be successfully simulated by the proposed method. The presented method does not have the boundary edge problem of the tetrahedral mesh-based method mentioned above. The volume-based method can smoothly regenerate the burned-out region, and thus, more realistic graphical rendering can be achieved as compared with the tetrahedral mesh-based method shown in Fig. 10 Moreover, deformation does not depend on the level of precision of the mesh in the proposed method. Even if it requires the additional step of barycentric mapping, less computation is required for an equivalent level of realism.

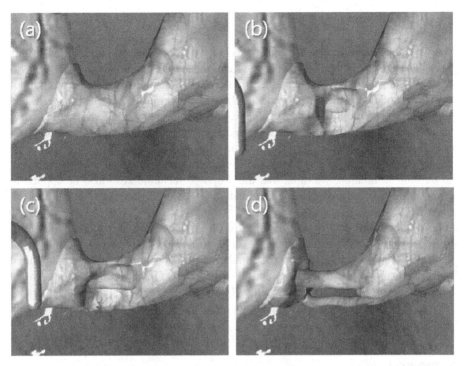

Fig. 9. Results of fat tissue removal simulation using volumetric model (Approach #2)

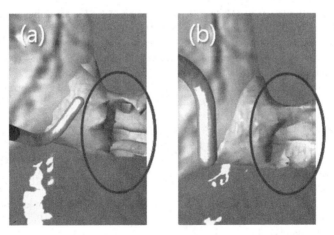

Fig. 10. Comparison of soft tissue removal simulations. (a) Tetrahedral mesh model-based approach and (b) volumetric model-based approach

4   Conclusion

A new technique of volumetric mesh carving with deformation is presented in this paper. The proposed method includes (1) carving by CPT and adaptive polygonization, (2) deformation by hexahedral FEM, and (3) barycentric mapping between models. The method can smoothly regenerate the carved region for deformable mesh, and thus it can overcome the boundary edge problem of the tetrahedral mesh-based carving method. The proposed method is successfully applied to fat tissue removal to identify the cystic duct and artery procedure in laparoscopic cholecystectomy. Although we applied the proposed method to fat tissue removal in a laparoscopic surgical training simulation, we think that the proposed technique can also be applied to any other kind of soft tissue carving simulation.

Acknowledgement. We would like to thank Prof. Helen Hong for modelling organs, Prof. Heewon Kye for texture mapping, and Prof. Woo Jung Lee for consulting of medical procedures and evaluation of simulation results. This research was supported by the Ministry of Culture, Sports and Tourism (MCST) and by the Korea Creative Content Agency (KOCCA) of the Culture Technology (CT) Research & Development Program of 2009. This work is also supported by the KIST Institutional Program (2E22610).

References

1. Zucker, K.A., Bailey, R.W., Gadacz, T.R., Imbembo, A.L.: Laparoscopic guided cholecystectomy. The American Journal of Surgery 161(1), 36–44 (2004)
2. Veldkamp, R., et al.: Laparoscopic surgery versus open surgery for colon cancer: Short-term outcomes of a randomised trial. The Lancet Oncology 6(7), 477–484 (2005)
3. SEP, SimSurgery Co., (2012), http://www.simsurgery.com/
4. LapSim, Surgical-Science Co. (2012), http://www.surgical-science.com/
5. LAP Mentor, Simbionix Co. (2012), http://www.simbionix.com/
6. LapVR, Immersion Co. (2012), http://www.immersion.com/
7. Cotin, S., Delingette, H., Ayache, N.: Real-time elastic deformations of soft tissues for surgery simulation. IEEE TVCG 5(1) (1999)
8. Montgomery, K., Bruyns, C., Brown, J., Sorkin, S., Mazzella, F.: SPRING: A general framework for collaborative, real-time surgical simulation. Medical Meets Virtual Reality 10, 23–26 (2002)
9. Kim, Y.J., Kim, K.H., Roy, F., Park, S.H.: Development of laparoscopic surgical training system with simulation open framework architecture (SOFA). In: Proc. ACCAS 2011, Bangkok, Thailand (2011)
10. SOFA (2012), http://www.sofa-framework.org/
11. Allard, J., Cotin, S., Faure, F., Bensoussan, P.J., Polyer, F., Duriez, C.: SOFA: An open source framework for medical simulation. Medical Meets Virtual Reality 15, 13–18 (2007)
12. WebSurg (2012), http://www.websurg.com/
13. Labelle, F., Shewchuk, J.R.: Isosurface stuffing: Fast tetrahedral meshes with good dihedral angles. In: Proc. ACM SIGGRAPH 2007, vol. 26(3) (2007)

14. Baldwin, M.A., Langenderfer, J.E., Rulkoetter, P.J., Laz, P.J.: Development of subject-specific and statistical shape models of the knee using an efficient segmentation and mesh-morphing approach. Computer Methods and Programs in Biomedicine 97(3), 232–240 (2010)
15. Sigal, I.A., Yang, H., Roberts, M.D., Downs, J.C.: Morphing methods to parameterize specimen-specific finite element model geometries. Journal of Biomechanics 43(2), 254–262 (2010)
16. Sigal, I.A., Whyne, C.M.: Mesh morphing and response surface analysis: quantifying sensitivity of vertebral mechanical behaviour. Annals of Biomedical Engineering 38(1), 41–56 (2010)
17. Kim, L.H., Park, S.H.: Haptic interaction and volume modeling techniques for realistic dental simulation. Visual Computing 22, 90–98 (2006)
18. Mauch, S.: A fast algorithm for computing the closest point and distance transform. Technical Report, http://www.its.caltech.edu/~sean/
19. Velho, L., Figureiredo, L.H.D., Gomes, J.: A unified approach for hierarchical adaptive tesselation of surfaces. ACM Transactions on Graphics 18(4), 329–360 (1999)
20. Nesme, M., Marchal, M., Promayon, E., Chabanas, M., Payan, Y., Faure, F.: Physically realistic interactive simulation for biological soft tissues. Recent Research Developments in Biomechanics 2, 117–138 (2005)
21. Park, J.S., et al.: Visible Korean Human: Its techniques and applications. Clinical Anatomy 19, 216–224 (2006)
22. Hubert, N.: GPU Gems 3., Lab Companion Series 3. Addison-Wesley (2008) ISBN 0321515269

Synthesis of Realistic Subcortical Anatomy with Known Surface Deformations

Yi Gao and Sylvain Bouix

Psychiatry Neuroimaging Laboratory, Harvard Medical School, Boston, MA 02115

Abstract. Statistical shape analysis is an actively studied field which has been playing an important role in the morphometric analysis of anatomical structures. Many algorithms have been proposed to compare the shape of anatomical structures across populations and a number of theoretical and technical advances have been developed on the subject. Unfortunately, there is very little work on the evaluation and validation of these new techniques. In contrast, comprehensive and objective evaluation frameworks have been designed for closely related fields such as image segmentation, registration or denoising, and play an important role in evaluating the quality of newly proposed algorithms. One possible reason may lie in the difficulty of generating a large set of synthetic shapes which are anatomically realistic, and another set of similar shapes with statistical difference from the previous group. In this work, we try to solve this shape synthesis problem, the outcome of which could be used for the purpose of evaluating shape analysis algorithms. Our method is based on two key components. First, a manifold learning algorithm is applied to a set of known control shapes, giving us the ability to generate an infinite number of new shapes. Second, a multi-scale clustering algorithm allows us to apply known, consistent and realistic deformations to input shapes surfaces. Our framework can thus provide arbitrarily many shapes (of the same organ/structure) with "ground truth" deformations. We present several synthetic, but anatomically derived, shape sets of varying complexity.

1 Introduction

Comprehensive and objective evaluation plays a very important role in the design and development of virtually any algorithm, technique, and system. In most of the research done in medical image analysis, such as image segmentation [8], registration [12], and denoising [2], the evaluation of the algorithms is an active topic, and is constantly applied on various newly developed techniques. Contrastingly, while statistical shape analysis is being widely studied and many ingenious algorithms have been proposed, an objective and comprehensive algorithm evaluation platform is still largely lacking, especially for 3D. This may be partially due to the difficulty of generating a large set of synthetic shapes which are anatomically realistic, and another set of similar shapes with *known and realistic* differences from the previous group. Previous work in the shape

J.A. Levine, R.R. Paulsen, Y. Zhang (Eds.): MeshMed 2012, LNCS 7599, pp. 80–88, 2012.
© Springer-Verlag Berlin Heidelberg 2012

based segmentation and/or shape analysis often construct a shape space from the training images using, for instance, the principle component analysis [3,11], principal geodesic analysis [9], kernel based methods [5], etc. Then, new shapes can be obtained by varying the coefficients in the learned shape space. However, on one hand, it is not easy to know where the deformation is in the newly generated shapes; on the other hand, it is not able to generate a population of shapes with consistent deformations. In this work, we try to solve this shape synthesis problem, the outcome of which could potentially be used for the purpose of shape analysis and evaluation.

Indeed, when analyzing real data, we often have a limited set of shapes to feed the algorithm. This is mainly due to the fact that, in practice, each shape is generated in a time consuming (semi-)manual segmentation process. Hence, an automatic and consistent way of generating potentially infinitely many shapes of the same organ/structure is needed. Furthermore, similarly to evaluating image denoising algorithms, where the random noise is added into the image to model a realistic degradation process, for shape analysis, it is also desired to introduce shape abnormalities. However, simply randomly perturbing vertex coordinates of the shape's surface will not give anatomically relevant deformations. The induced deformation should be in similar locations and magnitude across the population in order to model realistic shape changes.

To solve those problems, in this work we propose a method to synthesize of realistic subcortical anatomy with known surface deformations. Specifically, we address the above first problem by employing manifold learning techniques to generate arbitrarily many new shapes. In order to model shape abnormality, we apply a joint clustering algorithm, which parcellates the shape's surface into multi scaled regions which are consistently located across all shapes. A Log-Euclidean framework is then used to introduce smooth, invertible and anatomically realistic deformations to one or multiple regions defined by the clustering.

2   Methods: Synthesis of Realistic Subcortical Shapes

Assume we have a set of anatomical structures from a normal control population represented by binary images: $\tilde{S}_i : \Omega \subset \mathbb{R}^3 \to \{0, 1\}$, $i = 1, 2, \ldots, N$, where Ω is the common domain of the images. From these structures, our goal is to generate arbitrarily many similar shapes (Section 2.1), and induce anatomically relevant deformations to a sub group of them (Section 2.2).

2.1   Manifold Learning Shape Generator

Registration Following [14,6], we define "shape" as the geometric features of an object that are invariant to similarity transformations. Therefore, the first step of our pipeline is to align all training images using similarity transformations. To that end, we arbitrarily pick one shape and register all others to it by minimizing the energy with respect to each similarity transformation $T_j : \mathbb{R}^3 \to \mathbb{R}^3$:

$E(T_j) := \int_\Omega \left(\tilde{S}_j(T_j \circ \boldsymbol{x}) - \tilde{S}_i(\boldsymbol{x}) \right)^2 \mathrm{d}\boldsymbol{x}$. We denote the registered training shapes as $S_j := \tilde{S}_j \circ T_j : \Omega \to [0, 1]$, $j = 1, 2, \ldots, N$. We note that we could perform an unbiased population based registration, but our experiments do not show this as a necessary step for the purpose of generating new shapes from a learned manifold.

Manifold Learning Shape Generator. In a high dimensional shape space, the N training shapes S_i's most likely reside on a manifold rather than in a linear space [5]. In order to generate arbitrarily many shapes of the same category, one need to "sample" shapes by interpolating the training shapes on the manifold. However, due the high dimensional nature of the manifold, characterizing its topology for interpolation is difficult. To overcome this problem, we apply a local linear embedding method to map the high dimensional manifold to a lower dimensional space, and perform the computation therein [13]. Let (n_x, n_y, n_z) be the size of the binary volume S_i and let $\boldsymbol{V}_i \in \mathbb{R}^D$, where $D = n_x \cdot n_y \cdot n_z$, be a long vector representation of the binary image. First, we compute the weights $\boldsymbol{W} = \{W_i^j\} : j = 1, \ldots, k$ so that each vector V_i can be represented by its k nearest neighbors with minimal error:

$$\Psi(\boldsymbol{W}) := \sum_{i=1,\ldots,N} \left| \boldsymbol{V}_i - \sum_{j \in K_i} W_i^j \boldsymbol{V}_j \right|_D^2 \tag{1}$$

where K_i is the index set of $\boldsymbol{V}_i$'s k nearest neighbors, and $\sum_j W_i^j = 1, \forall i$. We then map $\boldsymbol{V}_i$ to $\boldsymbol{v}_i \in \mathbb{R}^d$, where $d \ll D$ such that the following error is minimized:

$$\Phi(\boldsymbol{v}_i) := \sum_{i=1,\ldots,N} \left| \boldsymbol{v}_i - \sum_{j \in K_i} W_i^j \boldsymbol{v}_j \right|_d^2 \tag{2}$$

Mapping the manifold to a locally linear lower dimensional space enables us to locally approximate the topology of the manifold with the Delaunay triangulation [4]. The local structure of the manifold (in low dimension) is thus characterized by the d-simplex (e.g. triangle in $2 - d$ or tetrahedron $3 - d$), and we can now generate a sample on the manifold by interpolating it on the d-simplex and then map it back to the high dimensional space. Details on how a new random sample is estimated are as follows. First, a d-simplex, along with its associated shapes $(\boldsymbol{V}_i, i=1,..,d)$, is randomly selected from the manifold, and a d-dimensional random vector $\boldsymbol{r} \in \mathbb{R}^d$ is generated such that each of $\boldsymbol{r}$'s components are uniformly distributed on $[0, 1]$. Then $\boldsymbol{r}$ is normalized so that $\|\boldsymbol{r}\|_1 = 1$. A new shape vector $\boldsymbol{V}^* \in \mathbb{R}^D$ can then be generated as $\boldsymbol{V}^* = \sum_{i=1}^d r_i \boldsymbol{V}_i$ and re-formatted to a volumetric image $U^* : \mathbb{R}^3 \to [0, 1]$. The above process can be repeated infinitely, and allows us to create arbitrarily large test data sets.

2.2 Abnormality Mesh Simulation

In the context of medical studies, most statistical shape analysis methods aim at examining whether there exist statistically significant shape differences between two populations of anatomical structures [6]. The hypothesis is that a disease acts upon the morphometry of the anatomy in a consistent manner and can be detected, localized and measured with the appropriate tools. The method described above is only able to generate large "new" data sets similar to the training data set. We thus need to design an algorithm to introduce artificial, yet realistic shape deformations to the data in order to mimic the action of a disease on an anatomical structure. In many cases, the anatomical abnormalities are hypothesized to be (i) located around similar regions across the shape population, and (ii) observable locally as a protuberance/depression or more globally as thinning/thickening of certain regions.

In what follows, we present a scheme which is able to introduce controlled local and global shape changes at similar regions across a population. This is achieved by applying a joint clustering algorithm to define a consistent parcellation across all shapes in the population. The shape are then deformed using diffeomorphic framework to simulate smooth and realistic shape abnormalities.

Mesh Joint Clustering. In order to find a common location among the population to induce a deformation, a joint clustering is performed among all shapes. As we will observe later, this not only addresses the common location requirement, but also allows us to control the extent of a shape change over the object.

Let $U_i : i = 1, \ldots, M$ be the generated sample shape binary maps and $C^i = \{c_1^i, \ldots, c_{L_i}^i\} \subset \mathbb{R}^3, i = 1, \ldots, M$ be their corresponding triangulated surface meshes, with L_i the number of vertices in mesh C^i. We first compute the outward normal vector $\mathcal{N}_j^i : C^i \to \mathbb{S}^2$ for each vertex ($j = 1, \ldots, L_i$). We then represent each surface as a 6 dimensional feature vector set $F^i = \{\boldsymbol{f}_j^i : j = 1, \ldots, L_i\}$ where $\boldsymbol{f}_j^i := (\boldsymbol{c}_j^i; \lambda \mathcal{N}_j^i) \in \mathbb{R}^6$ is a feature vector where λ weights the contribution of the unit normal in the clustering. Finally, the union of all feature vectors $F := \cup_i^M F_i$ is clustered using the k-means algorithm [7]. We incorporate the normal vector as a feature in order to ensure that different "sides" in an object are not clustered together, which could happen in very thin structures. The normal vector is a natural choice to separate two sides of a shape. It also allows to control the side on which an inflation or deflation may be introduced.

Using k-means also allows us to control the *scale* of the deformation, by simply changing the number of output clusters. If the purpose is to evaluate shape analysis algorithms' capability of discriminating *small* scale shape difference, the number of cluster parameter is set to be *large*, resulting in small regions on the surface. On the other hand, a small cluster number will give large patches on the shape surface which indicates global scale shape deformation.

Diffeomorphic Mesh Editing. Once the clustering is obtained any cluster (or combination of clusters) can be selected to be deformed. Both inward and outward deformations can be chosen as they can mimic true anatomical phenomena. For instance, in order to model a local bulge (on small scale) or thickening (on large scale), the deformation direction should be aligned with the outward normal. However, simply deforming the patch by pulling all cluster (patch) coordinates by an arbitrary amount in the normal direction has two significant problems. First, the deformation would not be smooth; and second, the deformed patch could collide or merge with other parts of the object, which would be anatomically unrealistic, as shown in Figure 5(b). To solve these problems, we use the Log-Euclidean registration framework of [1] to generate diffeomorphic deformations, which will be smooth and preserve the topology of the object.

Without loss of generality, let $G = \{c_j^i : y_j^i = l_0\} \subset \mathbb{R}^3$ (l_0 is the cluster label picked by the user) be the patch to be deformed by a vector $h \in \mathbb{R}^3$. Directly applying the vector h to the points of G is problematic. Instead, we smoothly extend the effect of the deformation to *all* surface points so as to make the entire deformation a diffeomorphism. This is done by first defining a weighting function: $w : \mathbb{R}^3 \to \mathbb{R}^+$ as

$$w(x) = \exp\left(-\frac{\min_{g \in G} |x - g|^2}{\sigma}\right) \qquad (3)$$

The function w indicates how strong the deformation vector will affect a spatial point located at x.

Although directly using w to modulate the deformation would result in a non-diffeomorphic transformation, one can use the Log-Euclidean approach described in [1], to generate a diffeomorphic mapping. To proceed, the transformation (here simply a translation) is first represented in homogeneous coordinates:

$$H = \begin{pmatrix} A & h \\ \mathbf{0}^{1\times3} & 1 \end{pmatrix} \in \mathbb{R}^{4\times4} \qquad (4)$$

The matrix logarithm of H, $\mathfrak{h}$, is then computed [10] and the weighting function w applied to $\mathfrak{h}$: $\mathfrak{z}(x) = w(x)\mathfrak{h}$.

The diffeomorphic transformation is obtained by simply applying the matrix exponential to $\mathfrak{z}$: $Z(x) = \mathrm{expm}(\mathfrak{z}(x))$, and all surface points can be safely transformed: $\tilde{c}_j^i = c_j^i + Z(c_j^i), \quad j = 1, \ldots, L_i; i = 1, \ldots, M$ \qquad (5)

We now have all the elements required to generate synthetic, yet realistic large test data sets for the purpose of evaluating shape analysis tools. If one wanted to mimic a population study with N "controls" and M "disease" sample shapes based on training data from a "control" group, one would first generate $N + M$ samples using the method described in section 2.1, then randomly choose M shapes and apply a desired transformation using the method outlined in this section.

3   Experiments and Results

In this section, we first demonstrate the manifold shape generation tool applied to binary maps representation of the hippocampus and the full striatum in Section 3.1. We then show how joint clustering parcellates each structure consistently across a population in Section 3.2. Finally in Section 3.3, shape abnormalities are simulated on the newly generated striatum shapes. All binary maps were selected from manual tracings of neuroanatomical structures in our MRI database normal controls. The training sample sizes were 25 for the hippocampus, and 27 for the striatum.

3.1   Manifold Learning Shape Generation

In this section, we present results of the manifold shape generator detailed in Section 2.1. Note that although we only show ten newly generated shapes for each structure, there is no limit to the number of new shapes the shape generator can produce.

First, the method is applied on the hippocampus, and ten generated shapes are shown in Figure 1. One can observe that the shapes vary quite a lot, in particular with regards to the roughness of the surfaces and the bending angle of the hippocampus body, yet maintain the "hippocampus look" without developing unwanted artifacts.

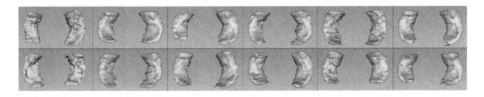

Fig. 1. Two training hippocampus shapes (leftmost column) and ten hippocampus shapes generated by the manifold learning

We tested the algorithm further using the striatum, a much more complex shape. As can be observed in Figure 2, even for such a convoluted shape, the newly generated samples are visually satisfying without topological error and possess detailed shape features found in the training sample.

Fig. 2. A training striatum shape (leftmost) and four striatum shapes generated by the manifold learning

3.2   Joint Shape Clustering

As detailed in Section 2.2, in order to simulate thinning or thickening of a particular region of the shape, one has to consider the surface normal orientation when clustering the surfaces. Indeed, as shown in Figure 3, if only point coordinates are used and 2 clusters are chosen, the clustering will separate the hippocampus along the longest axis of the shape and cluster a "head" and a "tail". Based on such clusters, constructing thinning or thickening deformations is challenging. However, when adding surface orientation to the clustering, we obtain the regions from different sides of the shape, which makes thinning/thickening effects easier to implement.

We also show the robustness of the clustering on the more complicated striatum in Figure 4. It can be seen that the different shapes are clustered consistently, enabling the application of consistently localized deformations as shown in the next section.

Fig. 3. Clustering of shape surface without orientation information (a), (b) and with orientation information (c) (d). See text for detail.

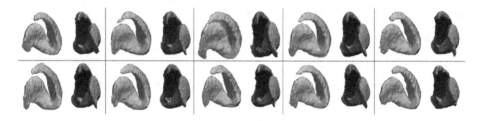

Fig. 4. Joint clustering of multiple striatums. It can be seen that different shapes are clustered consistently.

3.3   Shape Abnormality Simulation

In this experiment we demonstrate the power of our diffeomorphic deformation technique by simulating a thickening of the lateral side of the head of the caudate. This is particularly challenging because of the close proximity of the globus pallidus/putamen. Indeed, if a translation vector field is directly applied to the points in that region, the resulting surface will intrude into the medial side of the putamen (Figure 5(b)). Our proposed framework overcomes this problem by

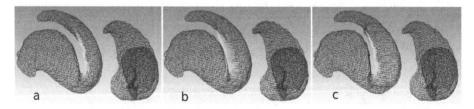

Fig. 5. In order to model a lateral swelling of the right caudate head, the yellow region in the original surface, shown in (a), is to be deformed. If an expansion vector field is directly applied, the surface protrudes into the putamen (b). Using the proposed method, the expansion becomes diffeomorphic (c) and the putamen retreats smoothly to avoid the collision.

providing a global diffeomorphic transformation derived from the desired local deformation. (Figure 5(c)).

Figure 6 shows examples of deformed striatum shapes mimicking a thickening or thinning of the head of the caudate. All shapes are very realistic and can be used to test and evaluating the statistical shape analysis algorithms.

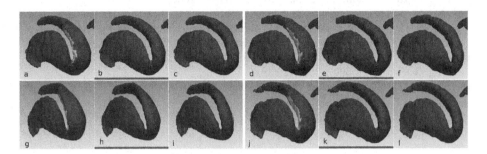

Fig. 6. Four sets of deformed shapes. The four sub-figures on the red bar (b,e,h,k) are four newly generated shapes from normal data. Those to their left, respectively, are thickening of the lateral side, shown in yellow color, of the right caudate. Those to their right are thinning of the medial side of the right caudate.

4   Conclusion and Discussion

We present a framework for the generation of anatomically inspired synthetic data sets for the purpose of evaluating shape analysis algorithms. A manifold learning technique, allows us to generate arbitrarily many shapes, and the combination of a joint clustering and diffeomorphic transformation generation can simulate realistic, robust and controlled deformations. With such large data set along with ground truth abnormalities, shape analysis techniques can be accurately evaluated, which will be the subject of our future work.

References

1. Arsigny, V., Commowick, O., Ayache, N., Pennec, X.: A fast and log-euclidean polyaffine framework for locally linear registration. JMIV 33, 222 (2009)
2. Buades, A., Coll, B., Morel, J.: Nonlocal image and movie denoising. IJCV 76, 123
3. Cootes, T., Taylor, C., Cooper, D., Graham, J., et al.: Active shape models-their training and application. Computer Vision and Image Understanding 61(1), 38–59 (1995)
4. Cormen, T., Leiserson, C., Rivest, R.: Introduction to algorithms. MIT Press (2001)
5. Dambreville, S., Rathi, Y., Tannenbaum, A.: A framework for image segmentation using shape models and kernel space shape priors. IEEE TPAMI 30, 1385 (2008)
6. Dryden, I., Mardia, K.: Statistical shape analysis. John Wiley & Sons (1998)
7. Duda, R., Hart, P., Stork, D.: Pattern classification (2001)
8. Fenster, A., Chiu, B.: Evaluation of segmentation algorithms for medical imaging. In: IEEE EMBS, p. 7186 (2005)

9. Fletcher, P., Lu, C., Pizer, S., Joshi, S.: Principal geodesic analysis for the study of nonlinear statistics of shape. IEEE Transactions on Medical Imaging 23(8), 995–1005 (2004)

10. Golub, G., Van Loan, C.: Matrix computations. Johns Hopkins Univ. Press (1996)

11. Leventon, M., Grimson, W., Faugeras, O.: Statistical shape influence in geodesic active contours. In: Proceedings of IEEE Conference on Computer Vision and Pattern Recognition, vol. 1, pp. 316–323. IEEE (2000)

12. Murphy, K., van Ginneken, B., Klein, S., Staring, M., de Hoop, B., Viergever, M., Pluim, J.: Semi-automatic construction of reference standards for evaluation of image registration. Medical Image Analysis 15(1), 71 (2011)

13. Roweis, S., Saul, L.: Nonlinear dimensionality reduction by locally linear embedding. Science 290(5500), 2323 (2000)

14. Small, C.G.: The statistical theory of shape. Springer (1996)

Robust Shape Correspondence via Spherical Patch Matching for Atlases of Partial Skull Models

Boris A. Gutman[1,2], Ryan McComb[2], Jay Sung[2], Won Moon[2],
and Paul M. Thompson[1]

[1] UCLA Laboratory of Neuro Imaging
[2] UCLA School of Dentistry

Abstract. Problems of dense partial correspondence for meshes of variable topology are ubiquitous in medical imaging. In particular, this problem arises when constructing average shapes and probabilistic atlases of partial skull models. We exploit the roughly spherical extrinsic geometry of the skull to first approximate skull models with shapes of spherical topology. The skulls are then matched parametrically via a non-local non-linear landmark search using normalized spherical cross-correlation of curvature features. A dense spherical registration algorithm is then applied for a final correspondence. We show that the non-local step is crucial for accurate mappings. We apply the entire pipeline to low SNR skull meshes extracted from conical CT images. Our results show that the approach is robust for creating averages for families of shapes that deviate significantly from local isometry.

Keywords: Shape Registration, Spherical Cross Correlation, Shape Atlas, Patch Matching.

1   Introduction

Registration of topologically variably shapes is an often-encountered problem in medical imaging. Unlike registration of topologically equivalent models, the problem requires additional flexibility and the ability to perform partial matching. A basic solution is the well-known iterative closest point algorithm (ICP) [1]. Applying the EM algorithm to the problem of point correspondence, ICP alternates between rigid alignment and local correspondence search. The major drawback of ICP is the very local nature of its search, and the use of Euclidian distance in the ambient space, which can be a crude approximation to true geodesic distance. A more general solution proposed by Bronstein et al. [2] is to generalize the multidimensional scaling algorithm (MDS) from Euclidian space to a general 2-manifold, replacing the Euclidian metric with geodesic distance. Such a framework naturally leads to full and partial matching between surfaces potentially differing in connectivity. A further improvement upon this framework was proposed in [3], where the geodesic distance is replaced with diffusion distances, while keeping polynomial complexity. Such a metric relies on the average path length between two points, rather than just the shortest, making it much more robust for cases of variable connectivity. The drawback here

J.A. Levine, R.R. Paulsen, Y. Zhang (Eds.): MeshMed 2012, LNCS 7599, pp. 89–100, 2012.
© Springer-Verlag Berlin Heidelberg 2012

lies in the assumption that locally the surfaces are sufficiently isometric, an assumption that cannot always be satisfied by anatomical shape models.

Another traditional alternative is to embed surfaces in a canonical space [4,5], and perform registration in this space. While this eliminates the requirements that the shapes be near-isometries, or that the search be purely local, it requires that we approximate our shapes with shapes of appropriate topology to enable their embedding. Since we are interested in creating a statistical average from a population, we must already assume a particular topology for the atlas, without necessarily knowing a "correct" topology a priori. Thus, a canonical space approach may be most appropriate for our needs.

There are also practical considerations. Our goal is to create a fast pipeline that is immediately useable in the clinic without the need to tune any parameters, and robust enough to handle meshes of any quality, like the four real skull meshes in figure 1. We would like to create a pipeline that is robust with respect to the quality of triangulation and segmentation, and low in complexity. For example, computing the Laplace-Beltrami eigenfunctions required for diffusion distances is highly sensitive to triangulation quality [6], and so may not be suitable for an initial correspondence search. On the other hand, a purely statistical model, the Active Appearance Model (AAM) [7] can be used to establish correspondence without relying on high mesh quality. AAM couples texture and spatial information to create a compact model of appearance. A correspondence search is then driven by maximizing the agreement between the new shape and the learned model. AAM works well when the new example to be registered is sufficiently similar to the training examples, but generally does not handle outliers very well.

For these reasons we choose to go back to a common canonical space – the 2-sphere. Having chosen this space, we must now ensure that our initial correspondence search is not restricted to be local, and is robust with respect to outliers and incomplete matches, as required by our data. A correlation-type search is ideally suited for this purpose: while the localization may be coarse, correlation is guaranteed to find a global optimum in the space of allowable transformations. This is the key idea of our approach.

Briefly, our method consists of the following steps. We first use a straight-forward spherical mapping, similar to the star-map to initialize a partial spherical parameterization of non-genus zero skull models. We then approximate our skull models with shapes of spherical topology with an approach similar to minimal surfaces, based on the spherical heat kernel. Next, the genus-zero shapes are registered parametrically with a novel weighted normalized cross-correlation (WNCC) algorithm. The idea is to use spherical maps of curvature features and a global search to optimize positions of multiple surface patches simultaneously. A dense initial correspondence is found with spherical splines with anchor points defined by patch centers [8]. An existing spherical registration algorithm is then applied for a final dense correspondence.

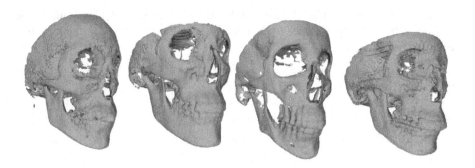

Fig. 1. Four partial skull models

The remainder of the paper is organized as follows. In the second section we describe briefly our initial spherical mapping and spherical shape approximation. In the third, we go through the mathematical preliminaries of weighted normalized cross-correlation on the 2-sphere. The fourth section is devoted to our non-local landmark correspondence search for multiple landmarks. We briefly touch on the approach for dense spherical correspondence. Section 5 presents results on 67 real skull models, and section 6 concludes the paper.

2 Spherical Parameterization

Our spherical parameterization is a slightly generalized star map. It is based on the principal axis of the shape. By principal axis, we mean the line through the center of mass, in the first principal direction of the shape's inertia matrix, parameterized by $\theta \in [0, \pi]$. Given a surface $\mathcal{M}$, we define the axial star map and a corresponding "filler" mask as

$$S_a(\theta, \varphi) = \begin{cases} Star_a(\theta, \varphi), & if\ \exists\ R\ s.\,t.\ \boldsymbol{a}(\theta) + R\boldsymbol{u}_G(\theta, \varphi) \in \mathcal{M} \\ \boldsymbol{a}(\theta) + \overline{r(\theta)}\boldsymbol{u}_G(\theta, \varphi), & otherwise \end{cases} \tag{1}$$

$$M(\theta, \varphi) = \begin{cases} 1, & if\ \exists\ R\ s.\,t.\ \boldsymbol{a}(\theta) + R\boldsymbol{u}_G(\theta, \varphi) \in \mathcal{M} \\ 0, & otherwise \end{cases} \tag{2}$$

Here, $\boldsymbol{a}(\theta)$ is the principal axis, $\boldsymbol{u}_G$ is a unit vector normal to the tangent direction of $\boldsymbol{a}(\theta)$, rotated around the tangent direction by φ. $Star_a(\theta, \varphi) = \boldsymbol{a}(\theta) + r\boldsymbol{u}_G(\theta, \varphi)$, $r = max\{R \in \mathbb{R} \mid \boldsymbol{a}(\theta) + R\boldsymbol{u}_G(\theta, \varphi) \in \mathcal{M}\}$, and $\overline{r(\theta)}$ is the mean radial extension at θ. Though simplistic, this mapping is a robust and fast initialization for our spherical approximations. The principal axis-based star map is well suited for skull models and leads to much smaller metric distortions than the usual centroid-based star map in practice.

To smooth the regions of the spherical shape which do not correspond to real data, we approximate heat kernel smoothing with boundary conditions. This is accomplished by applying successive heat kernels on the sphere. The following pseud-code describes the approximation. We assume that we have a set of N_σ monotonically decreasing radii of the heat kernel $\sigma(i)$, and a given tolerance ε for convergence at all levels of smoothing.

```
Inputs: Nσ, ε, σ(i), spherical map S:𝕊² → ℝ³, binary map
M:𝕊² → {0,1}
i = 0;
WHILE   (i < Nσ)
  Set σ = σ(i);
  j = 0;

  WHILE    (‖Sⱼ − Sⱼ₋₁‖ > ε)
    Compute Sσ = Kσ * Sⱼ₋₁
    Set Sⱼ  by  Sⱼ(p) = { Sσ(p)   if M(p) = 0
                          Sⱼ₋₁(p)    otherwise
    j = j + 1;
  ENDWHILE

  i = i + 1;
ENDWHILE
```

The result is similar to directly approximating minimal surfaces of the filler mask boundary curves. Because S_σ is computed very quickly on the sphere [9], the entire approximation is very fast and robust.

3   Weighted Normalized Cross Correlation on $\mathbb{S}^2$

To initialize a robust correspondence between highly variable noisy shapes, we develop a weighted normalized cross correlation on the sphere for use with multiple informative surface patches. Many of the details in this section are given for completeness – the main goal of this tool is to enable an initialization that is (a) robust, (b) fast, and (c) based only very loosely on statistical learning, to enable reasonable initialization for outlier cases.

We follow the normalized cross-correlation (NCC) algorithm on the 2-sphere presented in [10]. The basic idea is to exploit fast algorithms for Fourier transforms on the spherical domain and the group of rotations $SO(3)$. Briefly, Fourier series on the sphere, or spherical harmonics, form an orthonormal basis for L^2 functions on the sphere $f: \mathbb{S}^2 \to \mathbb{R}$, and can be expressed as

$$Y_l^m(\theta, \phi) = (-1)^m \sqrt{\tfrac{(2l+1)(l-m)!}{4\pi(l+m)!}} P_l^m(\cos\theta)e^{im\phi}, \qquad (3)$$

where P_l^m denotes associated Legendre polynomials. An L^2 function f on the sphere can be expressed in terms of its spherical harmonic coefficients $\widehat{f_{l,m}}$ as

$$f(\omega) = \Sigma_l \Sigma_{|m| \le l} \widehat{f_{l,m}} Y_l^m(\omega), \qquad (4)$$

which can be computed efficiently in $O(B^2 \log^2 B)$ operations [11], where B is the bandwidth of the transform. By analogue, Fourier series on *SO(3)*, also called Wigner D-functions, are expressed by

$$D_{m,n}^l(\alpha, \beta, \gamma) = e^{-im\alpha} d_{m,n}^l(\beta) e^{-in\gamma}, \tag{5}$$

with $d_{m,n}^l(\beta)$ denoting the Wigner *d*-function, and α, β, γ, the Euler angles. For brevity, we use $SO(3) \ni R = R(\alpha, \beta, \gamma)$. An L^2 function C on *SO(3)* can be expressed as

$$C(R) = \sum_l \sum_{|m| \leq l} \sum_{|n| \leq l} \overline{C_{m,n}^l} D_{m,n}^l(R), \tag{6}$$

with coefficients $\overline{C_{m,n}^l}$, as well as the inverse transform computable in $O(B^4)$ operations. For more details on the fast Fourier transform on *SO(3)* (SOFT), we refer the reader to [12].

Suppose that we wish to compute the inner product, or correlation, between a spherical function *I* and a rotated version of another function, or template *T*.

$$C(R) = \int_{\mathbb{S}^2} I(\omega) \Lambda(R) T(\omega) d\omega. \tag{7}$$

Alternatively, this can be expressed in terms of spherical harmonic coefficients as

$$C(R) = \sum_l \sum_{|m| \leq l} \hat{I}_{l,m} \overline{\Lambda(R) T_{l,m}}. \tag{8}$$

Here, $\Lambda(R)$ is the rotation operator on a spherical function. Using the fact that rotating spherical harmonics can be expressed in terms of the Wigner-D's as

$$\Lambda(R) Y_l^m(\omega) = \sum_{|n| \leq l} Y_l^n(\omega) D_{n,m}^l(R), \tag{9}$$

it can be shown with a little algebraic manipulation [12] that the Fourier coefficients of the correlation function satisfy

$$\overline{C_{m,n}^l} = \hat{I}_{l,-m} \overline{\hat{T}_{l,-n}} (-1)^{m-n}. \tag{10}$$

By analogue to fast Euclidian correlation, this is the key idea for a fast NCC on the sphere: all that is needed to compute the full correlation are two spherical Fourier transforms and one inverse SOFT transform. This immediately leads to an $O(B^4)$ spherical cross-correlation algorithm.

Suppose now the support of the template function *T* is not the entire sphere, but a proper subset, or patch $\mathcal{P} \subset \mathbb{S}^2$. In this case (7) would not be sufficient as a true measure of match quality, as it is biased by variability in local intensity. We would instead like to compute the normalized cross correlation

$$NC(R) = \frac{\int_{\mathbb{S}^2} (I(\omega) - \overline{I_{\mathcal{P}}})(\Lambda(R) T(\omega) - \overline{T}) d\omega}{\sqrt{\int_{\mathcal{P}} |I(\omega) - \overline{I_{\mathcal{P}}}|^2 d\omega \int_{\mathcal{P}} |T(\omega) - \overline{T}|^2 d\omega}}. \tag{11}$$

The difficulty, compared to Euclidian NCC, lies in computing the term $\int_{\mathcal{P}} |I(\omega) - \overline{I_{\mathcal{P}}}|^2 d\omega$, as the shape of the window $\mathcal{P}$ changes for every rotation. As suggested in [13] and done in [10], this can be done by computing two additional correlation functions between a binary mask of the support patch $M_{\mathcal{P}}$, and both the image I and its square:

$$\int_{\mathcal{P}} |I(\omega) - \overline{I_{\mathcal{P}}}|^2 d\omega = \int_{\mathbb{S}^2} I^2(\omega)\Lambda(R)M_{\mathcal{P}}(\omega)d\omega - \frac{\left[\int_{\mathbb{S}^2} I(\omega)\Lambda(R)M_{\mathcal{P}}(\omega)d\omega\right]^2}{\int_{\mathbb{S}^2} M_{\mathcal{P}}(\omega)d\omega}. \quad (12)$$

If in addition we wish to weigh our NCC with some weighting function $W: \mathcal{P} \subset \mathbb{S}^2 \to \mathbb{R}$, equation (11) becomes

$$NC(R, W) = \frac{\int_{\mathbb{S}^2} W(\omega)(I(\omega) - \overline{I_{\mathcal{P},W}})(\Lambda(R)T(\omega) - \overline{T_W})d\omega}{\sqrt{\int_{\mathcal{P}} W(\omega)|I(\omega) - \overline{I_{\mathcal{P},W}}|^2 d\omega \int_{\mathcal{P}} W(\omega)|T(\omega) - \overline{T_W}|^2 d\omega}}, \quad (13)$$

where $\overline{I_{\mathcal{P},W}} = \int_{\mathcal{P}} I(\omega)\Lambda(R)W(\omega)d\omega / \int_{\mathbb{S}^2} W(\omega)d\omega$, and $\overline{T_W}$ is defined analogously. Expanding the term $\int_{\mathcal{P}} W(\omega)|I(\omega) - \overline{I_{\mathcal{P},W}}|^2 d\omega$, it is clear that to compute it one simply has to replace $M_{\mathcal{P}}$ in (12) with W:

$$\int_{\mathcal{P}} W(\omega)|I(\omega) - \overline{I_{\mathcal{P},W}}|^2 d\omega = \int_{\mathbb{S}^2} I^2(\omega)\Lambda(R)W(\omega) - \frac{\left[\int_{\mathbb{S}^2} I(\omega)\Lambda(R)W(\omega)\right]^2}{\int_{\mathbb{S}^2} W(\omega)}. \quad (14)$$

With $\overline{T_W}$ and the other term in the denominator of (13) being constant, this makes the number of operations required for a spherical WNCC identical to the usual NCC. While this is a trivial extension of [10], we have not seen it in literature.

4   Non-local Correspondence Search with Multiple Patch Matching

Suppose we have selected multiple corresponding landmarks on several example skull models (figure 2), and wish to find their counterparts on a new skull. A direct approach would be to select a patch of a spherical curvature map around each landmark, and approximate its location with NCC over the new skull map. While this is straightforward, this approach fails in practice for several reasons.

First, a straightforward NCC does not take into account the plausibility of a given patch transformation, given that the two shapes are already rigidly aligned on the sphere. Second, NCC does not consider the relative stability of curvature features at any given point in a patch. And third, the approach does not take into account the relative positions of all other patches that are being matched, which could lead to highly improbable landmark placement. We develop an approach for multiple patch matching that addresses each of these issues in turn.

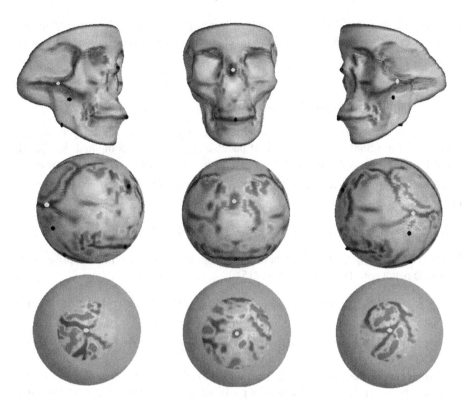

Fig. 2. Spherical Patches. First row: spherical skull model with landmarks marked by black and yellow dots. Second row: Spherical curvature map with corresponding landmarks. Third row: patches around landmarks marked with yellow dots above.

4.1 Single Patch Priors

To deal with the first issue, we modify each individual NCC with two prior terms for spatial congruence:

$$NC_{mod}(R) = NC(R) \left(\frac{a_\gamma - 1}{a_\gamma - \cos \gamma} \right) \left(\frac{a_p - 1}{a_p - \langle p_o, p_R \rangle} \right). \tag{15}$$

Here $a_\gamma, a_p \in (1, \infty)$ are parameter weights, p_o is the original spherical position of the patch, γ has the same meaning as in equation 5, and $p_R = R \circ \eta$ is the North Pole rotated by R. As all patches are moved to the North Pole for correlation, this represents the new position of p_o. The first term penalizes implausible patch orientations, while the second does the same for patch placement relative to the original position of the template. In practice, even this modification alone turns out to be sufficient for correct placement of skull patches in many cases.

To address the issue of spatially variable feature stability in a patch, we apply the weighted version of NCC. The weights in this case should reflect the variability at each patch point, which could be learned from examples. This is the only aspect of our approach that is at all akin to statistical learning: given multiple examples of the same patch, we weigh NC_{mod} with the inverse of the standard deviation of the template function T, i.e. $W(\omega) = \dfrac{1}{\sigma_T(\omega)}$.

4.2 Combining Multiple Patches

Finally, to address the problem of congruence *across* patches, we apply two more prior terms for a final combined score of match quality. Having computed WNCC for several patches T^i, $NC_{mod}^i(R^i, W^i)$, we would like to find the set of optimal patch rotations $\{R_{opt}^i\}_{i=1}^N$ for each of N landmarks. We define this optimal set as the maximal argument of the combined match score:

$$NC_{combined}(\{R^i\}_{i=1}^N) = \prod_i NC_{mod}^i(R^i, W^i) \prod_{j \neq i} C_{orient}(R^i, R^j) C_{dist}(R^i, R^j). \quad (16)$$

The two terms C_{orient}, and C_{dist} serve an analogous purpose to the two prior terms for single patch correlation in equation (15):

$$C_{orient}(R^i, R^j) = \exp\left[-a_{orient} \cos^{-1}\langle v_0^{i,j}, v_{R^i, R^j}^{i,j}\rangle\right], \quad (17)$$

$$C_{dist}(R^i, R^j) = \exp\left[-a_{dist}\left(\cos^{-1}\langle p_0^i, p_0^j\rangle - \cos^{-1}\langle p_{R^i}^i, p_{R^j}^j\rangle\right)^2\right]. \quad (18)$$

The arguments of the inner product in equation (17) represent tangent vectors of the geodesics between the original and new positions of landmarks i and j. The original tangent vector is transported to lie in the tangent space of $p_{R^i}^i$:

$$v_0^{i,j} = \mathcal{T}(p_0^i, p_{R^i}^i) \circ \frac{Proj_{T_{p_0^i}}(p_0^j - p_0^i)}{\left|Proj_{T_{p_0^i}}(p_0^j - p_0^i)\right|}, \quad (19)$$

$$v_{R^i, R^j}^{i,j} = \frac{Proj_{T_{p_{R^i}^i}}(p_{R^j}^j - p_{R^i}^i)}{\left|Proj_{T_{p_{R^i}^i}}(p_{R^j}^j - p_{R^i}^i)\right|}, \quad (20)$$

where by $Proj_{T_p}$ we mean the projection onto the tangent plane of p, and $\mathcal{T}(v, w)$ is the parallel transport operator along the great circle from v to w.

4.3 Search Strategies for Multiple Patch Placement

In order to optimize (16), we must select an appropriate search strategy. It is clear that an exhaustive search over all possible locations for every patch is implausible even for the coarsest tessellation of $SO(3)$ and $\mathbb{S}^2$. This is because an exhaustive search has exponential complexity. Given L possible locations on the sphere, and N patches, such a search requires $O(N^2 L^N)$ operations. A straightforward simplification is to select only the top few peaks from each individual correlation function. While this makes the search possible when there are only a few patches, this strategy also becomes impractical when N exceeds 10-15, depending on L.

A further reduction in complexity can be achieved by adopting a hierarchical search approach similar to fast sorting strategies. Instead of considering all N patches at once, we spatially cluster the patches into groups of K elements, and find the top L sets of locations for each cluster. We repeat this process so that the previous clusters form elements in the new clusters, again selecting only the top L sets of locations. This process is repeated until all patches are incorporated in a final search. The complexity of this strategy is $\mathcal{O}(N^2 L^K log_K N)$. For a reasonable L and K, e.g. L, $K = 6$, this makes the search quick even for relatively large N.

4.4   Dense Surface Correspondence

To initialize a dense correspondence, we extrapolate a spherical warp from landmark displacements using the spherical splines [8]. To achieve a final correspondence, we modify an existing, highly robust framework for unconstrained spherical mapping proposed by Freidel et al. [14], by adding L^2 terms to the cost. Using Freidel's notation, the cost function becomes

$$E = aE_{conformal} + bE_{area} + \sum_{i=1}^{n} w_i \int_{\mathbb{S}^2} \big(f_i(\omega) - g_i(\omega)\big)^2 d\omega, \qquad (21)$$

where f_i, g_i are scalar features of the moving and stationary spherical image. We use mean curvature κ and a smoothed filler mask $K_\sigma * M$. More details on this step may be found in [14] and [15].

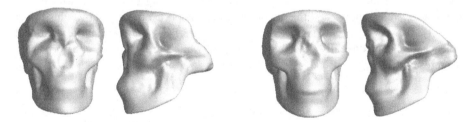

Fig. 3. Two skull averages. Left: local search only. Right: non-local initialization

5   Experiments

We applied our registration framework to 67 skull models of healthy subjects, acquired with a NewTom 3G conical CT scanner. The surface models were extracted from the CT images using Dolphin software. In the non-local step of our pipeline, we experimented with different numbers of landmarks and examples for each patch. A reasonable mapping for our data could be achieved with as few as 8 landmarks and only one example subject. However, for added robustness we use 25 landmarks and 10 subjects. We used circular patches of pre-set radius around each landmark, with the radius varying between $\pi/7$ and $\pi/5$. Landmark origins were set to be the geodesic average of the training landmarks. The average patch for each landmark was computed by warping each example curvature map to the average position. This was done by computing landmark displacement to the average and using spherical splines. The entire training process took less than 1 minute. We used the hierarchical search with $K=5$ elements per cluster and $L=10$ top sets of landmark placements. Using a bandwidth of B=64, our total time for the multiple patch matching stayed between 2 and 3 minutes, running on a Lenovo W520 ThinkPad with an Intel i7 2820QM processor. RAM requirements for 25 landmarks are approximately 500 MB, although using the hierarchical search allows this to be greatly reduced if required.

To assess the need for our non-local initialization step, we compared the proposed method to using only local correspondence of equation (21). We first computed shape averages using both methods, and computed average vertex-wise distance between the average and each shape after Procrustes alignment. A paired t-test revealed that the distance decreases significantly when the non-local step is applied, with $p = 0.026$. The vertex-wise distance decreased by 0.63 mm on average with the use of multiple patch matching. Training subjects were excluded from this comparison. The resulting atlases are shown in figure 3.

In the second part of the comparison, we assessed the compactness of our two atlases with Principal Components Analysis. A model is said to be more compact if a greater proportion of the total variance in the data is captured by a given number of principal components (PC) [16]. We plot the total percent of variance explained versus the number of PC's in figure 4, disregarding the first component as it primarily captures affine misalignment. Note that the curve resulting from the non-local step dominates, which shows that this model is more compact. Figure 5 shows this effect visually. By varying each shape atlas along its first 3 PC's, we see that the non-local atlas captures anatomically plausible variability, while the local-only atlas primarily captures error in registration.

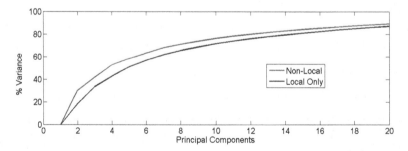

Fig. 4. Model compactness (% of explained variance vs. number of principal components). The non-local model is more compact.

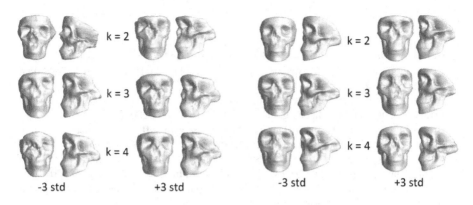

Fig. 5. Shape variation along principal components. Left: local only. Right: Non-local

6   Conclusion

We have presented a robust pipeline for quickly computing shape atlases from in-complete, highly variable, and noisy skull models. The key feature of our pipeline is a non-linear non-local correspondence search, made fast by exploiting analytic proper-ties of the sphere and the rotation group. Our approach is based on very few training data (as low as 1) and few manually labeled landmarks, which makes it more practical than models more rooted in statistical learning, such as the Active Appearance Model. The basic idea is to compute global correlation functions for patches around example landmarks for locating corresponding landmarks on new shapes automatically. We modify an existing fast normalized cross correlation algorithm on the sphere to enable its weighted version. The weighted NCC helps to further improve the robustness of our pipeline.

We have applied our pipeline to 67 human skull models, and showed that an ana-tomically plausible shape atlas is only achieved when the non-local initialization is used in shape registration. Our non-local search leads to statistically significant im-provements in distance to the average shape.

A major drawback of this framework is the admittedly ad-hoc nature of our prior terms for individual and combined match scores (eqns. 15 and 16), and the weight-ing function. A more principled derivation of prior terms may be possible if one assumes a binary spherical feature function. In such a case, the normalized cross-correlation is equivalent to a difference of conditional probabilities, which may enable us to cast this problem in a Bayesian framework, while keeping NCC as the main workhorse of the algorithm. In this case, probabilistic spatial priors could be learned from the training data to use in place of the average case. Another direction for future work would be to replace manual labeling with automatic selection of informative patches.

References

1. Granger, S., Pennec, X.: Multi-scale EM-ICP: A Fast and Robust Approach for Surface Registration. In: Heyden, A., Sparr, G., Nielsen, M., Johansen, P. (eds.) ECCV 2002, Part IV. LNCS, vol. 2353, pp. 418–432. Springer, Heidelberg (2002)
2. Bronstein, A., et al.: Generalized Multidimensional Scaling: A Framework for Isometry-Invariant Partial Surface Matching. PNAS 103(5), 1168–1172 (2006)
3. Bronstein, A., et al.: A Gromov-Hausdorff Framework with Diffusion Geometry for Topologically-Robust Non-Rigid Shape Matching. IJCV 89(2-3), 266–286 (2010)
4. Gu, X., Wang, Y., et al.: Genus Zero Surface Conformal Mapping and its Application to Brain Surface Mapping. IEEE Transactions on Medical Imaging 23(8), 949–958 (2004)
5. Yeo, T., et al.: Spherical Demons: Fast Diffeomorphic Landmark-Free Surface Registration. IEEE TMI 29(3), 650–668 (2010)
6. Reuter, M.: Laplace-Beltrami Spectra as 'Shape-DNA' of Surfaces and Solids. Comput. Aided Des. 38(4), 342–366 (2006)
7. Cootes, T.F., et al.: Active Shape Models—their Training and Application. Comput. Vis. Image Underst. 61(1), 38–59 (1995)
8. Zou, G., Hua, J., Muzik, O.: Non-rigid Surface Registration Using Spherical Thin-Plate Splines. In: Ayache, N., Ourselin, S., Maeder, A. (eds.) MICCAI 2007, Part I. LNCS, vol. 4791, pp. 367–374. Springer, Heidelberg (2007)
9. Chung, M.: Heat Kernel Smoothing on the Unit Sphere. In: ISBI 2006, pp. 992–995 (2006)
10. Huhle, B., et al.: Normalized Cross-Correlation using SOFT. In: LNLA, pp. 82–86 (2009)
11. Healy, D., et al.: FFTs for the 2-Sphere-Improvements and Variations. J. Fourier Anal. App. 9(4), 341–385 (2003)
12. Kostelec, P., et al.: FFTs on the Rotation Group. J. Fourier Anal. App. 14(2), 145–179 (2008)
13. Sorgi, L., Daniilidis, K.: Normalized Cross-Correlation for Spherical Images. In: Pajdla, T., Matas, J. (eds.) ECCV 2004. LNCS, vol. 3022, pp. 542–553. Springer, Heidelberg (2004)
14. Freidel, I., et al.: Unconstrained Spherical Parameterization. J. Graphics, GPU and Game Tools 12(1), 17–26 (2007)
15. Gutman, B., et al.: Shape Matching with Medial Curves and 1D Group-wise Registration. In: ISBI (2012)
16. Davies, R., et al.: A Minimum Description Length Approach to Statistical Shape Modeling. IEEE TMI 21(5), 525–538 (2002)

Feature-Preserving, Multi-material Mesh Generation Using Hierarchical Oracles

Max Kahnt, Heiko Ramm, Hans Lamecker, and Stefan Zachow

Medical Planning Group, Zuse Institute Berlin,
Takustraße 7, D-14195 Berlin-Dahlem, Germany
lastname@zib.de
http://www.zib.de/en/visual/medical-planning.html

Abstract. This paper presents a method for meshing multi-material domains with additional features curves. This requirement arises for instance in situations where smooth objects (e.g. anatomical structures) are combined with technical objects (e.g. implants, surgical screws). Our approach avoids the tedious process of generating a single consistent input surface by means of an implicit representation, called *oracle*. Input features are preserved in the output mesh and termination of the algorithm is proved for certain conditions. We show that our method provides good element quality while at the same time keeping the number of elements in the output mesh low.

1 Introduction

Problems that can be described by partial differential equations (PDEs) are generally solved by finite element (FE) methods. Due to their geometric flexibility, tetrahedral FE meshes (tetmeshes) are well suited to discretise complex shapes. A challenge lies in generating tetmeshes with preferably few elements to keep the complexity of the FE computations low, while accurately approximating a given geometry. Concurrently, the elements must be of good shape in order to ensure stability [14]. Satisfying both criteria at a time is generally not possible, hence a compromise must be found.

In this paper we focus on meshing of multi-material domains that represent a combination of both smooth and non-smooth geometries. Applications comprise the combination of anatomical and mechanical structures like bone/implant compounds, e.g. to predict implant wear [10], or the necessity that feature curves are represented explicitly. In such scenarios, an accurate representation of the material interfaces and the non-smooth regions (sharp edges) is desirable.

Usually, the geometry of anatomical structures is derived via image segmentation as in Zachow et al. [16], while mechanical parts are represented analytically, e.g. as CAD models. In a first step, a boundary representation of the multi-material compound is generated, which is then "stuffed" with tetrahedra. This typically requires an explicit fusion of the objects to be discretised before meshing, for instance using a single voxel- or surface-representation. Inconsistencies resulting from object overlaps are resolved easily within a voxel grid like used

J.A. Levine, R.R. Paulsen, Y. Zhang (Eds.): MeshMed 2012, LNCS 7599, pp. 101–111, 2012.

by Zhang et al. [17]. But the resulting mesh typically suffers from artificially introduced inaccuracies, for instance lost information about sharp edges. Alternatively, a consistent surface triangulation that separates the different objects (called domains) can be computed. Regions where boundary intersections introduce small angles or narrow inter-boundary distances occur exhibit small or badly shaped triangles which are not suited for generating useful FE meshes.

An alternative approach, which does not require an explicit boundary representation, was introduced by Oudot et al. [11] and Pons et al. [12]. This Delaunay-based method requires only the implementation of a so-called "oracle" which returns the following information: (1) the material a point belongs to, (2) one intersection of a line segment with a boundary, if it exists. However, for geometries with non-smooth boundaries (sharp edges), this approach tends to introduce many small elements while still not recovering the feature curves adequately.

Boltcheva et al. [4] address feature curves that occur at the junctions of 3 or more materials in segmented image data. They sample them a-priori according to a user-given density parameter. Avoiding any point insertion too close to these samples, the junctions are preserved throughout the mesh generation process. In their approach, the point density along the feature curves is determined at the beginning of the algorithm which opposes the self-adjusting criteria-driven Delaunay refinement.

Very recently, Dey et al. [6] propose a method that meshes piecewise-smooth complexes approximately defined by multi-label datasets. They provide a method to extract the feature curves. These are incorporated in the mesh generation process as a set of line segments protected by spheres eventually to be refined on encroachment.

The resulting mesh quality of meshes generated by Delaunay refinement schemes can be improved in terms of dihedral angle. Foteinos and Chrisochoides [8] employ a refinement criterion that heuristically removes most slivers. Cheng et al. [5] and Edelsbrunner et al. [7] propose methods to post-process such meshes.

We propose a method to extend the oracle-based approach by Oudot et al. [11] to preserve a user-given set of line segments. We prove that our algorithm terminates while preserving any set of line segments not exhibiting angles below 60°. Our implementation provides a hierarchical oracle that allows for an intuitive setup if simple Boolean operations describe the mutual relations of separate input domains. As each input domain is handled transparently through the oracle, they can be of distinct type, e.g. voxel representation or triangular surface, and an explicit fusion step can be omitted. A study on bone/implant compounds demonstrates that our method simplifies the mesh generation process and provides high quality FE meshes.

2   Preserving 1D Feature Lines

Delaunay triangulations of an ε-sample have been shown to appropriately approximate smooth surfaces, both geometrically and topologically. Boissonnat and

Oudot [3] use these results to construct a surface mesh generator with provable properties. From an initial point set, successive refinements lead towards a reliable surface approximation. They point out that their method is general enough to handle various kinds of input, e.g. analytical implicit surface descriptions, level sets in 3D images, point set surfaces and polyhedra, as long as some simple properties can be fulfilled to build up *an oracle* and provide an appropriate sizing field. Oudot et al. [11] extend the method to the volumetric case. They add higher dimensional refinement rules to the surface meshing method. The resulting algorithm fully contains the surface mesh generation method and consecutively addresses the volumetric cells. Eventually the volumetric algorithm falls back on the surface refinement rules. Finally, Pons et al. [12] propose an approach for oracle-based multi-material volume meshing. A material is assigned to each Delaunay tetrahedron according to the corresponding Voronoi vertex, i.e. the tetrahedron circumcenter. Moreover, they propose parameters to tune element size and shape criteria globally or per material to simplify the application of their algorithm.

Our method extends the set of rules proposed by Oudot et al. [11] to preserve a set of constrained line segments, in the following called segments. The segments are maintained in the conforming sense, i.e. if the algorithm attempts to insert a point that conflicts with a constrained segment, it is split beforehand. Oudot et al. [11] append a meshing layer to the algorithm of Boissonnat and Oudout [3] to tackle the volumetric elements. Analogously, we prepend a meshing layer to the method of Pons et al. [12] that handles the constrained segments. Both, the surface and the volumetric layer of the algorithm are modified to eventually fall back on the constrained segment refinement rules. The geometric and topological guarantees given by a dense sampling of the material interfaces hold for smooth surfaces, see Amenta and Bern [2]. While this does not necessarily conflict with our extension, its application admittedly is most interesting at non-smoothnesses. We provide the application to non-smooth geometries in a similar manner as already is done for the original algorithm: For instance, the non-smoothness of polyhedral input is hidden within the oracle.

2.1 Strategy to Preserve Constrained Segments in the Oracle Method

Let E a set of segments to be preserved with P_E the set of their endpoints. A segment s is called *constrained* if it is a segment to be preserved, i.e. iff $s \in E$. Note that the set E is modified during the course of the algorithm when a segment is split. Point insertions triggered by the necessity to split a constrained segment remove the respective segment $s = (a, b)$ with endpoints a, b and splitting point m from E. As a replacement the subsegments (a, m) and (m, b) resulting from the split are inserted into E. Their preservation, resp. the preservation of their subsegments, recursively guarantees the preservation of s in the conforming sense. We will denote $E_0 = E$ the initial set and E_i the result of the i-th split of a segment.

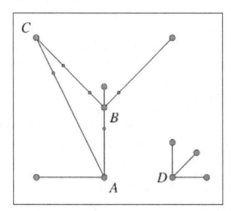

Fig. 1. The type of star vertices. Small points are added later. A, B, C, D are star vertices because they all have at least two adjacent points in the initial set of endpoints. The other points are non-star vertices.

A segment s with endpoints a, b and midpoint m is said to be *encroached* by a point p if $\|p - m\| < \|a - m\|$, i.e. the point is in the open diameter ball of the segment. This is a common notion when dealing with conforming triangulations [13]. This encroachment definition differs from the encroachment notions for tetrahedra and Delaunay facets, because it is triggered also on point insertions not necessarily extinguishing the segment from the Delaunay triangulation. The converse is true though: If there is no point within the diametral sphere, the corresponding segment is a simplex of the Delaunay triangulation.

The vertices $p_i \in P_E$ that are endpoints of at least two constrained segments on initialization, are called *star vertices*. It is a property of the input set of vertices, i.e. no refinement point added has this property and no *star vertex* can lose it during the course of the algorithm, For each *star vertex* $p_i \in P$ let $l_{\min,i}$ the length of its shortest incident constrained segment in E. A constrained segment is called *bad*, if (1) it is incident to a star vertex p_i and has length larger than $\frac{l_{\min,i}}{3}$, (2) it is incident to a star vertex and is longer than some other segment incident to the same star vertex, or (3) if it is encroached by some point.

We chose $\frac{l_{\min,i}}{3}$ heuristically, assuring that the initial splits do not create arbitrarily small subsegments. For an initial constrained segment s that is incident to two star vertices, the medial subsegment resulting from the splits at each of its ends according to (1) is not the shortest subsegment of s. We maintain the notation of Oudot et al. [11] where σ specifies the sizing field, α the angle bound of a facet and B the minimal radius-edge ratio.

2.2   Algorithm Preserving Constrained Segments

The first part of the algorithm aims at recovering the constrained segments in the Delaunay triangulation of the initial point set. To avoid non-terminating

---

Rule set for algorithm preserving constrained segments

T1 If a constrained segment e is bad
  T1.1 if e is incident to a star vertex p_i and has length $> \frac{l_{\min,i}}{3}$, insert the point
    at distance $\frac{l_{\min,i}}{3}$ from p_i on e
  T1.2 else insert the midpoint of e
T2 If a facet f does not have its three vertices on ∂O or has a surface Delaunay ball
  $B(c,r)$ with ratio $\frac{r}{\sigma(c)} > \alpha$, then:
  T2.1 if c is included in a segment diameter ball $B(c',r')$, insert c'
  T2.2 else insert c
T3 If a tetrahedron t with circumcentre c has a circumradius r greater than $\sigma(c)$ or
  radius-edge ratio $\frac{r}{l_{\min}}$ greater than B, then
  T3.1 if c is included in a segment diameter ball $B(c'',r'')$, insert its center c''
  T3.2 else if c is included in a surface Delaunay ball $B(c',r')$ and c' is included in
    a segment diameter ball $B(c'',r'')$, insert c''
  T3.3 else if c is included in a surface Delaunay ball $B(c',r')$ insert c'
  T3.4 else insert c

---

recursive insertions around star vertices, incident segments are trimmed to a uniform length on their first refinement triggering.

Rules T2 and T3 are analogues to the meshing rules proposed by Oudot et al. [11]. They only differ in the fallback strategy eventually refining constrained segments on encroachment. This strategy assures the preservation of the constrained segments since they cannot be encroached by a point actually inserted into the triangulation whenever T1 is fulfilled.

We explicitly prove termination of the algorithm for a decomposed version of the RULE SET T:
The initial conformation step is independent of the actual geometry a mesh is to be generated for. After a finite number of point insertions all constrained segments are guaranteed to not being encroached in the Delaunay triangulation of the successively built point set.

In a second step, we generalise the termination proof of Oudot et al. [11] to our extended method. We follow the common idea of deriving an insertion radius lower bounding the mutual distance of any two points in the resulting mesh. In this context, lower bounds on the applicable parameters are deduced. Our proofs point out the existence of finite values for the minimal facet angle bound α and the minimal radius-edge ratio bound B, depending on the configuration of the constrained segments and the sizing field σ. Our proofs only apply to constrained segment configurations not exhibiting angles below $\frac{\pi}{3}$. There are no general negative proofs on termination though, hence motivating the use of the method also for a more practical choice of parameters.

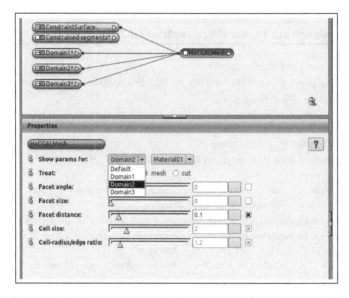

Fig. 2. Mesh generator module in ZIBAmira. Inputs (top): The separate domains represent distinct objects and a mesh is required for their fusion. They are connected sequentially to the mesh generator according their priority at regions of mutual overlap. Additionally a set of constrained segments is connected to the meshing module. In its current implementation, this set is a set of line segments constituting a piecewise linear surface path defined on the *ConstraintSurface* wich does not serve any further purposes; Parameters (bottom): quality criteria can be bounded by constants, defined separately for each material. It is possible to treat a material as a *cut geometry*: all points within this material are handled as points outside of any domain with same or lower priority.

3   Implementation

An implementation of Oudot et al. [11] and Pons et al. [12] is available in CGAL since version 3.5. We integrated CGAL as a module into ZIBAmira-2012.03 [15] (http://amira.zib.de). Our current implementation is based on CGAL 3.7 [1].

3.1   Hierarchical Oracle

An oracle has been implemented that defines the domain to be meshed. It allows to implicitly perform Boolean operations, because the mesh generation algorithm itself does only require the two kinds of query operations introduced by Boissonnat and Oudot [3]. The hierarchical oracle essentially maintains a priority list of input domains, such that point queries are passed to lower priority domains if they are outside all higher prioritized inputs. That way the oracle is a black box that performs the Boolean operations on the input domains without explicitly computing the intersections and implicitly resolving inconsistencies in data type and shape. The data types that can currently be handled are (1) watertight triangular surface meshes with exactly two triangles joining at an edge, (2) labeled uniform voxel grids, and (3) implicit spheres given by their resp. midpoint and radius.

The features that are to be preserved are defined by a connected set of piecewise linear segments. In ZIBAmira these can be defined as surface path sets on triangulated surfaces. If specific points of the domain boundary are known a-priori these can be added to the initial point set in order to speed up the mesh generation process or simply to preserve them. The ZIBAmira module offers a port to connect a geometry containing these points.

4   Experiments

We tested our method in a simulation study concerning the computation of strains occurring in bone/implant compounds. Galloway et al. [9] generated FE meshes for implanted tibiae (see Figure 3). We randomly selected one hundred virtual total knee replacement settings from that study, including geometric representations of the tibia and the tibial component. For each implant, the region where protruding bone has been removed was given and sharp edges were marked as line segments to be preserved. The one hundred datasets were then meshed with our implementation and the method of Pons et al. [12] (available in CGAL 3.7). For both methods the desired quality criteria were determined heuristically and chosen as follows: (1) maximal radius-edge ratio of 1.1 for all materials, (2) maximal circumradius of 1 mm for implant and 3 mm for bone, and (3) maximal facet distance of 0.1 mm to approximate the surfaces for implant and 2 mm for bone material. Despite lacking the theoretical guarantee of termination for this choice of parameters, all models were generated successfully without further tweaking. The results of both approaches were postprocessed by the sliver removal methods available in CGAL 3.7, see [5], [7].

The tetrahedral meshes generated with our implementation met the quality criteria with 437,000 tetrahedra on average (range 295,000 to 707,992). The number of tetrahedra generated with Pons approach was significantly larger with an average number of 900,898 tetrahedra per mesh (range 614,234 to 1,533,011). For the meshes generated by our method, the average minimal dihedral angle was $8.72°(\pm 1.31°)$ after post-processing.

5   Discussion

As shown in the experiments, our method generates fewer elements than the method by Pons et al. with the same quality criteria applied. We attribute this to the fact that for the original method geometric accuracy is achieved by unguided refinement of the mesh in areas where the quality criteria are not met. Our method specifically aims at reconstructing the requested features first due to a more targeted point insertion during the refinement process in those areas (see fig. 5).

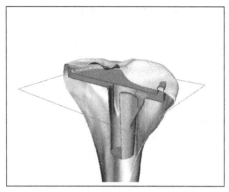

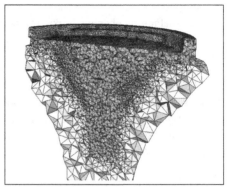

Fig. 3. Tibia implantation scenario. Above the orange rectangle the protruding bone shall be removed. Implant, cutting plane and bone enter the hierarchical oracle.

Fig. 4. Resulting mesh. High geometric accuracy at implant boundary and sharp features. Mesh size grades down where elements are far from the implant-bone material interface.

Termination of the algorithm has not been proven for arbitrary constrained segment configurations. The algorithm terminates if the minimal angle in the set of constrained segments α_0 is greater or equal to $\frac{\pi}{3}$ and parameters α, B have been chosen appropriately. Conversely our algorithm does not terminate if the specified quality parameter α, B directly contradict the preservation of the constrained segments, e.g. $B < \frac{1}{2\sin\alpha_0}$ where α_0 is the minimal angle in E. The termination proof in its current form does not yield lower bounds for α, B in case α_0 is too small.

If the surface is not sampled densely enough, constrained segments might not be present in the resulting mesh. They are guaranteed by our algorithm to be not encroached and hence are represented in the final Delaunay triangulation. But the resulting mesh is the union of all Delaunay cells restricted to the materials and an insufficiently dense surface sampling might cause a lack of surface elements also involving the local segments. This problem is more general and not exclusively related to constrained segments. But their explicit definition offers a way to develop further refinement criteria depending on their actual presence in the resulting mesh (i.e. we call a segment bad if it is not in the resulting mesh, or equivalently, if there is no incident tetrahedron assigned to a material).

A set of constrained segments is not suited to accurately represent smooth feature curves. In practice they are more likely to be approximations of the feature curves. If features are explicitly tagged but are not close enough to the material interface provided through the oracle w.r.t. the desired or self-induced element sizing, then they eventually are not part of the discretised boundary. In such settings the inaccurate constrained segments are inconsistent to the "oracled" surface.

Our approach pushes off the problem of localizing the features as we do not restrict to a certain input type. Moreover feature curves might address distinct properties of the mesh. Among them are sharp edges (where small dihedral

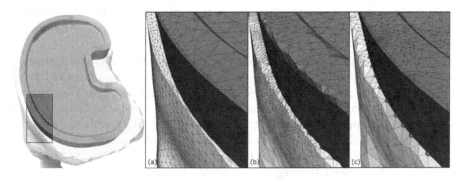

Fig. 5. (a) The advancing-front approach preserves the surface triangulation, which encloses the volumes to fill with tetrahedra. It generates distorted elements in regions where implant and bone surface leave small gaps. (b) The Pons approach inserts many elements in the vicinity of these gaps to accurately recover the geometry of the implant. With the radius-edge ratio specified, that even leads to smaller elements on the bone surface. (c) These problems do not occur with the *guided* point insertion in our method.

angles are ultimately introduced), multi- material interfaces where 3 or more materials meet and multi-material interfaces resulting from the implicit fusion process. Our approach only covers some of these cases as described above.

In the original oracle-based method, non-smoothness is hidden within the oracle e.g. when meshing polyhedral domains. It does not disturb the mesh generator if some quantities can be estimated/faked appropriately. If sharp features are given explicitly, the dihedral angles at these junctions might jeopardise the termination. We did not investigate such effects.

Our proof of termination is not optimal w.r.t. the lower bounds on the parameters α and B. Furthermore post-processing has not been adjusted to respect the constrained segments.

Lastly, the advantages of the preservation of features and the effortless fusion of different domains through the hierarchical oracle can only be used in combination if the features are not a result of the fusion process itself, i.e. they must be known a-priori.

6   Conclusion

In this work we extend the oracle-based meshing approach. It is based on an abstract domain representation and does not require time-consuming preprocessing of the input data. We coupled the ZIBAmira software with an extension of the oracle-based meshing approach. ZIBAmira allows to load, align and visualise the data describing the domains to generate a mesh for. Feature curves can be defined as so-called path sets. The hierarchical oracle currently allows triangle meshes, label images and implicit spheres as input. The overlaps and mutual inconsistencies of the data can be solved without the need to explicitly compute a consistent representation. The hierarchical oracle overrides the tedious and error-prone process deriving a single multi-material surface or comparable. Quality parameters such as element size and shape bounds can be applied material-wise. The resulting mesh will respect the desired criteria and additionally preserve the feature curves as prescribed.

Future work will be directed towards generalizing constraint configurations and finding improved termination bounds. Smooth feature curves shall be incorporated in the meshing approach. It would be nice to have an algorithm extracting the features with the current oracle methods only or with a new oracle assumption as simple as the existing. This would eventually enable to specifically address features that evolve from fusion implicitly. The recent method by Dey et al. [6] seems to be advantageous to our approach but also does not solve this issue that comes up when using our hierarchical oracle.

Acknowledgement. We thank the anonymous referees for their comments that helped improve the presentation of the paper. Heiko Ramm is supported by the EU Project MXL. Hans Lamecker is supported by the DFG-MATHEON Project F2.

References

1. Alliez, P., Rineau, L., Tayeb, S., Tournois, J., Yvinec, M.: 3D mesh generation. In: CGAL User and Reference Manual. CGAL Editorial Board, 3.7 edn. (2010), http://www.cgal.org/Manual/3.7/doc_html/cgal_manual/packages.html#Pkg:Mesh_3
2. Amenta, N., Bern, M.: Surface reconstruction by Voronoi filtering. In: SCG 1998: Proceedings of the Fourteenth Annual Symposium on Computational Geometry, pp. 39–48. ACM, New York (1998)
3. Boissonnat, J., Oudot, S.: Provably good sampling and meshing of surfaces. Graphical Models 67(5), 405–451 (2005)
4. Boltcheva, D., Yvinec, M., Boissonnat, J.-D.: Mesh Generation from 3D Multi-material Images. In: Yang, G.-Z., Hawkes, D., Rueckert, D., Noble, A., Taylor, C. (eds.) MICCAI 2009, Part II. LNCS, vol. 5762, pp. 283–290. Springer, Heidelberg (2009)
5. Cheng, S., Dey, T., Edelsbrunner, H., Facello, M., Teng, S.: Silver exudation. Journal of the ACM (JACM) 47(5), 883–904 (2000)
6. Dey, T., Janoos, F., Levine, J.: Meshing interfaces of multi-label data with delaunay refinement. In: Engineering with Computers, pp. 1–12 (2012)
7. Edelsbrunner, H., Li, X., Miller, G., Stathopoulos, A., Talmor, D., Teng, S., Üngör, A., Walkington, N.: Smoothing and cleaning up slivers. In: Proceedings of the Thirty-second Annual ACM Symposium on Theory of Computing, pp. 273–277. ACM (2000)
8. Foteinos, P., Chrisochoides, N.: High-quality multi-tissue mesh generation for finite element analysis. In: MeshMed, Workshop on Mesh Processing in Medical Image Analysis (MICCAI), pp. 18–28 (September 2011)
9. Galloway, F., Kahnt, M., Seim, H., Nair, P.B., Worsley, P., Taylor, M.: A large scale finite element study of an osseointegrated cementless tibial tray. In: 23th Annual Symposium International Society for Technology in Arthroplasty (2010)
10. Ong, K., Kurtz, S.: The use of modelling to predict implant behaviour. Medical Device Technology 19(5), 64–66 (2008)

11. Oudot, S., Rineau, L., Yvinec, M.: Meshing volumes bounded by smooth surfaces. In: Proceedings of the 14th International Meshing Roundtable, pp. 203–219. Springer (2005)
12. Pons, J.-P., Ségonne, F., Boissonnat, J.-D., Rineau, L., Yvinec, M., Keriven, R.: High-Quality Consistent Meshing of Multi-label Datasets. In: Karssemeijer, N., Lelieveldt, B. (eds.) IPMI 2007. LNCS, vol. 4584, pp. 198–210. Springer, Heidelberg (2007)
13. Shewchuk, J.: Mesh generation for domains with small angles. In: Proceedings of the Sixteenth Annual Symposium on Computational Geometry, pp. 1–10. ACM (2000)
14. Shewchuk, J.: What is a good linear finite element? interpolation, conditioning, anisotropy, and quality measures (preprint). University of California at Berkeley (2002)
15. Stalling, D., Westerhoff, M., Hege, H.-C.: Amira: A highly interactive system for visual data analysis. In: Hansen, C.D., Johnson, C.R. (eds.) The Visualization Handbook, pp. 749–767. Elsevier (2005)
16. Zachow, S., Zilske, M., Hege, H.: 3D reconstruction of individual anatomy from medical image data: Segmentation and geometry processing. In: Proceedings of 25. ANSYS Conference & CADFEM Users' Meeting, Dresden (2007)
17. Zhang, Y., Hughes, T.J.R., Bajaj, C.L.: An automatic 3D mesh generation method for domains with multiple materials. In: Computer Methods in Applied Mechanics and Engineering (2009)

Partition Cortical Surfaces into Supervertices: Method and Application

Gang Li, Jingxin Nie, and Dinggang Shen

Department of Radiology and BRIC, University of North Carolina at Chapel Hill, USA

Abstract. Many problems in computer vision and biomedical image analysis benefit from representing an image as a set of superpixels or supervoxels. Inspired by this, we propose to partition a cortical surface into a collection of small patches, namely supervertices, with quasi-uniform size and coverage, compactness, and also smooth boundaries that align sulcal fundi or gyral crest curves on cortical surfaces. The ultimate goal of supervertices partition of the cortical surfaces is to use supervertices as primitives for cortical surface analysis, such as the extraction of sulcal fundi or gyral crest curves by linking boundaries of supervertices, and also the parcellation of cortical surfaces by labeling supervertices instead of vertices. We formulate the supervertices partition as an energy minimization problem and optimize it with graph cuts. Specifically, our energy function encourages the supervertices with compact shapes and smooth boundaries at flat cortical regions and also the supervertices with boundaries aligned with the sulcal fundi or gyral crest curves at highly bended cortical regions. The method has been successfully applied to cortical surfaces of brain MR images in NAMIC and MSC datasets. Both qualitative and quantitative evaluation results demonstrate its validity. We also show an application, i.e., extraction of gyral crest curves on cortical surfaces by linking boundaries of supervertices.

Keywords: Superpixels, supervertices, cortical surface partition, sulcal fundi, gyral crest curves, graph cuts.

1   Introduction

Superpixels/superpvoxels, which aims to partition images into a collection of small compact and perceptually-meaningful atomic regions with uniform appearance and conforming to local structures [1-8, 22], have been extensively studied and widely used for image segmentation [9-11, 23] and recognition [1, 12, 13] in fields of computer vision and biomedical image analysis, due to their benefits of computational efficiency and long-range spatial support of superpixel primitives over pixel primitives [1]. Inspired by those superpixels/supervoxels in images, we propose to partition cortical surfaces into a set of small patches, namely supervertices, with quasi-uniform size and coverage, compactness, and also smooth boundaries that align sulcal fundi or gyral crest curves, as shown in Fig. 1(d), since many anatomical regions are bounded by sulcal fundi or gyral crest curves on cortical surfaces [14, 20, 21]. Thus, all vertices in a

J.A. Levine, R.R. Paulsen, Y. Zhang (Eds.): MeshMed 2012, LNCS 7599, pp. 112–121, 2012.

supervertex are likely belonging to the same anatomical region. The supervertices partition of cortical surfaces has many potential applications in cortical surface analysis. For example, the extraction of sulcal fundi or gyral crest curves on cortical surfaces, which have been extensively used as landmark constraints for brain warping [15] and for studying the considerable variability of cortical folding across individuals, could be achieved by linking boundaries of supervertices. And also the cortical surface parcellation could be considered as a problem of labeling supervertices, which is more efficient and provides more useful long-range spatial context support over labeling vertices, since the local geometries of different sulci and gyri might be quite similar.

In this paper, we formulate the supervertices partition on cortical surfaces as an energy minimization problem and optimize it using graph cuts. The energy function consists of a data term and a smoothness term. The data term is determined by the curvature-weighted geodesic distance [20] from the uniformly distributed seeds on the cortical surface. And the smoothness term is determined by local geometric information. The energy function encourages the supervertices with compact shapes and smooth boundaries at flat cortical regions and also the supervertices aligned with sulcal fundi or gyral crest curves at highly bended cortical regions. The proposed method has been successfully applied to cortical surfaces of human brain MR images in NAMIC and MSC datasets. Both qualitative and quantitative evaluation results demonstrate its validity. We also show an application of supervertices partition, i.e., extraction of gyral crest curves on cortical surfaces by automatically linking boundaries of supervertices.

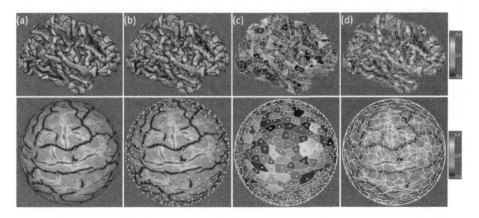

Fig. 1. An illustration of supervertices partition of an inner cortical surface. (a) A cortical surface color-coded by the maximum principal curvature (Note that herein we use the inward normal vector field). (b) The initially placed seed points (white points) of supervertices. (c) The supervertices partition results by our method, including 640 supervertices, represented by different colors. (d) The boundaries (white curves) of supervertices overlaid on the maximum principal curvature map. The top row images show the original cortical surfaces and the corresponding results; while the bottom row images show the cortical surfaces mapped onto spheres and their corresponding results. The color bar of the maximum principal curvature is provided on the right, and the red and blue colors indicate sulci and gyri, respectively. As we can see, the boundaries of supervertices align well with the sulcal fundi or gyral crest curves at highly bended cortical regions.

2   Method

Given a triangulated cortical surface with the correct topology and accurate geometry, in our method, partitioning the cortical surface into supervertices is considered as a labeling problem: assigning a supervertex label to each vertex by taking into account the spatial contextual information. The energy function of supervertices partition of cortical surfaces is formulated as:

$$E = E_d + \lambda E_s \tag{1}$$

where λ is a non-negative weighting parameter, determining the tradeoff between the data term E_d and the smoothness term E_s. λ is set as 0.1 in the paper. The definition of the data and smoothness terms will be detailed in the following sections.

Assuming we aim to partition a cortical surface into L (user-specified number) supervertices, inspired by the methods in [3, 4, 7], where uniformly distributed seeds are placed in images for generating superpixels, we first place L uniformly distributed seeds on the cortical surface, with one seed corresponding to one supervertex label and serving as the initial center of one supervertex. However, since the cortical surface is highly convoluted and folded, it is not easy to place uniformly distributed seeds on the cortical surface directly. Therefore, the cortical surface is first mapped onto a sphere as shown in Fig 1(a) by minimizing the metric distortion between the cortical surface and the spherical representation using FreeSurfer [16], and then the seeds are uniformly placed on its spherical representation; at last, the seeds on the sphere are mapped back to the original cortical surface as shown in Fig 1 (b). To avoid seeds accidentally falling on sulcal fundi or gyral crest curves, the position of each seed is perturbed locally to stay at a relatively flat cortical region. Based on the seeds of supervertices, then we compute the data and smoothness terms and minimize the energy function to achieve the supervertices partition. After that, the seed of each supervertex is repositioned to the geometric center of the supervertex based on the current supervertices partition results, and further perturbed locally. The two steps of supervertices partition and seed repositioning are iteratively performed until the change between two iterations is less than a threshold, or enough number of iterations has been conducted.

2.1   Data Term

The data term represents the sum of the set of data costs on all vertices:

$$E_d = \sum_x D_x(l_x) \tag{2}$$

where $D_x(l_x)$ represents the cost of labeling a vertex x as a possible supervertex label l_x. Given current seed positions of supervertices, one intuitive way to partition a cortical surface into supervertices is to assign the supervertex label to each vertex based on the closest geodesic distance on the cortical surface to the L seeds. However, the boundaries of supervertices obtained by this way might not align sulcal fundi or gyral crest curves at highly bended cortical regions. To deal with this problem, the data term is defined based on the curvature-weighted geodesic distances [20] from seeds. Given a supervertex label, the data term is defined as:

$$D_x(l_x) = 1.0 - e^{-\alpha|g_{l_x}(x)|} \tag{3}$$

where $g_{l_x}(x)$ is the curvature-weighted geodesic distance between the vertex x and the seed corresponding to the supervertices label $l_x \in \{0, ..., L-1\}$. And α is a non-negative parameter and set as 0.2 in the paper. The curvature-weighted geodesic distance is computed by using the fast marching method on the triangular surface mesh [17, 20]. Generally, the fast marching method is a numerical approach for solving Eikonal equation:

$$|\nabla T(x)|F(x) = 1, x \in M \tag{4}$$

which describes the evolution of closed curves on a surface manifold as a function of arrival time $T(x)$ with the marching speed $F(x)$ at a point x on the curve, with the constraint x staying on the surface manifold M. The curvature-weighted geodesic distance from a seed is computed by solving the Eikonal equation on the surface. The marching speed $F(x)$ at a vertex x is defined based on curvatures as:

$$F(x) = e^{-\beta|c(x)|} \tag{5}$$

where $c(x)$ is the maximum principal curvature at vertex x, which is the principal curvature with the larger magnitude in the two principal curvatures at each vertex on the cortical surface, and β is a non-negative parameter and set as 3.0 in the paper. Given a seed, if the geodesic path between the seed and a vertex passes through sulcal bottoms and gyral crests, where the magnitudes of the maximum principal curvatures are large values [20, 21] and the marching speeds are designed as small values, the weighted geodesic distance between the seed and the vertex will be large, thus the cost of labeling the vertex as the current supervertex is large. Otherwise, the weighted geodesic distance will be small, and the cost of labeling the vertex as the current supervertex is small. From each seed, the fast marching is performed to compute curvature-weighted geodesic distance from the seed. To reduce the computational cost, the fast marching is only performed in a local region around each seed, since vertices extremely far away from the current seed are unlikely belonging to the current supervertex and thus set as large distance values accordingly. Each vertex has L curvature-weighed geodesic distances from L seeds placed on the cortical surface. Since our designed energy function encourages the supervertices with smooth boundaries at flat cortical regions and the supervertices with boundaries aligning with sulcal fundi or gyral crest curves at highly bended cortical regions, different initializations using seed points with different distributions will affect the boundaries of supervertices at flat cortical regions but not the boundaries of supervertices around sulcal fundi and gyral crest curves. Considering that different cortical regions are normally bounded by sulcal fundi or gyral crest curves [14, 20, 21], therefore, for our applications, such as sulcal fundi or gyral crest curves extraction and cortical surface labeling, the final results are unlikely very sensitive to the initialization.

2.2   Smoothness Term

The smoothness term, imposing spatial smoothness on supervertices, represents the sum of the cost of labeling a pair of spatial neighboring vertices on a cortical surface:

$$E_s = \sum_{\{x,y\} \in N} V_{x,y}(l_x, l_y) \tag{6}$$

where N indicates the set of neighboring vertex pairs in the cortical surface, and $V_{x,y}(l_x, l_y)$ indicates the cost of labeling a pair of neighboring vertices x and y as l_x and l_y, respectively. Herein, the one-ring neighborhood in the triangular surface mesh is adopted to define neighboring vertex pairs. And $V_{x,y}(l_x, l_y)$ is defined as:

$$V_{x,y}(l_x, l_y) = w(x, y) \cdot (1 - \delta(|l_x - l_y|)) \tag{7}$$

$$w(x, y) = 0.25 \times (1 + \mathbf{n}(x) \cdot \mathbf{n}(y)) \cdot (e^{-|c(x)|} + e^{-|c(y)|}) \tag{8}$$

where $w(x, y)$ represents the spatially adaptive weight between two neighboring vertices, and $\mathbf{n}(\cdot)$ is the normal direction. The central idea behind the above setting is that the two neighboring vertices belonging to the two adjacent yet different cortical regions generally meet at sulcal fundi or gyral crest curves, where the magnitudes of maximum principal curvatures and the angle between their normal directions are large, in contrast to the flat cortical regions. Therefore, the cost of discontinuous labeling of supervertices is set as a small value for a pair of neighboring vertices belonging to two adjacent yet different cortical regions. Thus, at sulcal bottoms or gyral crests, the boundaries of supervertices will align sulcal fundi or gyral crest curves.

2.3   Energy Minimization

The alpha-expansion graph cuts method [18] is adopted to efficiently solve the energy minimization problem. In the method, the cortical surface is represented as an undirected weight graph $\mathbf{G} = (\mathbf{V}, \mathbf{E})$, where $\mathbf{V}$ is the set of nodes, including all vertices on the cortical surface and the terminals represented by L labels corresponding to L supervertices. $\mathbf{E}$ is the collection of edges, consisting of the edges formed by neighboring vertices (called n-links), and edges formed by vertices to terminals (called t-links). In the constructed graph, D_x describes the edge weight of t-links, and $V_{x,y}$ describes weights of n-links. A cut is a set of edges by removing which the linked nodes are divided as disjoint sets, and meanwhile each node connects to only one terminal corresponding to its supervertex label. The cost of a cut is the sum of the weights on the edge set. The graph cuts can guarantee a strong local minimum for certain multiple-label energy functions [18].

3   Results

To validate the proposed supervertices partition method on cortical surfaces, we applied the method to two MRI datasets: the NAMIC dataset [19] which includes 39 subjects with manually labeled gyral based regions on cortical surfaces by experts [14], and the MSC dataset [15] which include 12 healthy subjects with manually traced sulcal curves on cortical surfaces by experts. All cortical surfaces are generated by FreeSurfer software [16], and each hemisphere contains around 130000 vertices.

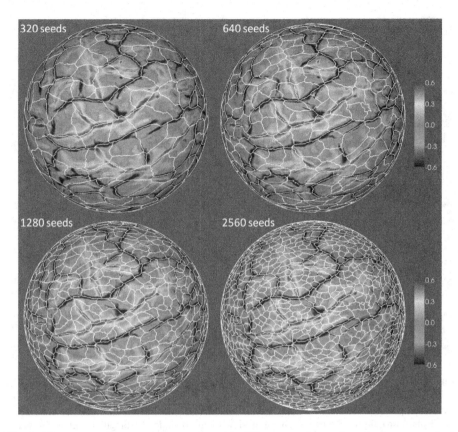

Fig. 2. The supervertices partition results with different numbers of seeds L on a cortical surface. All results are mapped onto spheres for better inspection. The white curves represent boundaries of supervertices. The color bar of the maximum principal curvature is provided on the right, with red colors indicating sulci and blue colors indicating gyri.

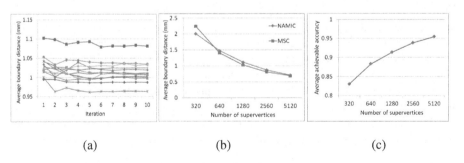

        (a)   (b)   (c)

Fig. 3. The performance of supervertices partition on NAMIC and MSC datasets. (a) The change of average boundary distance with respect to the iteration numbers, on 12 subjects with 1280 supervertices in MSC dataset. One curve indicates a subject. (b) Average boundary distance. (c) Achievable segmentation accuracy on NAMIC dataset.

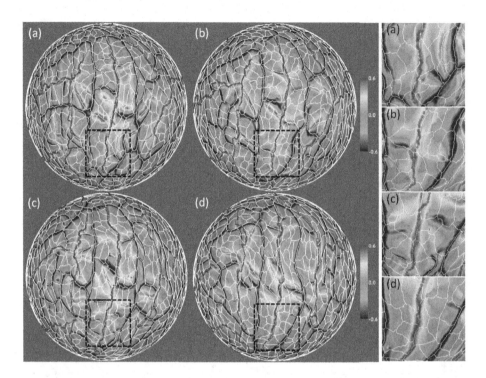

Fig. 4. The boundaries of supervertices (white curves) by 1280 seeds and the manually delineated sulcal fundi curves (purple curves) on 4 subjects in MSC dataset, overlaid on the maximum principal curvature maps. Red colors indicate sulci, and blue colors indicate gyri. The rightmost column shows the zooming view of the bounded rectangular regions by black colors in the left column.

Fig. 1 shows an illustration of supervertices partition on an inner cortical surface with 640 seeds. As we can see, the boundaries of supervertices align well with sulcal fundi or gyral crest curves at highly bended cortical regions. Fig. 2 shows the supervertices partition results with different number of seeds on a cortical surface. All results are mapped onto spheres for better inspection. To quantitatively evaluate how well the boundaries of supervertices align with sulcal fundi or gyral crest curves, we adopt two measurements: average distance measurement and achievable segmentation accuracy, as widely used in validation of superpixels. Denote the parcellated regions in the ground truth as $T = \{T_1, T_2, ..., T_n\}$ and supervertices partition as $= \{P_1, P_2, ..., P_L\}$ on a cortical surface. And also denote $A(\cdot)$ as the area of a region. The average distance measurement is defined as:

$$\frac{1}{|\delta T|} \Sigma_{\mathbf{x} \in \delta T} \min_{\mathbf{y} \in \delta P} \|\mathbf{x} - \mathbf{y}\| \tag{9}$$

where δT and δP represent the union sets of ground truth boundaries/curves and supervertices boundaries, respectively. And $|\delta T|$ indicates the size of δT. To compute the achievable segmentation accuracy, which measures the highest achievable accuracy of cortical surface parcellation by using supervertices as units, we label each supervertex with the label of ground truth parcellation that has the largest overlap. The achievable segmentation accuracy is defined as:

$$\frac{\sum_j max_i A(P_j \cap T_i)}{\sum_i A(T_i)} \tag{10}$$

Fig. 3(a) shows the average distance along with iterations on left hemispheres of MSC dataset with 1280 supervertices. As we can see, the iterations generally converge in 5 or 6 iterations. Fig. 3(b) and (c) shows the two measurements on left hemispheres of NAMIC and MSC datasets. Since the ground truth of cortical surface parcellation is not available in MSC dataset, only average distance measurements are computed in this dataset. Larger number of supervertices generally produces more accurate results. However, since the average edge length in cortical surfaces generated by FreeSurfer is around 1mm, supervertices with 1280 seeds, which achieve 1mm distance measurement and 92% segmentation accuracy, might be accurate enough for our potential applications. Fig. 4 shows the boundaries of supervertices by 1280 seeds and the manually delineated sulcal curves (purple curves) on 4 randomly selected subjects in MSC dataset. As we can see, the boundaries of supervertices align well with sulcal fundi curves, suggesting that sulcal fundi curves could be extracted by linking boundaries of supervertices.

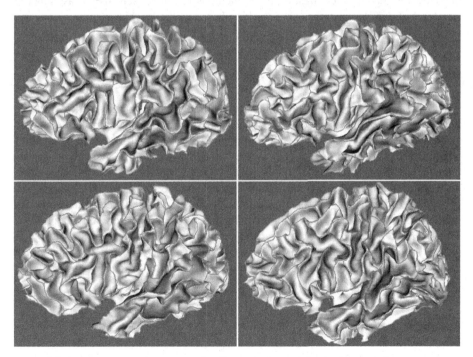

Fig. 5. The extracted gyral crest curves (orange curves) by automatically linking boundaries of supervertices on cortical surfaces of 4 subjects in MSC dataset.

4   Application

To demonstrate the potential application of supervertices partition for cortical surface analysis, we show that the extraction of gyral crest curves on cortical surfaces can be achieved by linking boundaries of supervertices. Herein, we adopt the supervertices partition with 1280 seeds. All boundaries of supervertices with the average maximum principal curvature being smaller than a low threshold such as -0.3 are labeled as strict segments of gyral crest curves, and all boundaries with the average maximum principal curvature being smaller than a high threshold such as -0.2 are labeled as candidate segments. From a strict segment, the curve linking is performed by adding the adjacent strict or candidate segments with the minimum transition angle between the two segments. Fig. 5 shows the extracted gyral crest curves (orange curves) on 4 inner cortical surfaces of left hemispheres from MSC dataset. As we can see, the extracted gyral crest curves on cortical surfaces are quite visually reasonable. The advantage of our method is that: a clear energy function based on curvature information is formulated to force boundaries of supervertices to align with the sulcal fundi or gyral crest curves at highly bended cortical regions, thus the extracted gyral crest curves by linking boundaries of supervertices are relatively accurate and robust, in contrast to many skeletonization-based methods which are sensitive to asymmetric structures of gyri and also the curve-tracking-based methods which require computing sensitive high-order curvature information.

5   Conclusion

This paper presents an energy minimization method for partitioning cortical surfaces into supervertices. The method encourages supervertices with compact shapes and smooth boundaries at flat cortical regions and also supervertices with boundaries aligning sulcal fundi or gyral crest curves at highly bended cortical regions. The method has been successfully applied to cortical surfaces of NAMIC and MSC datasets. In the future, we will quantitatively compare our extracted gyral crest curves by linking boundaries of supervertices with those by other methods and also investigate more potential applications of supervertices partition on cortical surfaces. Moreover, we will also study supervertices partition by using other cortical attributes, such as structural connectivity information derived from diffusion MRI and functional connectivity information derived from functional MRI, instead of using only the geometric information as used in this paper.

References

1. Ren, X., Malik, J.: Learning a classification model for segmentation. In: ICCV, pp. 10–17 (2003)
2. Moore, A.P., et al.: Superpixel lattices. In: CVPR, pp. 1–8 (2008)
3. Levinshtein, A., et al.: TurboPixels: Fast superpixels using geometric flows. IEEE Trans. PAMI 31, 2290–2297 (2009)

4. Veksler, O., Boykov, Y., Mehrani, P.: Superpixels and Supervoxels in an Energy Optimization Framework. In: Daniilidis, K., Maragos, P., Paragios, N. (eds.) ECCV 2010, Part V. LNCS, vol. 6315, pp. 211–224. Springer, Heidelberg (2010)
5. Liu, M., et al.: Entropy rate superpixel segmentation. In: CVPR, pp. 2097–2104 (2011)
6. Zhang, Y., et al.: Superpixels via pseudo-Boolean optimization. In: ICCV, pp. 1387–1394 (2011)
7. Zeng, G., et al.: Structure-sensitive superpixels via geodesic distance. In: ICCV, pp. 447–454 (2011)
8. Wang, J., Wang, X.: VCells: Simple and efficient superpixels using edge-weighted centroidal Voronoi tessellations. IEEE Trans. PAMI 34, 1241–1247 (2012)
9. Vazquez-Reina, A., Avidan, S., Pfister, H., Miller, E.: Multiple Hypothesis Video Segmentation from Superpixel Flows. In: Daniilidis, K., Maragos, P., Paragios, N. (eds.) ECCV 2010, Part V. LNCS, vol. 6315, pp. 268–281. Springer, Heidelberg (2010)
10. Andres, B., et al.: 3D segmentation of SBFSEM images of neuropil by a graphical model over supervoxel boundaries. Med. Image Anal. 16, 796–805 (2012)
11. Lucchi, A., et al.: Supervoxel-based segmentation of mitochondria in EM image stacks with learned shape features. IEEE Trans. Med. Imaging 31, 474–486 (2012)
12. Fulkerson, B., et al.: Class segmentation and object localization with superpixel neighborhoods. In: ICCV, pp. 670–677 (2009)
13. Tighe, J., Lazebnik, S.: SuperParsing: Scalable Nonparametric Image Parsing with Superpixels. In: Daniilidis, K., Maragos, P., Paragios, N. (eds.) ECCV 2010, Part V. LNCS, vol. 6315, pp. 352–365. Springer, Heidelberg (2010)
14. Desikan, R.S., et al.: An automated labeling system for subdividing the human cerebral cortex on MRI scans into gyral based regions of interest. Neuroimage 31, 968–980 (2006)
15. Pantazis, D., et al.: Comparison of landmark-based and automatic methods for cortical surface registration. Neuroimage 49, 2479–2493 (2010)
16. http://surfer.nmr.mgh.harvard.edu/
17. Kimmel, R., Sethian, J.A.: Computing geodesic paths on manifolds. PNAS 95, 8431–8435 (1998)
18. Boykov, Y., et al.: Fast approximate energy minimization via graph cuts. IEEE Trans. PAMI 21, 1222–1239 (2001)
19. http://www.insight-journal.org/midas/item/view/2467
20. Li, G., et al.: An automated pipeline for cortical sulcal fundi extraction. Med. Image Anal. 14, 343–359 (2010)
21. Li, G., et al.: Automatic cortical sulcal parcellation based on surface principal direction flow field tracking. Neuroimage 46, 923–937 (2009)
22. Achanta, R., et al.: SLIC superpixels compared to state-of-the-art superpixel methods. IEEE Trans. PAMI (in press)
23. Levinshtein, A., et al.: Optimal image and video closure by superpixel grouping. IJCV 100, 99–119 (2012)

Automatic Boundary Evolution Tracking via a Combined Level Set Method and Mesh Warping Technique: Application to Hydrocephalus*

Jeonghyung Park[1], Suzanne M. Shontz[2], and Corina S. Drapaca[1]

[1] The Pennsylvania State University, University Park, PA 16802, USA
[2] Mississippi State University, Mississippi State, MS 39762, USA
jxp975@cse.psu.edu, sshontz@math.msstate.edu, csd12@psu.edu

Abstract. Hydrocephalus is a neurological disease which causes ventricular dilation due to abnormalities in the cerebrospinal fluid (CSF) circulation. Although treatment via a CSF shunt in the brain ventricles has been performed, poor rates of patient responses continue. Thus, to aid surgeons in hydrocephalus treatment planning, we propose a geometric computational approach for tracking hydrocephalus ventricular boundary evolution via the level set method and a mesh warping technique. In our previous work [1], we evolved the ventricular boundary in 2D CT images which required a backtracking line search for obtaining valid intermediate meshes. In this paper, we automatically detect the ventricular boundary evolution for 2D CT images. To help surgeons determine where to implant the shunt, we also compute the brain ventricle volume evolution for 3D MR images using our approach.

1 Introduction

Hydrocephalus is a neurological disease characterized by abnormalities in the cerebrospinal fluid (CSF) circulation, resulting in ventricular dilation. The CSF is formed within the cerebral ventricles by the choroid plexuses and the brain parenchyma, circulates through the ventricles and within the subarachnoid space surrounding the brain, and drains into the venous blood by passing through the arachnoid villi located in the dura matter [18]. Currently, it is believed that hydrocephalus may be caused by increased CSF production, by obstruction of CSF circulation or of the venous outflow system, or due to genetic factors. The efforts in treatment have been principally through CSF flow diversion. Within limits, the dilation of the ventricles can be reversed by either CSF shunt implantation or by performing an endoscopic third ventriculostomy (ETV) surgery, resulting in a relief from the symptoms of hydrocephalus. However, despite the technical advances in shunt technology and endoscopy, the two treatments show no statistically significant difference in the efficacy for treating hydrocephalus

---

* The work of the first author was funded by NSF CAREER Award OCI-1054459; the work of the second author was funded in part by NSF CAREER Award OCI-1054459 and NSF grant CNS-0720749.

J.A. Levine, R.R. Paulsen, Y. Zhang (Eds.): MeshMed 2012, LNCS 7599, pp. 122–133, 2012.
© Springer-Verlag Berlin Heidelberg 2012

[24]. ETV performs well only in some clinical cases of hydrocephalus [13], whereas shunt failure happens in over 60% of patients [16]. There is therefore an urgent need to design better therapy protocols for hydrocephalus.

An important step in this direction is the development of predictive theoretical and computational models of the mechanics of hydrocephalus. The Monro-Kellie hypothesis [17,20] reduces the dynamics of the cranium to a competition for space among CSF, blood, and brain parenchyma. This idea leads to numerous pressure-volume models [22] (and references within) where the CSF is contained within one compartment surrounded by compliant walls representing the brain parenchyma. However, these models provide little insight towards a more fundamental understanding of the mechanisms of hydrocephalus. In [15], Hakim proposed to model the brain parenchyma as a porous sponge of viscoelastic material. Nagashima [21] extended this model by applying Biot's theory of consolidation and carried out finite element simulations of the resulting mathematical model. This introduced one of the two current models of brain biomechanics, namely the poroelastic model [23,25], in which the brain is a porous linearly elastic sponge saturated in a viscous incompressible fluid. The second modeling approach considers the brain parenchyma to be a linear viscoelastic material [19,26]. Unlike the linear viscoelastic and poroelastic models which are based on the assumption of small strain theory, the quasi-linear viscoelastic model proposed in [14] was the first to successfully predict the large ventricular displacements in hydrocephalus. Most of the above-mentioned mechanical models, however, use either a cylindrical or a spherical geometry for the brain.

In order for mechanical models of brain to be of clinical relevance their corresponding computational algorithms and software must incorporate the structural geometry of the brain as seen in medical images as well as efficient and robust numerical solvers. In our recent work [1,12], we used nonlinear constitutive laws and two-dimensional medical images of brains to simulate the response of hydrocephalic brains to treatments. In this paper, we generalize the results from [1] and propose an automatic computational pipeline for the evolution of the brain ventricles that involves the following steps: image denoising, threshold-based image segmentation, prediction of the ventricular boundaries via the level set method, generation of computational meshes of the brain, mesh deformation based using the finite element-based mesh warping (FEMWARP) method, and mesh quality improvement of the deformed meshes. We will present three-dimensional changes in the geometry of the lateral ventricles of a normal brain during simulated development of hydrocephalus, in the particular case when hydrocephalus is due to the occlusion of the interventricular foramina. The interventricular foramina (or foramina of Monro) are channels that connect the lateral ventricles with the third ventricle of the brain, and allow the CSF produced in the lateral ventricles to flow into the third ventricle and then to the rest of the brain.

2   Computational Techniques for Motion of Geometric Models and Meshes in Biomedical Simulations

Level-set methods (LSM) (e.g., [9,27,28,29,30]) are computational techniques for tracking evolving curves or surfaces and have been used extensively in medical imaging and in other fields. The level set approach delineates region boundaries using closed parametric curves (or surfaces, etc.) that deform according to motion prescribed by a partial differential equation (PDE). The problem of how to move the curves is formulated as a front evolution problem. The final contour position is influenced by the speed of the deformation, which may be controlled by local curvature of the contour, the intensity gradient in an image, shape, the initial position of the contour [9], and the intrinsic physics of the problem. One important advantage of LSM is that deforming shapes undergoing topological changes can easily be tracked. This makes the LSM ideal for tracking the evolution of hydrocephalic brain ventricles.

Persson *et al.* developed a moving mesh technique [31,32] for image-based problems which is based on the incorporation of level sets into an adaptive mesh refinement technique which uses a Cartesian or octree background mesh to determine the mesh motion. Alternatively, mesh warping algorithms compute the mesh deformation from the source domain to the target domain based upon interpolation and/or extrapolation of the vertex coordinates. Several mesh warping techniques for biomedical applications have been developed (e.g., [33,34,35,36]). However, none of these techniques were designed to handle the large deformations the ventricles undergo due to hydrocephalus.

3   Introduction to the Level Set Method and FEMWARP

In this section, we describe the particular level set and mesh warping methods we employ in our geometric computational pipeline.

3.1   The Chan and Vese Level Set Method for Curve Evolution

The Chan and Vese method [37] evolves level set curves using minimization of an energy functional of Mumford-Shah type.

Let u_0 denote a given image with domain Ω and C denote a parametrized curve. Let ϕ be a Lipschitz function which implicitly represents C. The zero-level curve of the function at time t of the function $\phi(t, x, y)$ is used to evolve C based on a prescribed speed and direction.

Let c_1 and c_2 be constants depending on C which are the averages of u_0 inside and outside of C, respectively, and let $F(c_1, c_2, \phi)$ denote the energy functional to be minimized by computing the Euler-Lagrange equations and then solving the resulting PDE. Let $\mu \geq 0, \nu \geq 0, \lambda_1$, and λ_2 be fixed parameters, and let $H_\epsilon, \delta_\epsilon$ be regularized Heaviside functions and one-dimensional Dirac measures, respectively. The curve evolution is obtained by minimizing the following regularized energy functional:

$$F_\epsilon(c_1, c_2, \phi) = \mu \int_\Omega \delta_\epsilon(\phi(x,y))|\nabla\phi(x,y)| \ dx \ dy$$
$$+\nu \int_\Omega H_\epsilon(\phi(x,y)) \ dx \ dy$$
$$+\lambda_1 \int_\Omega |u_0(x,y) - c_1|^2 \ H_\epsilon(\phi(x,y)) \ dx \ dy \tag{1}$$
$$+\lambda_2 \int_\Omega |u_0(x,y) - c_2|^2 \ (1 - H_\epsilon(\phi(x,y))) \ dx \ dy.$$

The Chan and Vese technique is also known as the active contours without edges method, since the stopping criteria does not depend on the gradient of the image but rather on a particular segmentation of the image in which the given image is approximated by a piecewise constant function. We solve the energy minimization problem for (1) using the Matlab implementation by Wu in [40].

3.2 The Shontz and Vavasis Finite Element-Based Mesh Warping (FEMWARP) Algorithm

FEMWARP is a topology-preserving, tetrahedral mesh warping approach which was proposed by Baker [38] and was developed by Shontz and Vavasis [39].

First, FEMWARP represents each interior vertex in the mesh as a specific linear combination of its neighbors by computing the global stiffness matrix A for the boundary value problem $\triangle u = 0$ on Ω with $u = u_0$ on $\partial\Omega$ is formed, where Ω is the mesh domain, and A is computed based on piecewise linear finite elements on the mesh. Because only A is kept, any u_0 may be prescribed.

Let x be a vector containing the x-coordinates of the initial mesh vertices (and similarly for the y and z coordinates). It follows that

$$A_I[x_I, y_I, z_I] = -A_B[x_B, y_B, z_B], \tag{2}$$

where A_I and A_B are the submatrices of A with the rows indexed by interior vertices and the columns indexed by interior and boundary vertices, respectively.

Second, FEMWARP solves the above linear system, i.e., (2) with a new right-hand side vector based on the new boundary vertex positions (i.e., $[\hat{x}_B, \hat{y}_B, \hat{z}_B]$) (established by the level set method in our case) for the new coordinates of the interior vertices of the deformed mesh. In particular, we solve (3)

$$A_I[\hat{x}_I, \hat{y}_I, \hat{z}_I] = -A_B[\hat{x}_B, \hat{y}_B, \hat{z}_B] \tag{3}$$

for $[\hat{x}_I, \hat{y}_I, \hat{z}_I]$.

4 Ventricular Boundary Deformation with the Level Set Method and FEMWARP for Hydrocephalus Treatment

To track the evolution of the brain ventricles during treatment of hydrocephalus, we propose a combined level set/mesh warping algorithm. Our approach is designed as a computational pipeline and includes the following steps: image denoising, image segmentation, obtaining boundary vertices via the LSM, mesh

---

Algorithm 1. Mesh warping with the level set method

1: **Input:** medical images with source and target ventricular boundaries
2: Image denoising using mask filters
3: Image segmentation via thresholding method
4: Obtain ventricular boundary vertices from segmented source and target med-
    ical images via level set method
5: Generate initial mesh with A using Triangle
6: **LOOP 1**: Deform mesh from source to target using FEMWARP
7: **if** mesh is valid **then**
8:    Mesh quality improvement on the deformed mesh
9:    return mesh
10: **else**
11:    Backtracking line search with small-step FEMWARP until mesh is valid
12: **end if**
13: Go to **LOOP 1**

---

generation, LSM and mesh warping, and mesh quality improvement. Pseudocode for our combined level set/mesh warping algorithm is given in Algorithm 1. More details for each step of the algorithm are given in [1].

We performed two simulations based on our combined level set/mesh warping algorithm shown in Algorithm 1. The first simulation was ventricular boundary deformation for 2D CT images via the LSM. Unlike our previous study [1], the evolution of the ventricular boundary was automatically detected via the LSM in the first simulation. The second simulation was the ventricular boundary evolution of 3D brain images. The motion of the 3D brain ventricles was simulated based on the LSM with a constant speed movement. The Solaris machine employed for the simulations was an UltraSPARC-III CPU with a 750MHz processor, 1GB SDRAM of memory, and an 8MB L2 cache.

4.1   Simulation 1: Automatic Boundary Detection via Level Set Method

Three CT images [2], i.e., pre-treatment, period 1 (6 months later), and period 2 (1 year later) of hydrocephalus treatment via shunt insertion, are used as inputs for this simulation. In our previous study, the LSM was applied only to obtain the ventricular boundary vertices in the segmented images. The intermediate boundary deformation from pre-treatment to period 1 and from period 1 to period 2 was determined by using a backtracking line search.

In this simulation, however, the intermediate boundary vertices were obtained by applying the LSM instead of using a backtracking line search. When detecting the boundary vertices in an image, the LSM sets up an initial boundary contour starting as a zero curve. This initial contour moves toward the ventricular boundary in the image based on the movement computed by the LSM.

In each iteration, the LSM moves the initial contour toward the next target boundary. The contours of each iteration represent the deformation of the brain ventricles. Thus, by tracking the boundary movement via the LSM, the intermediate boundary vertices for the deformation are obtained. Since the variation of the boundary movement between intermediate steps is very small, the automatic intermediate boundary detection steps generate valid meshes and use of a backtracking line search is not required.

Image denoising was performed as the first step of the simulation. For the pre-treatment, period 1 and period 2 CT images, 3×3, 6×6, and 4×4 mask filters were applied [8]. When segmenting the denoised images, threshold-based segmentation method was performed [7] with threshold values of 20, 77, and 45 for the pre-treatment, period 1, and period 2 images. After segmentation, the ventricles in the segmented images were represented as zero-valued pixels, and the remaining parts were represented as one-valued pixels.

From the segmented pre-treatment image, the LSM was applied to obtain the boundary vertices of the ventricles in the image. The contour for the zero function obtained by the LSM matched the boundary of the ventricles in the segmented pre-treatment image. The ventricular boundary obtained from the segmented pre-treatment image was used as an initial contour of the LSM for boundary detection of the segmented period 1 image. For each ventricular boundary vertex, the next vertex is selected from the boundary vertices a fixed Euclidean distance from the given vertex. The coordinates of the boundary vertices are computed and ordered by repeating this process. The LSM moved the contour in the inward normal direction with a constant speed of $13.2e^{-12}$ to detect the boundary of the ventricles in the segmented period 1 image. Since the movement was slow, all intermediate steps computed by the LSM generated valid meshes. The level set method evolved until the average of the absolute distance between the previous and the current contour vertices was smaller than 10^{-9}.

Similar to the process of obtaining the boundary of the ventricles in the segmented period 1 image, the ventricular boundary of the segmented period 2 image was obtained. The ventricular boundary of the segmented period 1 image was used as an initial contour of the LSM to obtain the ventricular boundary of the segmented period 2 image.

An initial mesh for the segmented pre-treatment image was generated using Triangle [3]. By using the boundary vertices obtained automatically from the LSM, mesh deformation for the ventricles was performed. Mesh deformation with intermediate steps from pre-treatment to period 1, and from period 1 to period 2 was performed by FEMWARP algorithm [39].

Figure 1 shows initial, intermediate, and final meshes generated during ventricular mesh deformation via the LSM with automatic intermediate boundary detection. The boundary deformation in the figure was obtained in reverse (i.e., from the period 2 segmented image to the pre-treatment image). Since the LSM detects expanding boundaries better than shrinking ones, the intermediate boundaries were easily obtained and valid meshes were generated without the use of a backtracking line search. After each intermediate mesh deformation step, average mesh quality improvement was performed by feasible Newton

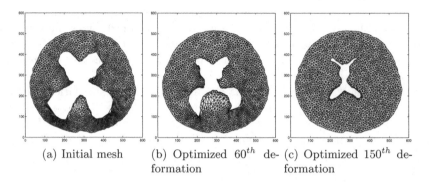

(a) Initial mesh   (b) Optimized 60th de-   (c) Optimized 150th de-
                     formation   formation

Fig. 1. (a) The mesh having the ventricular boundary vertices matched to pre-treatment ventricular boundary vertices. The mesh contained 2187 vertices and 4026 elements. ((b) and (c)) the deformed meshes generated by the FEMWARP algorithm [39]. The 60th and 150th intermediate mesh deformation results matched exactly to the boundary vertices for the ventricles in the segmented period 1 and period 2 images. Mesh quality improvement was performed to improve the mesh quality at each step of the hydrocephalus ventricular deformation.

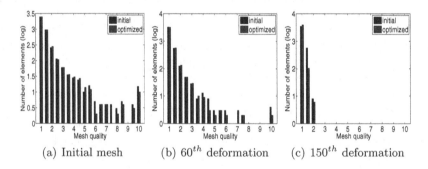

(a) Initial mesh   (b) 60th deformation   (c) 150th deformation

Fig. 2. Inverse mean ratio mesh quality distribution for meshes generated in Simulation 1. Quality distribution for (a) the initial mesh, (b) the 60th deformation, and (c) the 150th deformation.

method [5] in Mesquite [4]. The inverse mean ratio [5] mesh quality distribution for the intermediate meshes are shown in Figure 2.

4.2   Simulation 2: 3D Ventricular Mesh Deformation via Level Set Method and FEMWARP

We obtained a 3D MR image of the normal brain containing 181 2D brain MRI slices from [6]. The goal of this experiment was to simulate 3D ventricular deformation from the normal to hydrocephalic state. In this simulation, the intermediate boundaries were computed by expanding the volume of the normal brain ventricles using LSM [9], as no target image is available in this dataset. The boundary of the expanded ventricles was used as an intermediate boundary of ventricular deformation. If a target MR image were available, our approach could also be used to simulate hydrocephalus treatment.

In order to obtain the brain ventricle volume, the 3D brain is created by segmenting the 3D MRI. First, all 181 2D MR images were denoised using a 3×3 mask filter [8]. After image denosing was performed, the images were segmented based on threshold value of 50 [7]. In each segmented image, the white parts represent the brain tissue, and the black parts represent the brain ventricles, which will be deformed via the LSM. The segmented 2D images were stacked on top of each other to create a segmented 3D MRI [10]. By extracting the portion of the image represented as voxels with a value of zero in the reconstructed 3D MR image, the brain ventricle volume was obtained and is shown in Figure 3(a).

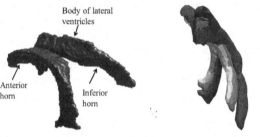

(a) Brain ventricle volume (b) Brain ventricle volume
evolution

Fig. 3. (a) The brain ventricle volume obtained from the segmented 3D MR image. (b) The brain ventricle volume evolution via the LSM [9].

To obtain the boundary vertices of the volumetric brain ventricles, the Matlab function isosurface was used. With the boundary vertex information, the initial mesh for the 3D brain MR image was generated by Tetgen [11]. After obtaining the ventricular boundary vertices, the ventricular boundary deformation was computed via the LSM. The boundary obtained from the segmented 3D MR image was used as an input zero surface of the LSM. To evolve the ventricular boundary, the LSM [9] moved the boundary of the 3D ventricles along their interior normals with a constant speed of 0.01. Once the ventricular boundary surface was evolved, the normals of the previous boundary vertices were computed. The next position of each boundary vertex was computed by selecting the point where the normal meets the evolved surface. In this simulation, the ventricular boundary evolution was terminated after 10 iterations since the expanded ventricle brain volume was similar to the hydrocephalic state. The evolved brain ventricular volumes are shown in Figure 3(b).

When computing the new contour position, the mesh was deformed via FEMWARP [39]. Also, mesh quality improvement for the intermediate step was performed once the deformed mesh was obtained. The optimized mesh was used as input in the computation of the next intermediate deformation step. Figure 4 shows the initial, intermediate, and final meshes obtained during 3D brain ventricle boundary deformation. In each iteration, the mesh deformed by

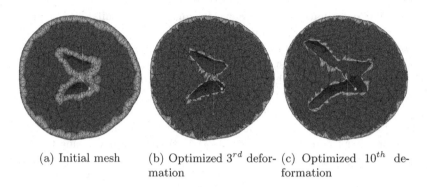

(a) Initial mesh   (b) Optimized 3rd defor-   (c) Optimized 10th de-
mation   formation

Fig. 4. (a) The mesh having the ventricular boundary vertices matched to the 3D normal brain MRI. ((b) and (c)) the deformed meshes generated by the FEMWARP algorithm [39]. Each evolved surface was computed via the 3D LSM with constant speed of 0.01. The mesh contained 8200 vertices and 40,783 elements. The blue-colored brain represents the part to be deformed. Mesh quality improvement was performed to improve the mesh quality at each step of the brain ventricular volume deformation.

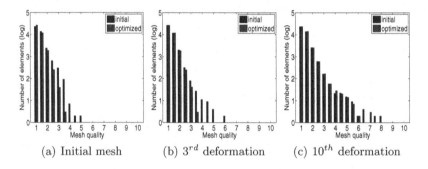

(a) Initial mesh   (b) 3rd deformation   (c) 10th deformation

Fig. 5. Inverse mean ratio mesh quality distribution for meshes generated in Simulation 2. Quality distribution for (a) the initial mesh, (b) the 3rd deformation, and (c) the 10th deformation.

FEMWARP [39] was valid; hence, a backtracking line search was not required. Feasible Newton [5] mesh quality improvement via Mesquite [4] was performed after each boundary deformation step. The brain ventricle volume was expanded three times bigger than its initial volume. Figure 5 shows the inverse mean ratio [5] mesh quality distribution for the intermediate meshes. Unlike the previous simulation, since the brain ventricle volume was enlarging to establish hydrocephalus, the mesh parts to be deformed and analyzed shrunk. Thus, the mesh quality distribution for the 10th iteration is worse than that of the previous iterations. In spite of this, the mesh quality was constantly monitored to ensure the mesh quality was good enough for simulation.

5   Conclusions

In our previous research [1], we develop an image-based ventricular evolution tracking method via the LSM [9] and FEMWARP [39]. In this paper, we proposed two new techniques: the automatic ventricular boundary deformation for 2D CT images and the brain ventricle volume deformation for 3D MR image via the LSM and FEMWARP. This approach can be used for any types of medical images such as CT, MR, and ultrasound. Compared to our previous work [1], the ventricular boundary deformation for 2D CT images was computed automatically via the LSM. There were no invalid meshes in deformed meshes generated by the automatic boundary detection process via the LSM. Thus, no backtracking line search was required. Simulation results showed that the 2D ventricular boundary deformation via FEMWARP with the ventricular boundaries obtained from the automatic LSM boundary detection was successfully performed.

Also, deformation of the brain ventricle volume for a 3D MRI was performed, which is an extension of our previous work [1]. Since no target MR images are available to us, a 3D normal brain MRI was used for computing the ventricle volume evolution for the simulation. To evolve the brain ventricle volume, the LSM computed the evolved boundaries. By using the evolved brain ventricle boundary, the brain ventricle volume deformation was performed via FEMWARP successfully. Unlike our previous work, no actual topological changes occurred when 3D brain ventricular volume deformation was performed. Through our approach, we aid neurosurgeons in easily determining where to place the shunt and thus in obtaining better prognosis of hydrocephalus treatment. We will extend our geometric computational approach to incorporate the mechanics of hydrocephalus. We will also apply our technique to patient 3D MRIs.

References

1. Park, J., Shontz, S., Drapaca, C.: A combined level set/mesh warping algorithm for tracking brain and cerebrospinal fluid evolution in hydrocephalic patients. In: Zhang, J. (ed.) Image-based Geometric Modeling and Mesh Generation. Lecture Notes in Computational Vision and Biomechanics. Springer (to apppear, 2012)
2. West, J.: Application of the level set method to hydrocephalus: Simulating the motion of the ventricles. Master's thesis, University of Waterloo (2004)
3. Shewchuk, J.: Triangle: Engineering a 2D quality mesh generator and delaunay triangular. In: Lin, M.C., Manocha, D. (eds.) FCRC-WS 1996 and WACG 1996. LNCS, vol. 1148, pp. 203–222. Springer, Heidelberg (1996)
4. Brewer, M., Diachin, L., Knupp, P., Leurent, T., Melander, D.: The Mesquite mesh quality improvement toolkit. In: Proc. of the 12th International Meshing Roundtable, Sandia National Laboratories, pp. 239–250 (2003)
5. Munson, T.: Mesh shape-quality optimization using the inverse mean-ratio metric. Math. Program 110, 561–590 (2007)
6. Cocosco, C.A., Kollokian, V., Kwan, R.K.-S., Evans, A.C.: BrainWeb: Online interface to a 3D MRI simulated brain database, NeuroImage, In: Proc. of 3rd International Conference on Functional Mapping of the Human Brain, vol.5(4), Part 2/4, S425, (1997).

7. Zhu, S., Xia, X., Zhang, Q., Belloulata, K.: An image segmentation algorithm in image processing based on threshold segmentation. In: Proc. of the 2007 Third International IEEE Conference on Signal-Image Technologies and Internet-Based System, pp. 673–678 (2007)

8. Fabijanska, A.: Variance filter for edge detection and edge-based image segmentation. In: Proc. of 7th International Conference on Perspective Technologies and Methods in MEMS Design, pp. 151–154 (2011)

9. Sethian, J.: Level Set Methods and Fast Marching Methods: Evolving Interfaces in Computational Geometry, Fluid Mechanics, Computer Vision, and Materials Science, Cambridge Monographs on Applied and Computational Mathematics (1999)

10. Narayanan, K., Karunakar, Y.: 3-D reconstruction of tumors in MRIs. International Journal of Research and Reviews in Signal Acquisitionand Processing 1(2) (2011)

11. Si, H.: TetGen: A Quality Tetrahedral Mesh Generator and 3D Delaunay Triangulator Version 1.4 (2006)

12. Roy, S., Heltai, L., Drapaca, C.S., Costanzo, F.: An immersed finite element method approach for brain Biomechanics. To Appear in the Proc. of SEM (2012)

13. Choi, J.U., Kim, D.S., Kim, S.H.: Endoscopic surgery for obstructive hydrocephalus. Yonsei Med. J. 40(6), 600–607 (1999)

14. Drapaca, C.S., Tenti, G., Rohlf, K., Sivaloganathan, S.: A quasi-linear viscoelastic constitutive equation for the brain: Application to hydrocephalus. J. Elasticity 85, 65–83 (2006)

15. Hakim, S., Venegas, J., Burton, J.: The physics of the cranial cavity, hydrocephalus and normal pressure hydrocephalus: Mechanical interpretation and mathematical model. Surg. Neurol. 5, 187–210 (1976)

16. Hydrocephalus statistics (2008), http://www.ghrforg.org/faq.htm

17. Kellie, G.: Appearances observed in the dissection of two individuals; death from cold and congestion of the brain. Trans. Med-Chir. Soc., 1–84 (1824)

18. Milhorat, T.H.: Pediatric Neurosurgery. Contemporary Neurology Series 16 (1978)

19. Miller, K., Chinzei, K.: Constitutive modeling of brain tissue - experiment and theory. J. Biomech. 30, 1115–1121 (1997)

20. Monro, A.: Observations on Structure and Functions of the Nervous System. Creech and Johnson, Edinburgh (1783)

21. Nagashima, T., Tamaki, N., Matsumoto, S., Horwitz, B., Seguchi, Y.: Biomechanics of hydrocephalus: A new theoretical model. Neurosurg. 21(6), 898–904 (1987)

22. Sivaloganathan, S., Tenti, G., Drake, J.: Mathematical pressure volume models of the cerebrospinal fluid. Appl. Math. Comput. 94, 243–266 (1998)

23. Tenti, G., Sivaloganathan, S., Drake, J.: Brain biomechanics: steady-state consolidation theory of hydrocephalus. Can. App. Math. Q. 7(1), 111–124 (1999)

24. Tuli, S., Alshail, E., Drake, J.: Third ventriculostomy versus cerebrospinal fluid shunt as a first procedure in pediatric hydrocephalus. Pediatr. Neurosurg. 30(1), 11–15 (1999)

25. Tully, B., Ventikos, Y.: Coupling poroelasticity and CFD for cerebrospinal fluid hydrodynamics. IEEE Trans. Biomed. Eng. 56(6), 1644–1651 (2009)

26. Wilkie, K., Drapaca, C.S., Sivaloganathan, S.: A theoretical study of the effect of ventricular pressure pulsations on the pathogenesis of hydrocephalus. Submitted to Appl. Math. Comput. (2009)

27. Osher, S., Sethian, J.: Fronts propagating with curvature dependent speed: Algorithms based on Hamilton-Jacobi formulations. J. Comput. Phys. 79, 12–49 (1988)

28. Vese, L., Chan, T.: A multiphase level set framework for image segmentation using the Mumford and Shah model. Int. J. Comput. Vision 50, 271–293 (2002)

29. Osher, S., Fedkiw, R.: Level Set Methods and Dynamic Implicit Surfaces. Applied Mathematical Sciences, vol. 153. Springer (2003)
30. Mitich, A., Ayed, I.: Variational and level set methods in image segmentation. Springer Topics in Signal Processing, vol. 5. Springer (2010)
31. Persson, P.: Mesh size functions for implicit geometries and PDE-based gradient limiting. Engineering with Computers 22, 95–109 (2006)
32. Strang, G., Persson, P.: Circuit simulation and moving mesh generation. In: Proc. of Int. Symp. on Comm. and Inform. Tech., ISCIT 2004 (2004)
33. Bah, M., Nair, P., Browne, M.: Mesh morphing for finite element analysis of implant positioning in cementless total hip replacement. Med. Eng. Phys. 31, 1235–1243 (2009)
34. Baldwin, M., Langenderfer, J., Rullkoetter, P., Laz, P.: Development of subject-specific and statistical shape models of the knee using an efficient segmentation and mesh-morphing approach. Comput. Meth. Prog. Bio. 97, 232–240 (2010)
35. Liu, Y., D'Arceuil, H., He, J., Duggan, M., Gonzalez, G., Pryor, J., de Crespigny, A.: A nonlinear mesh-warping technique for correcting brain deformation after stroke. Magn. Reson. Imaging 24, 1069–1075 (2006)
36. Sigal, I., Yang, H., Roberts, M., Downs, J.: Morphing methods to parameterize specimen-specific finite element model geometries. J. Biomech. 43, 254–262 (2010)
37. Chan, T., Vese, L.: Active contours without edges. IEEE T. Image. Process. 10 (2001)
38. Baker, T.: Mesh movement and metamorphosis. In: Proc. of the Tenth International Meshing Roundtable, Sandia National Laboratories, pp. 387–396 (2001)
39. Shontz, S., Vavasis, S.: Analysis of and workarounds for element reversal for a finite elementbased algorithm for warping triangular and tetrahedral meshes. BIT, Numerical Mathematics 50, 863–884 (2010)
40. Wu, Y.: Matlab implementation of the Chan Vese active contour without edges method (2011), http://www.mathworks.com/matlabcentral/fileexchange/23445

Simplified Reeb Graph as Effective
Shape Descriptor for the Striatum

Antonietta Pepe[1,*], Laura Brandolini[2,*], Marco Piastra[2], Juha Koikkalainen[3],
Jarmo Hietala[4], and Jussi Tohka[1]

[1] Tampere University of Technology, P.O. Box 553, 33101, Tampere, Finland
[2] Universitá di Pavia, via Ferrata 1, Pavia, Italy
[3] VTT Technical Research Centre of Finland, P.O. Box 1300, FIN-33101 Tampere, Finland
[4] University of Turku, FIN-20700 Turku, Finland and Turku PET Centre, Finland

Abstract. In this work, we present a novel image and mesh processing pipeline
for the computation of simplified Reeb graphs for closed triangle meshes of the
human striatum extracted from 3D-T1 weighted MR images. The method uses
active contours for computing the mesh partition and the simplified Reeb graph.
Experimental results showed that simplified Reeb graphs, as obtained by our
pipeline, provide an intrinsic, effective, and stable descriptor of striatal shapes to
be used as an automatic tool for inter-subject mesh registration, mesh decomposition, and striatal shapes comparison. Particularly, the nodes of simplified Reeb
graphs proved to be robust landmarks to guide the mesh registration. The quality of the inter-subject mesh registration obtained by the use of simplified Reeb
graphs slightly outperformed the one obtained by surface-based registration techniques. In addition, we show the stability of the resulting mesh decomposition,
and we propose its use as an automatic alternative to the manual sub-segmentation
of the striatum. Finally we show some preliminary results on the inter-group comparisons among neuroleptic-naive schizophrenic patients and matched controls.

Keywords: Simplified Reeb Graph, Surface Registration, Mesh Decomposition,
Striatum, Schizophrenia, MRI.

1 Introduction

Human striatum is an highly innervated group of nuclei in the brain, and the primary
receiver of afferent nerves from the cerebral cortex and thalamus to the basal ganglia
[1]. Striatum is implicated, via the cortico-striato-thalamo-cortical circuitry, in motor
processes, such as spatial orientation and movement selection, and in a number of
non-motor processes such as cognitive functions, learning, attention, memory, moti-
vation, reward, and addiction [2,3,4]. Striatum can be anatomically divided into three
primary regions: caudate, putamen, and nucleus accumbens. Different striatal regions
are thought to receive projections from different cortical regions [5]. Particularly, caudate appears to have greater connectivity to prefrontal regions, and thus to be more
critical in cognitive and memory functions than putamen [2]. Putamen appears to have

---

* These two authors contributed equally to the work.

J.A. Levine, R.R. Paulsen, Y. Zhang (Eds.): MeshMed 2012, LNCS 7599, pp. 134–146, 2012.

connectivity with more posterior cortical regions than the caudate, and thus to be crucial to motor processing, and to subserve cognitive functions more limited to stimulus-response [2,3]. Striatal structures, due to their cognitive and motor functions, are of high interest in schizophrenia. In this disease, cognitive functions are impaired. Furthermore, parkinsonian and extrapyramidal (dyskinesias) signs have been reported in neuroleptic-naïve patients presenting schizophrenia [6]. The nucleus accumbens is a central part of limbic and prefrontal cortico-striato-pallidal-thalamic circuits, and it is involved in cognitive, emotional and psychomotor functions, which are often disturbed in schizophrenia [1].

In addition to volumetric studies [7,1], local and global morphometric approaches have been proposed for the analysis of the striatal shape and its aberrations in health and schizophrenia. Among the local shape approaches, [8] used the deformation fields required to warp an individual image to a reference template image as a basis for the analysis of localized shape changes; while [4] presented methods for the analysis of detailed 3D surface models after their macroscopic differences were removed (surface registration or matching). Deformation and surface based methods provide spatially localized shape information that is relatively straightforward to interpret; however, they usually require the establishment of the point correspondence among surfaces [9]. Except if ad-hoc strategies are used [10], the establishment of the point correspondence is computationally demanding, and it often requires remeshing.

Global shape approaches have been used in medical imaging for the compact representation and analysis of neuroanatomical shapes. Particularly, [11] used medial representation to study shape differences in schizophrenia; [12] used spherical harmonic description to study the shape changes in striatum with bipolar disorder; [9] used Laplace-Beltrami eigenvalues for shape comparisons of hippocampus based on selected eigenfunctions. Furthermore, [13] proposed an algorithm for mesh partitioning and skeletonization using a shape diameter function.

In this paper we propose the adoption of Reeb graphs as compact descriptors for the striatal shape. Indeed, Reeb graphs are more robust than other skeletal descriptors since they are less sensitive to small and localized changes on the mesh [14].

The definition of a Reeb graph [15] for a closed and connected surface is based on the concept of Morse function [16,17], which is a scalar function defined on the surface, having only *maxima*, *minima* and *saddles* as critical points. In particular a Morse function does not have *degenerate saddles* (see definitions in [18]). The Reeb graph is related to the level lines of the Morse function on the surface; each point in the Reeb graph corresponds to a connected component of a level line of the Morse function. More precisely, the nodes in the Reeb graphs correspond to the connected component containing critical points and the arcs correspond to sets of connected components containing only regular (i.e. non-critical) points of the Morse function. As a remarkable property, the number of loops of the Reeb graph of a closed, connected surface is equal to the *genus* of the surface [19]. In practical applications, Reeb graphs are complemented by a geometric embedding by which each point in the Reeb graph is positioned at the centroid of the corresponding connected component. In addition, the extraction of the Reeb graph is often seen as part of a *mesh decomposition* (also referred as *mesh partitioning* or *surface segmentation* procedure), in which the connected components containing critical points of the Morse function serve as the boundaries of different surface *segments*.

The discrete variants of Reeb graphs have been broadly applied in recent years in different fields of computer vision with the role of compact shape descriptors [18], starting from the seminal works [20,21]. In [22], an interesting definition is given in terms of level-set diagrams, for 0-genus surfaces. [30] uses a geodesic function defined on the surface for object recognition. The concept in [22] is further expanded in [23], where the definition of a Morse function intrinsic to the surface was proposed, although with a random choice of the starting vertex as seed. The latter method uses evolving contours that also compute the mesh partitioning into segments, but the method may incur in critical contour configurations, especially in the case of coarser meshes. [24] proposed an on-line algorithm for Reeb graphs construction that takes into account all the simplicial elements of the mesh; the algorithm was validated with several different Morse functions but it does not compute a mesh partitioning. [25] described an approach based on dynamic graphs that are directly constructed from the critical points of the Morse function; the method however does not extract the level lines and this makes it difficult to compute the geometric embedding. In [26] Reeb graphs were applied to produce mesh decomposition with the use of average geodesic distance calculated from a small set of evenly-spaced vertices (base vertices), but no embedding is proposed for the graphs. [27] proposed an approach based on critical points and their isocontours, which is particularly suited for large meshes with small genus, for which 'smooth' Morse functions can be defined. The algorithm proposed in [28], which is derived from that in [23], uses evolving *active* contours for computing a mesh partitioning into segments, hence a *simplified* version of the Reeb graph in which each node corresponds to the centroid of an entire segment and the arcs describe the adjacency relations between segments.

In this paper, we adopt a variation of [28] to compute the simplified Reeb graph (SRG) for closed triangle meshes extracted from 3D T1-weighted brain MR images of the human striatum. This algorithm is particularly robust with respect to mesh density (number of vertices in the mesh) and to surface genus [28]. The goal of this work, behind the one of proposing the use of SRG as a compact descriptor of the striatal shape, was to explore the effectiveness of such a descriptor for the purpose of automatic inter-subject mesh registration (a), automatic mesh decomposition (b), and for the inter-group striatal shapes comparison (c).

(a) To assess the significance of the SRG-based registration as compared to other surface-based registration techniques (registration performed i.e. by establishing the point correspondence among the surface vertices on the entire mesh), we used a test set collected from neuroleptic-naive patients presenting schizophrenia and matched controls. The quality of the SRG based striatal mesh registration slightly outperformed the one obtained by surface-based registration techniques.

(b) Striatal structures, each of which is implicated in different functions, are differently affected in schizophrenia [7]. Striatal sub-segmentation is challenging as the signal intensity alone is not sufficient to distinguish among its sectors [29], and manual or semi-automatic methods are still regarded as the gold standard. We present here an automatic striatal mesh decomposition into its three primary anatomical regions (caudate, putamen and nucleus accumbens). The sub-segmentation is obtained as a direct result of the SRG extraction and it does not involve any registration to labelled images or any a priori information on the striatal surface. Our results, albeit not quantitatively validated, appeared as a promising, robust and repeatable alternative to the laborious manual methods.

(c) In this work we found that, despite their compactness, SRG are sensible to shape variations of the striatum. This result inspires further investigations on the use of the SRG descriptor for the detection and analysis of neuroanatomical morphological differences within and between groups.

2 Methods

2.1 Computing the Simplified Reeb Graph

Computing the Morse Function A critical aspect in extracting the Reeb graphs from surfaces is the choice of a proper Morse function [31,23]. The Morse function we adopted is based on the concept of *geodesic distance* on a mesh [32,33], i.e. the length of the shortest path connecting each two vertices. We first find the two *diameter vertices*, which are the pair of vertices at maximum geodesic distance. We then compute two distance functions, one for each of the diameter vertices, and we determine the *local maxima* and *minima* of each distance function (*local extrema*). The local extrema are then merged, with some tolerance: pairs of local extrema from each of the two functions are merged into a common *feature point* if they are not farther away than a certain predefined tolerance, otherwise they are simply discarded. By definition, the value of the Morse function of choice at each vertex is the geodesic distance to the closest feature point (see fig. 1(a)). The main advantage of this Morse function, which is a variant of those proposed in [23] and [22], is that the feature points correspond to prominent points of the shape and the resulting Morse function is intrinsic to the surface, in that it is independent from rotation and scaling.

Segmentation and Construction of the SRG. An *active contour* is a discrete, connected, closed line, made of vertices and edges, that represents the advancing front between the vertices that have been visited and the rest of the mesh. Active contours are initialized at each feature point (see fig. 1(b)), i.e. a minimum of the Morse function of choice. Active contours are then evolved in the direction of ascending values of the Morse function in a synchronized fashion (see fig. 1(c)); at each step, the vertex having the lowest value in all active contours is selected as the *candidate vertex* and the corresponding active contour is evolved. If the candidate is not a critical vertex, the selected active contour is just advanced locally, in the neighborhood of the vertex itself. The update is more complex if the candidate is a critical vertex, in particular a saddle. In fact, two types of event can occur at a saddle vertex:

– a *split* - the active contour is self-intersecting and is therefore split into two new active contours;

– a *merge* - the active contour came in touch with another one and the two are merged into a new active contour.

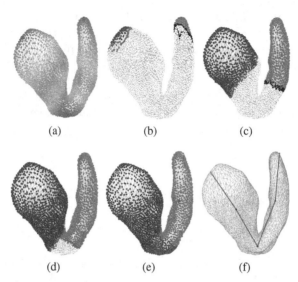

Fig. 1. Vertices colors represent increasing values (from dark red to dark blue) of the Morse function; feature points are magnified and represented in red. (a). Active contours start at each feature point (b) and they are evolved in the direction of ascending values of the Morse function (c). Two active contours merge in a new one (d). Each node in the SRG is either a feature point or the centroid of a segment (e), arcs of the SRG describe adjacency relations (f).

The update is straightforward when the candidate vertex is a maximum, as the selected active contour simply vanishes. The algorithm terminates when all active contours have vanished. The partition of the mesh into *segments* is constructed incrementally during the evolution of active contours. Away from critical vertices, all newly visited vertices are added to the corresponding segment. When either a split or a merge event occurs, all segments are closed and new segments are created. More precisely, when a split event occurs the splitting segment is closed and two new segments are created, whereas when a merge event occurs, the two merging segments are closed and a new segment is created (see fig. 1(d)). The overall mesh partitioning is described by the collection of all segments thus obtained. The simplified Reeb graph contains a node corresponding to the centroid of each of the segments (see fig. 1(e)) and the arcs represent the adjacency relations between the segments. The graph is completed by the nodes representing the feature points, together with an arc between each of them and the centroid of the segment in which they are contained (see fig. 1(f)).

The algorithm also contains special provisions for dealing with irregular cases, not described above, that occur more frequently with coarse meshes and/or with higher genus. See [28] for details.

2.2   Striatum Shape Processing

Material. In this study, we used 3-D T1-weighted MR brain images of 40 subjects (22 normal controls, and 18 neuroleptic-naïve patients presenting first-episode schizophrenia or schizoaffective disorder) previously described in [34]. This study was performed

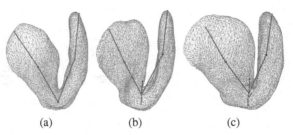

(a)   (b)   (c)

Fig. 2. SRG obtained by applying the proposed algorithm to three examples of striatal shapes

in accordance with the Declaration of Helsinki. The ethic committee of the Turku Central Hospital supervised and approved the experimental procedure. A written informed consent was collected from all of the participants enrolled in the study. MRI brain scans were acquired using a 1.5 T Siemens Magnetom (Erlangen, Germany) as detailed in [34]. The voxel size of the MR images was $1.5 \times 1.5 \times 1.0$ mm^3 and the size of the images varied from $256 \times 256 \times 150$ to $256 \times 256 \times 170$ voxels.

MRI to Mesh. MR images were manually segmented using a 3D software tool for interactive construction of individualized surface models with topologically correct triangulation [35,4]. With this 3D tool, the striatum (not including the tail of the caudate) was manually segmented in each MRI volume by non-rigid deformation of a same triangulated surface model to the edges of the striatum. The obtained striatal surfaces were decomposed into two mesh surfaces representing the left and right striatum separately.

Computing SRG. The SRG-algorithm (Section 2.1) was applied to each mesh to obtain a simplified Reeb graph and a mesh partitioning. A typical aspect of discrete Morse functions is that, depending on both the shape and the triangulation, they may have several extra maxima which generate extra branches in the Reeb graph (see Fig. 2). Nevertheless, given that all the striatum meshes have genus 0, the extracted Reeb graphs are guaranteed to contain no loops. In this specific case, this means that all extra branches had a common root and that the corresponding segments could be safely merged with the root segment. This also entailed recomputing the centroid of the root segment after the extra segments had been merged. As a result of this procedure, all the SRG had the same number of nodes.

2.3 SRG-Based Registration of Striatal Meshes

We developed an iterative algorithm for the 7-parameter linear registration of striatal surfaces by matching their SRG descriptors using Full Procrustes Superimposition [36] (FPS). The algorithm is composed of three consecutive steps:

Step 1: One of the N graphs $x_i, i = 1, ..., N$, is randomly selected as a reference x^r. All other graphs x_i are registered to x^r by minimization of the sum of square differences $\sum_{j=1}^{V} \|x_j^r - (s_i \mathbf{R}_i x_{i,j} + \mathbf{t}_i)\|^2$ w.r.t. $s_i, \mathbf{t}_i, \mathbf{R}_i$ using FPS. Here $V = 5$ is the number of nodes in each graph; x_j^r and $x_{i,j}$ are the 3D coordinates of the j-th node of the reference graph and of the i-th individual graph, respectively; $s_i, \mathbf{t}_i, \mathbf{R}_i$ are the isotropic scaling factor, translation vector, and rotation matrix, for the i-th graph respectively.

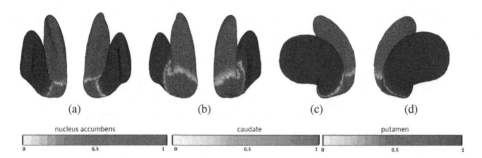

(a)	(b)	(c)	(d)

nucleus accumbens   caudate   putamen

Fig. 3. Probabilistic maps of the left and right striatal mesh decomposition, for the whole database, depicted in frontal (a), posterior (b), and lateral (c and d) views. Maps were obtained by calculating the probability of each surface vertex to be assigned to each mesh sector. Notice how the mesh decomposition of the striatal shapes into three sectors actually corresponds to the anatomical sub-segmentation of human striatum into nucleus accumbens (violet), caudate (green) and putamen (red).

Step 2: After step 1, each graph is aligned to x^r. To make sure that the quality of the SRG superimposition is not affected by the particular choice for the reference graph[1], a further iterative registration routine is implemented:

> (i) Calculate the mean shape of the SRG which were registered to x^r as the arithmetic mean of the registered graphs. If $\tilde{x}_i$ denotes the i-th registered graph, the mean shape is $\tilde{x}_j^m = (1/N) \sum_{i=1}^{N} \tilde{x}_{i,j}, \forall j = 1, ..., V$.
>
> (ii) Pre-registered graphs ($\tilde{x}_i$) are aligned to $\tilde{x}^m$ by minimizing $\sum_{j=1}^{V} \|\tilde{x}_j^m - (\tilde{s}_i \tilde{\mathbf{R}}_i \tilde{x}_{i,j} + \tilde{\mathbf{t}}_i)\|^2$ w.r.t. $\tilde{s}_i, \tilde{\mathbf{t}}_i, \tilde{\mathbf{R}}_i$ using FPS.
>
> (iii) The mean shape of the graphs is updated and the transformation $T(\tilde{s}, \tilde{\mathbf{t}}, \tilde{\mathbf{R}})$ is composed to the one calculated at the previous stages.

Points (ii) and (iii) are repeated until a maximum number of iterations is achieved or until there are no improvements to the SRG superimposition.

Step 3: The composed transformation $T(\tilde{s}, \tilde{\mathbf{t}}, \tilde{\mathbf{R}})$ that best matches each SRG to the mean graph shape is applied to the corresponding meshes (the ones from which the SRG were extracted from).

3   Results

3.1   Assessment of SRG-Based Surface Decomposition

As a result of the automatic SRG extraction and consequent mesh decomposition, three distinct mesh sectors were obtained for each striatal surface. By visual inspection, results of the mesh decomposition were consistent within (left and right striatum) and

---

[1] Particularly, the registration accuracy might be significantly impaired if the reference graph is not a good representative of the mean SRG in the dataset.

Table 1. Accuracy of the SRG-based registration compared to the surface-based registration. The accuracy of the striatal mesh registration was evaluated with two measures derived from the Hausdorff distance.

	SRG-based		surface-based			
	FPS^2		FPS ^{2}		Arun	
	Left	Right	Left	Right	Left	Right
HD_1 [mm]	3.4751	2.9124	3.4187	3.0510	3.4264	3.1653
HD_2 [mm]	4.8307	4.1326	4.8512	4.3999	4.9386	4.6012

between subjects, for the whole database. An example of mesh decomposition produced by our pipeline is depicted in Fig. 1.(e).

A probabilistic map of the resulting striatal decomposition was then obtained by calculating the probability of each surface vertex to be assigned to each mesh sector in the whole database. This mesh decomposition into three sectors corresponded to the anatomical sub-segmentation of human striatum into nucleus accumbens, caudate and putamen (depicted in Fig. 3 in violet, green and red colors, respectively).

3.2 Assessment of SRG-Based Registration of Striatal Meshes

The SRG-based registration routine described in Section 2.3 was used for the linear alignment of striatal surfaces (left and right striatum separately). For comparison, the same striatal meshes were also linearly aligned to each other with the same method illustrated in Section 2.3 but applied to the whole mesh: the linear transformation is extracted using all the vertices of the mesh, and is then applied to the corresponding SRG. For further comparison, a second surface-based registration routine similar to the one in [4] was also applied: a mean mesh was calculated and all the individual meshes were affinely registered to that using Arun's method [37]; the mean mesh was finally registered back to the previously (affinely) registered meshes using again [37]. Examples of the SRG and striatal meshes, prior and after registration, are shown in Fig. 4.

Since a ground truth for the striatal surface registration was not available, we quantitatively compared the results of the SRG-based registration of striatal meshes to the aforementioned (using FPS and Arun's method) more traditional surface-based methods. Results were quantitatively validated using the Hausdorff Distance (HD) (see Table 1). The HD [38] provides a measure of the maximum symmetrical distance between two surfaces and thus can be used to validate the surface registration. Particularly, two measures based on the HD (denoted as d) were computed:

– HD_1: mean of the HD computed between each registered surface and the mean surface mesh, $\frac{1}{N}\sum_{i=1}^{N} d(\tilde{x}_i, \tilde{x}^m)$. HD_1 can be interpreted as a measure of the dispersion of the registered surfaces as compared to the mean shape, and therefore as a measure of the remaining mis-alignment.

– HD_2: mean of the HD computed for each mesh with respect to each other mesh $\frac{1}{N(N-1)/2}\sum_{i=1}^{N}\sum_{l=i+1}^{N} d(\tilde{x}_i, \tilde{x}_l)$. HD_2 can be interpreted as a measure of the

---

^{2} Similar results were obtained if the optimization of the transformation was obtained (the absolute orientation problem) using Horn's quaternion-based closed form solution [39].

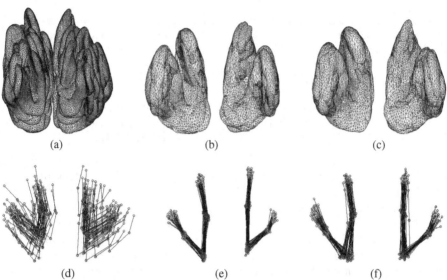

(a)   (b)   (c)

(d)   (e)   (f)

Fig. 4. Results of the SRG-based and surface-based registration performed on the whole database consisting of 40 subjects. In the first column, striatal meshes in the native space (a) are shown with their corresponding SRG (d). In the second column, the SRG in the native space (d) are aligned by SRG-based registration (e) and the obtained transformations are applied to the corresponding meshes (a) to obtain (b). In the third column, meshes in the native space (a) are aligned by a surface-based registration using FPS (c) and the obtained transformations are applied to the corresponding SRG graphs (d) to obtain (f).

mean maximal difference between each pair of surfaces in the database (after their alignment), and therefore also as a measure of the shape variability within the given dataset.

The registration accuracy obtained by the use of SRG was qualitatively (see Fig. 4) and quantitatively (as measured by the HD, see Table 1) comparable to, and in some cases outperforming, the registration accuracy obtained by more classical surface-based approaches.

In the surface-based registration algorithms, optimal registration parameters in the presence of point correspondence are estimated using all surface vertices. The establishment of the point correspondence is however computationally demanding, especially for dense surfaces, and it often requires remeshing (which could in turn influence shape comparisons done on surfaces [9]). On the other hand, our experimental results suggest that using a surface representation of the striatal shapes, although its importance for characterizing non-rigid motion remains unquestionable, is overly redundant in case of 7-parameter linear motion if an SRG descriptor of that shape can be extracted. The SRG-based registration proposed here only requires triangulated closed meshes and it is not limited to meshes having a same number of vertices. As a consequence, the implications of these results might be extended to other shapes than the human striatum, although further testing is required.

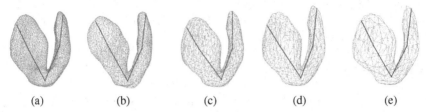

(a)	(b)	(c)	(d)	(e)

Fig. 5. The SRG is robust to mesh resolution. These are SRG of the same mesh progressively decimated: 3293 vertices (a), 1647 vertices (b), 824 vertices (c), 413 vertices (d), 207 vertices (e).

3.3   Stability of the SRG to Mesh Resolution

The SRG is stable to different mesh resolutions. Applying the SRG algorithm to meshes progressively decimated we can see that the resulting segmentation is robust and stable, and the corresponding SRG are consistent in that they contain the same number of nodes (see Fig. 5).

3.4   Shape Representation

The robustness of SRG to mesh resolution, besides confirming the legitimacy of using the nodes of the graph as robust landmarks to guide the registration, also motivated their use as descriptors for group-specific mean shapes. Particularly, the analysis of the mean SRG obtained in schizophrenia and control groups (Fig. 6) showed that, despite the compactness of the SRG descriptor, it is sensible to mesh variations. The use of simplified Reeb graphs as a tool for studying the intra-group shape variability (or for discriminating among groups based on their shapes) was out of the scope of this work

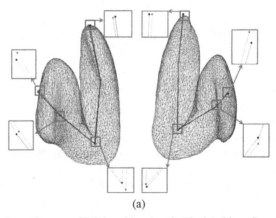

(a)

Fig. 6. The figure shows the mean SRG in schizophrenia (depicted in red) and in normal controls (depicted in black) overlaid to the mean striatal surface in frontal view. This is an illustration of the potentialities of the SRG as a descriptor for group-specific mean shapes, although we are aware that the role of this descriptor as a tool to discriminate among groups has not been validated, and no medical conclusions should be derived from it.

and has not been explored further. Nevertheless, our results inspires further investigations on the use of the SRG descriptor for the detection and analysis of neuroanatomical morphological differences within and between groups.

4   Conclusions

In this work, we presented an image and mesh processing pipeline that uses SRG as a faithful and effective shape descriptor for the striatal shapes extracted from 3D T1-weighted MR images. To the best of our knowledge, this is the first study proposing this kind of shape descriptor for the human striatum. Due to its geometrical and topological properties, SRG is robust to small local variations on the mesh, and as such, effective as a basis for inter-subject registration, shape representation, and mesh decomposition of striatal surfaces.

The results presented showed that the registration obtained with the proposed method is qualitatively comparable and quantitatively (as measured by the Hausdorff distance) outperforming the surface-based registration, while being computationally simpler. Indeed, the SRG-based registration does not require neither the computation of the point correspondence among mesh vertices, nor is limited to meshes having a same number of vertices. The results show also the efficacy of SRG for mesh partitioning: albeit not quantitatively validated, the sub-segmentation of the striatal surfaces into caudate, putamen, and nucleus accumbens are qualitatively meaningful. Finally, the results showed that, despite its compactness, SRG can be used as a compact descriptor for group specific mean-shapes of the human striatum.

Acknowledgments. This work was supported by the Academy of Finland grant number 130275 and 129657.

References

1. Lauer, M., Senitz, D., Beckmann, H.: Increased volume of the nucleus accumbens in schizophrenia. J. Neural Transmission 108, 645–660 (2001)
2. Brickman, A., Buchsbaum, M., Shihabuddin, L., Hazlett, E., Borod, J., Mohs, R.: Striatal size, glucose metabolic rate, and verbal learning in normal aging. Cognitive Brain Res. 17(1), 106–116 (2003)
3. Grahn, J., Parkinson, J., Owen, A.: The cognitive functions of the caudate nucleus. Prog. Neurobiol. 86(3), 141–155 (2008)
4. Koikkalainen, J., Hirvonen, J., Nyman, M., Lötjönen, J., Hietala, J., Ruotsalainen, U.: Shape variability of the human striatum - effects of age and gender. NeuroImage 34(1), 85–93 (2007)
5. Seger, C.: How do the basal ganglia contribute to categorization? their roles in generalization, response selection, and learning via feedback. Neurosci. Biobehav.l R. 32(2), 265–278 (2008)
6. McCreadie, R., Srinivasan, T., Padmavati, R., Thara, R.: Extrapyramidal symptoms in unmedicated schizophrenia. J. Psychiat. Res. 39(3), 261–266 (2005)
7. Buchsbaum, M.S., Shihabuddin, L., Brickman, A., Miozzo, R., Prikryl, R., Shaw, R., Davis, K.: Caudate and putamen volumes in good and poor outcome patients with schizophrenia. Schizophr. Res. 64(1), 53–62 (2003)

8. Volz, H., Gaser, C., Sauer, H.: Supporting evidence for the model of cognitive dysmetria in schizophrenia - a structural magnetic resonance imaging study using deformation-based morphometry. Schizophr. Res. 46(1), 45–56 (2000)

9. Reuter, M., Wolter, F., Shenton, M., Niethammer, M.: Laplace - beltrami eigenvalues and topological features of eigenfunctions for statistical shape analysis. Comput. Aided Design 41(10), 739–755 (2009)

10. Pepe, A., Zhao, L., Tohka, J., Koikkalainen, J., Hietala, J., Ruotsalainen, U.: Automatic statistical shape analysis of local cerebral asymmetry in 3d t1-weighted magnetic resonance images. In: Paulsen, R.R., Levine, J.A. (eds.) Proc. of MICCAI 2011 MedMesh Workshop, pp. 127–134 (2011)

11. Vetsa, Y.S.K., Styner, M., Pizer, S.M., Lieberman, J.A., Gerig, G.: Caudate Shape Discrimination in Schizophrenia Using Template-Free Non-parametric Tests. In: Ellis, R.E., Peters, T.M. (eds.) MICCAI 2003, Part II. LNCS, vol. 2879, pp. 661–669. Springer, Heidelberg (2003)

12. Hwang, J., Lyoo, I., Dager, S., Friedman, S., Oh, J., Lee, J.Y., Kim, S., Dunner, D., Renshaw, P.: Basal ganglia shape alterations in bipolar disorder. Am. J. Psychiatry 163(2), 276–285 (2006)

13. Shapira, L., Shamir, A., Cohen-Or, D.: Consistent mesh partitioning and skeletonization using the shape diameter function. Visual Comput. 24, 249–259 (2008)

14. Shi, Y., Lai, R., Krishna, S., Dinov, I., Toga, A.: Anisotropic laplace-beltrami eigenmaps: Bridging reeb graphs and skeletons. In: Proc. of CVPR 2008 Workshop, Anchorage, AK, USA, pp. 1–7. IEEE Computer Society Press (2008)

15. Reeb, G.: Sur les points singuliers d une forme de pfaff completement integrable ou d une fonction numerique. Comptes rendus de l'Academie des Sciences 222, 847–849 (1946)

16. Milnor, J.: Morse theory, vol. 51. Princeton Univ Pr. (1963)

17. Banchoff, T.: Critical points and curvature for embedded polyhedral surfaces. T. Am. Math. Mon. 77(5), 475–485 (1970)

18. Biasotti, S., Giorgi, D., Spagnuolo, M., Falcidieno, B.: Reeb graphs for shape analysis and applications. Theor. Comput. Sci. 392, 5–22 (2008)

19. Cole-McLaughlin, K., Edelsbrunner, H., Harer, J., Natarajan, V., Pascucci, V.: Loops in reeb graphs of 2-manifolds. In: Proc. of the 19th SoCG, SCG 2003, pp. 344–350. ACM, New York (2003)

20. Shinagawa, Y., Kunii, T., Kergosien, Y.: Surface coding based on morse theory. IEEE Comput. Graph. Appl. 11, 66–78 (1991)

21. Shinagawa, Y., Kunii, T.: Constructing a reeb graph automatically from cross sections. IEEE CG&A 11, 44–51 (1991)

22. Lazarus, F., Verroust, A.: Level set diagrams of polyhedral objects. In: Proc. of the 5th Symposium on Solid Modeling, pp. 130–140. ACM (1999)

23. Tierny, J., Vandeborre, J., Daoudi, M.: 3d mesh skeleton extraction using topological and geometrical analyses. In: Proc. of the 14th Pacific Graphics 2006, Taipei, Taiwan, pp. 85–94 (2006)

24. Pascucci, V., Scorzelli, G., Bremer, P.-T., Mascarenhas, A.: Robust on-line computation of reeb graphs: simplicity and speed. ACM Trans. Graph. 26 (July 2007)

25. Doraiswamy, H., Natarajan, V.: Efficient algorithms for computing reeb graphs. Comp. Geom. 42(6-7), 606–616 (2009)

26. Berretti, S., Del Bimbo, A., Pala, P.: 3d mesh decomposition using reeb graphs. Image Vision Comput. 27(10), 1540–1554 (2009); Special Section: Computer Vision Methods for Ambient Intelligence

27. Patane, G., Spagnuolo, M., Falcidieno, B.: A minimal contouring approach to the computation of the reeb graph. IEEE TVCG 15, 583–595 (2009)

28. Brandolini, L., Piastra, M.: Computing the reeb graph for triangle meshes with active contours. In: Proc. of ICPRAM 2012, vol. 2, pp. 80–89. SciTePress (2012)
29. Fischl, B., Salat, D., Busa, E., Albert, M., Dieterich, M., Haselgrove, C., van der Kouwe, A., Killiany, R., Kennedy, D., Klaveness, S., Montillo, A., Makris, N., Rosen, B., Dale, A.: Whole brain segmentation: automated labeling of neuroanatomical structures in the human brain. Neuron. 33, 341–355 (2002)
30. Ben Hamza, A., Krim, H.: Geodesic Object Representation and Recognition. In: Nyström, I., Sanniti di Baja, G., Svensson, S. (eds.) DGCI 2003. LNCS, vol. 2886, pp. 378–387. Springer, Heidelberg (2003)
31. Ni, X., Garland, M., Hart, J.: Fair morse functions for extracting the topological structure of a surface mesh. ACM Trans. Graph. 23, 613–622 (2004)
32. Novotni, M., Klein, R.: Computing geodesic distances on triangular meshes. In: Proc. of WSCG 2002, pp. 341–347 (2002)
33. Dijkstra, E.: A note on two problems in connexion with graphs. Numer. Math. 1, 269–271 (1959)
34. Laakso, M., Tiihonen, J., Syvälahti, E., Vilkman, H., Laakso, A., Alakare, B., Räkköläinen, V., Salokangas, R., Koivisto, E., Hietala, J.: A morphometric mri study of the hippocampus in first-episode, neuroleptic-naïve schizophrenia. Schizophr. Res. 50(1-2), 3–7 (2001)
35. Lötjönen, J., Reissman, P.-J., Magnin, I., Katila, T.: Model extraction from magnetic resonance volume data using the deformable pyramid. Med. Image Anal. 3(4), 387–406 (1999)
36. Kendall, D.G.: A survey of the statistical theory of shape. Statist. Sci. 4(2), 87–99 (1989)
37. Arun, K., Huang, T., Blostein, S.: Least-squares fitting of two 3-d point sets. IEEE Trans. Pattern. Anal. Mach. Intell. 9(5), 698–700 (1987)
38. Huttenlocher, D., Klanderman, G., Rucklidge, W.: Comparing images using the hausdorff distance. IEEE Trans. Pattern Anal. Mach. Intell. 15, 850–863 (1993)
39. Arun, K., Huang, T., Blostein, S.: Closed-form solution of absolute orientation using unit quaternions. J. Opt. Soc. Am. A. 4(4), 629–642 (1987)

Topology Aware Quad Dominant Meshing for Vascular Structures

Dominik Sibbing, Hans-Christian Ebke, Kai Ingo Esser, and Leif Kobbelt

Computer Graphics and Multimedia,
RWTH Aachen University Germany
{sibbing,ebke,esser,kobbelt}@cs.rwth-aachen.de
www.graphics.rwth-aachen.de

Abstract. We present a pipeline to generate high quality quad dominant meshes for vascular structures from a given volumetric image. As
common for medical image segmentation we use a Level Set approach to
separate the region of interest from the background. However in contrast
to the standard method we control the topology of the deformable object
– defined by the Level Set function – which allows us to extract a proper
skeleton which represents the global topological information of the vascular structure. Instead of solving a complex global optimization problem
to compute a quad mesh, we divide the problem and partition the complex model into *junction* and *tube* elements, employing the skeleton of
the vascular structure. After computing quad meshes for the *junctions*
using the Mixed Integer Quadrangulation approach, we re-mesh the *tubes*
using an algorithm inspired by the well known Bresenham Algorithm for
drawing lines which distributes irregular elements equally over the entire
tube element.

Keywords: Level Sets, Quad dominant meshes.

1 Introduction

Modern medical imaging techniques like, e.g, Magnetic Resonance Imaging (MRI)
or X-ray computed tomography (CT) are able to capture many details of anatomical structures. Often however the relevant information is hidden by additional
data, simultaneously collected during the scan. Besides this, a pure image based
representation is often insufficient for subsequent processing. Mesh based representations on the other hand open the door to a broad range of applications, like
physical simulation (fluid simulation, deformable objects), high quality render-
ings (global illumination and shadows) or even modeling and animation. Such
polygonal meshes often have to fulfill some application specific quality requirements. Compared to commonly used unstructured triangular representations,
shape-adaptive quad meshes have proven to be visually more pleasant, require
fewer elements, produce much more stable results for Finite Elements Methods
and enable the implementation of intuitive modeling metaphors.

J.A. Levine, R.R. Paulsen, Y. Zhang (Eds.): MeshMed 2012, LNCS 7599, pp. 147–158, 2012.
© Springer-Verlag Berlin Heidelberg 2012

In this paper we focus on angiogram data obtained from an MRI scanner. The task is to compute a quad dominant mesh representing the vascular structure embedded in a volume image. Since we are using a variant of the Level Set method which is able to control the topology of the deformable object, the topology of our extracted mesh is a plausible interpretation of the topology of the vascular structure. We employ this topological information to break down the difficult global quad meshing task of the entire vessel tree into a set of simpler sub-tasks namely the individual meshing of *junctions* and *tube* elements. Our *tube* meshing approach is not only faster than a global mesh generation approach but it is also able to effectively adapt the quad's aspect ratio and thereby needs fewer polygons to approximate the surface.

1.1 Related Work

Direct volume rendering is a technique to visualize the relevant information contained in a volumetric image in real-time [1]. A transfer function is used to highlight the region of interest and blend out uninteresting regions. Although this technique produces visually pleasant images, it offers not the same flexibility provided by polygonal meshes.

Image segmentation. Can be performed robustly by Active Contours like Level Sets where the surface of an deformable object evolves over time [2]. For the segmentation task a speed function for the evolution of the deformable model has to be defined, such that the region of interest is conquered before non interesting regions are conquered. In naive implementations this evolution process might produce a high genus object with many holes. Since our re-meshing approach is based on the topology of the vessel structure, we want our segmentation to represent this topology as realistically as possible. This is why we use a variant of the Level Set method which is able to control the topology of the deformable object [3].

Vascular structure surface reconstruction techniques can be differentiated into *model based* and *model free* approaches. Model based approaches usually assume that the vessels have a circular section at every point. While this simplification commonly leads to fast runtime performance it makes the reconstruction less accurate. Examples of model based methods are the ones presented by Felkel et al. [4] as well as Yim et al. [5], both of which produce quad dominant meshes.

In contrast, model free approaches attempt to reconstruct the original vascular structure's profile without simplifying assumptions, yielding more realistic results at the cost of a higher runtime. Many existing methods in this domain either produce triangle meshes (e.g. [6]) or are limited to certain structural configurations. For instance, the method introduced in [7] only works satisfactory on bifurcations (as opposed to general *n*-furcations).

In [8] Kälberer et al. extended the QuadCover approach to tube-like surfaces, where directional information is computed from the principal curvature of the input mesh, which can be sensitive to surface noise. In this paper we also focus on the topologically correct extraction of the branching structure. Since the skeleton based segmentation approach is not sensitive to a noisy mesh surface, we can even deal with rather rough surfaces at a low resolution, which are commonplace when computing polygonal meshes from volumetric images.

Quad re-meshing Many approaches have been proposed to compute quad (dominant) meshes for triangular input meshes. To compute a quad mesh for an arbitrary input mesh Ray et al. [9] utilized two given orthogonal vector fields to compute a globally smooth parametrization from which the quad layout can be extracted. Similar to this early approach other techniques have been proposed which formulate the quad meshing problem as a global parametrization problem [10,11,12,13]. Once this parametrization is known, the basic idea is to map the canonical integer grid of the parameter domain back onto the surface in order to obtain a quad mesh.

Finding a parametrization that leads to a sensible, geometrically sound singularity structure, that produces quads aligned with the curvature of the surface and that exhibits low distortion is a challenging and time consuming global optimization problem. The solution to this problem for the mesh of the entire vascular structure would come at prohibitive runtime costs. By segmenting the vessel structures, we can efficiently compute a quad covered surface. At the same time the boundaries originating from the segmentation give us directional information for orienting the quads. For a recent survey on quad meshing see [14].

2   Mesh Generation Pipeline

The input to our algorithm is an angiogram, which is typically stored as a volumetric image. The image intensities are represented by a real valued function

$$f : \mathbb{R}^3 \to \mathbb{R}$$

mapping each point $\mathbf{x}$ in 3D space to an intensity value $f(\mathbf{x})$. We first identify the voxels belonging to the interior of the vascular structure by using a variant of the Level Set method, while an adapted Marching Cubes algorithm is applied to extract a triangular mesh the topology of which is a plausible interpretation of the topology of the vascular structure (Section 2.1).

For this mesh we generate a skeleton consisting of nodes along the vessels' center-lines connected by simple line segments. Since the skeleton naturally represents the topology of the vascular structure we can easily identify branches, endpoints and connecting tube segments and thus partition the triangular mesh according to those classifications (Section 2.2) and thereby split the hard global quad meshing task into easier local sub-tasks: for junctions and endpoints we employ the Mixed Integer Quadrangultion approach by Bommes et al. [12]. Since tube segments are topological cylinders, we can use a simpler meshing technique (Section 2.3).

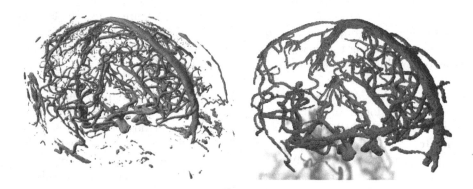

Fig. 1. Left: Direct volume rendering of the angiogram data. Right: Level Set volume at an early time of arrival. An adapted version of the Marching Cubes Algorithm extracts a noisy mesh with genus zero, which is the input to the subsequent stages of the re-meshing pipeline.

2.1   Separating the Vascular Structure from the Background

Deformable models are well established for 2D and 3D image segmentation [15]. Such models are initialized in the interior of the region of interest, in our case the vascular structure. Forces, acting on the surface of the deformable model, change its shape over time. Interior forces preserve surface smoothness while exterior forces are applied such that the surface is dragged towards the border of the region of interest. Level Sets can be considered as the Eulerian point of view of this idea: to each specific point $\mathbf{x} \in \mathbb{R}^3$ a time of arrival $\eta(\mathbf{x})$ is assigned. A point $\mathbf{x}$ is said to lie on the surface if its time of arrival matches a certain value t, i.e. the surface is represented by all points $\mathbf{x}$ with $\eta(\mathbf{x}) = t$.

Although there are many fast implementations of this segmentation method [2], most of them are oblivious to topological changes of the evolving surface. If the surface touches itself, it is possible that additional tunnels or handles are produced. This actually changes the topology of the model which may lead to unnatural anatomical structures. In our setting this would mean that the algorithm generates, e.g., unwanted branches or connections in the vascular structure. Bischof et al. [3] suggested to tag edges between voxels as *cut edges* whenever the front touches itself. An adapted version of the Marching Cubes Algorithm [16] inserts additional faces at those *cut edges* to separate the two fronts at sub-voxel accuracy. Thus, topological changes of the model are effectively prevented and the resulting surface is guaranteed to be genus zero.

The evolution of the Level Set function is implemented using the Fast Marching Method [3,2]. Voxels are classified into *conquered*, *front* and *free* voxels. At the beginning some voxels are marked as *conquered* and their time of arrival is set to $\eta = 0$. For this initialization step and as depicted in Figure 1, we visualize the vascular structure using direct volume rendering and allow the user to click on a vessel. The picked pixel position together with the position of the eye defines a ray which can be traced through the volume to identify possible

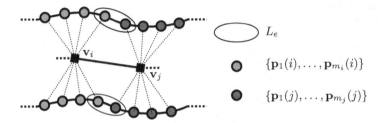

Fig. 2. Vertices approximately lying around the center of an edge are used to estimate the thickness of the structure

intersections with the visible surface. The midpoint between the first two intersections is likely to lie in the interior of a vessel and we use the surrounding voxels for the initialization.

In each iteration of the Fast Marching Method one *front* voxel $\mathbf{x}$ with smallest time of arrival $\eta(\mathbf{x})$ is marked as *conquered*. Then every *free* neighboring voxel $\mathbf{y}$ of $\mathbf{x}$ is marked as *front* and the time of arrival of all *front* neighbors are updated according to

$$\eta(\mathbf{y}) = \min\{\eta(\mathbf{y}), \eta(\mathbf{x}) + cost(\mathbf{x}, \mathbf{y})\}$$

The resulting segmentation is very sensitive to the design of the cost function. In our setting we define the cost function to be

$$cost(\mathbf{x}, \mathbf{y}) = (1 - f(\mathbf{y}))^2 + \nabla f(\mathbf{y}) \cdot \frac{(\mathbf{y} - \mathbf{x})}{\|(\mathbf{y} - \mathbf{x})\|}$$

Intuitively we allow the surface to grow fast into homogenous regions of high intensity, which is characteristic for vessels represented in angiogram data. If the conquering of a voxel (*free* → *front*) causes a topology change of the *front* surface, we mark the corresponding edge such that the resulting mesh preserves its genus zero topology (see [3] for details).

After all voxels have been conquered we use the Marching Cubes Algorithm to extract a triangular mesh representing the Level Set at some (user defined) early time of arrival. The resulting mesh is shown in the right image of Figure 1. The topology of this mesh is already close the topology of the vascular structure but it may still contain many geometric noise artifacts as it is common for meshes extracted with the Marching Cubes Algorithm. We use mesh smoothing [17] and an isotropic re-meshing technique [18] to generate a high quality triangle mesh which is passed on to the next steps of our pipeline.

2.2 Skeleton Extraction and Segmentation

In order to efficiently compute a quad dominant mesh given the previously computed triangular mesh $\mathcal{M}$, we segment this mesh into simpler elements, namely into *junctions* and *tubes*, and separately compute quad meshes for each part (we consider an endpoint as a special *junction* with only one neighbor). While in

Input: $T = (V, E)$
Output: a set of cuts $\{(e, \alpha)\} \subset E \times [0, 1)$
$S := \{\}$
for *each junction* $\mathbf{v}_j \in V$ **do**
    let $r = \max_{e=(j,k) \in E}\{r(e)\}$
    grow from $\mathbf{v}_j$ the connected subgraph $(V_J, E_J) \subseteq T$ with
        $\|\mathbf{v} - \mathbf{v}_j\| \leq 1.5r \quad \forall \mathbf{v} \in V_J$
    find the cut edges $C_J = ((i, k), \alpha) \subset E \times [0, 1)$ with
        $\mathbf{v}_i \in V_J, \mathbf{v}_k \notin V_J, \|(\mathbf{v}_i - \mathbf{v}_j) + \alpha(\mathbf{v}_k - \mathbf{v}_i)\| = 1.5r$
    add (V_J, E_J, C_J) to S   // "collect junction segments"
end
while $\exists (V_1, E_1, C_1), (V_2, E_2, C_2) \in S$ *with*   // "merge overlapping"
    $\exists (e, \alpha) \in C_1$ *so that* $e \in E_2$ *or*
    $\exists (e, \alpha) \in C_2$ *so that* $e \in E_1$ *or*
    $\exists ((i, j), \alpha) \in C_1, ((j, i), \beta) \in C_2$ *so that* $\alpha + \beta > 1$ **do**
    remove (V_1, E_1, C_1) and (V_2, E_2, C_2) from S
    merge (V_1, E_1, C_1) and (V_2, E_2, C_2) and add the result to S
end
return $\{C \mid \exists V, E : (V, E, C) \in S\}$

Algorithm 1. Skeleton Segmentation

general the segmentation of a two manifold surface is a rather difficult task, the segmentation of an embedded skeleton naturally emerges from the branchings and neighborhood relations between its vertices.

We employ the skeleton extraction algorithm suggested in [19] to compute a graph structure $T = (V, E)$ encoding the branching behavior of the vascular structure. The set $V = \{1, \ldots, n\}$ are the indices of the skeleton vertices and the (undirected) edges $E = \{(i, j) \mid i \text{ is connected to } j\}$ encode the neighbor relations. Since the mesh $\mathcal{M}$ resulting from the previous step is genus zero, T is a tree (no cycles). The idea of the skeleton extraction is to iteratively perform a number of smoothing steps on the input mesh to shrink it nearly to a one dimensional structure. A sequence of edge collapses finally generates the tree T, where nodes are connected by line segments. As described in [19] the procedure stores a set of associated parent vertices $S_i = S(\mathbf{v}_i) = \{\mathbf{p}_1(i), \ldots, \mathbf{p}_{m_i}(i)\} \in \mathcal{M}$ for each skeleton node $\mathbf{v}_i$, which we use to estimate the radius $r(e)$ for an edge $e = (i, j)$ as the average orthogonal distance to the surrounding parent vertices:

$$r(e) = r(i, j) = \frac{1}{|L_e|} \sum_{\mathbf{p} \in L_e} \|(Id - \mathbf{d}\mathbf{d}^T)(\mathbf{p} - \mathbf{v}_i)\|$$

Here $\mathbf{d}$ is the normalized vector pointing from $\mathbf{v}_i$ to $\mathbf{v}_j$ and $L_e = \{\mathbf{p} \in S(\mathbf{v}_i) \mid \exists \mathbf{q} \in S(\mathbf{v}_j) : (\mathbf{p}, \mathbf{q}) \in \mathcal{M}\} \cup \{\mathbf{p} \in S(\mathbf{v}_j) \mid \exists \mathbf{q} \in S(\mathbf{v}_i) : (\mathbf{p}, \mathbf{q}) \in \mathcal{M}\}$ is the set of all parent vertices of $\mathbf{v}_i$ (or $\mathbf{v}_j$) who have neighbors in $\mathcal{M}$, that are parents of the node $\mathbf{v}_j$ (or $\mathbf{v}_i$), see Figure 2.

Given the tree T and the radii $r(e)$ the idea for the mesh segmentation is rather simple. We start a growing procedure from all junctions and walk over the tree nodes until we reach a point whose distance to the junction is larger than a

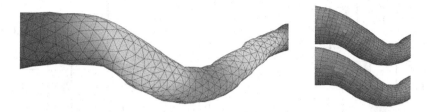

Fig. 3. Left: Harmonic field with boundary conditions zero (color coded as blue) at the left interface and one (color coded as red) at the right interface. Right: Since we can change the number of equally distributed rings, it is very easy to control the anisotropy of the quad elements. In the upper part we set the scaling factor to $s = 1$ while the lower part is an example for $s = 3$. This significantly reduces the total number of elements in the mesh.

multiple of the vessel radius (in our settings we use 1.5 times the maximal radius of the edges adjacent to the junction). With the edge direction at this point as normal vector, a plane is defined which cuts the mesh into two components.

Algorithm 1 shows the details of this procedure. Observe that this procedure merges simple *junctions* to more complex *junctions* by removing cuts whenever neighboring *junctions* lie close together. Each resulting cut plane intersects a set of edges of the original triangular mesh. By splitting those edges we get a 2D polygon lying in the respective plane. Cloning those new vertices finally splits the triangular mesh into two parts. We call the two versions of the cloned 2D polygon an interface between adjacent mesh segments. The final result of the segmentation is a set of meshes $\mathcal{M}_1, \ldots, \mathcal{M}_k$ where two adjacent mesh segments share a common interface. Thereby segments labeled as *junction* exhibit a number $\neq 2$ of interfaces to neighboring *tube* segments which have exactly two interfaces (Figure 5(b)).

2.3 Quad Dominant Re-meshing

Junctions. The first step is to compute quad meshes for all *junctions*. For this we use the Mixed Integer Quadrangulation proposed by Bommes et al. [12]. We avoid the difficult search for good feature directions to align the quads and simplyrequire the quads to align with the boundary defined by the interfaces. This automatically produces quads which are radially arranged around the interfaces of *tube* segments (cf. Figure 5(c)).

Tubes. Before we start re-meshing the *tubes* we resample the interfaces of a *tube* such that number and positions of the vertices lying on an interface match the number and positions of the vertices after quad meshing of the neighboring *junction* segments. Assume that after this step the left interface has n_l and the right interface has n_r vertices, where without loss of generality $n_l \leq n_r$.

Since the tube segments are topological cylinders there is a natural and simple way to generate quad meshes for them by intersecting a sequence of rings around

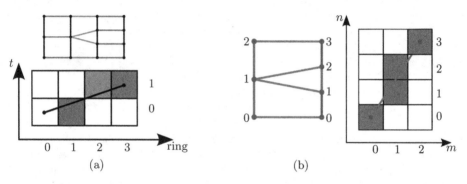

Fig. 4. (a) Identification of transition rings: The first step of the Bresenham Algorithm does not change y, so there will be no transition (green lines). In the second step we go north east, so a transition from $m = 3$ to $n = 4$ vertices occurs (blue lines). (b) Connection pattern between two rings with a different number of samples from $m = 3$ to $n = 4$ vertices.

the tube with a set of trajectories along the tubes. The only complication arises from the fact that the number of samples (= number of trajectories) at the left and right interface may be different since they are implied by the quad meshes that have been generated independently for the two neighboring junction segments.

Our procedure works in three steps. First, the rings are defined by equidistant iso-contours of a harmonic scalar field computed on the tube. Second, the number of samples is determined for each ring such that they coincide with the prescribed interfaces on both sides and in between we place a number of transition rings where the number of samples per ring changes. In the third step we connect the samples of neighboring rings to form quad elements whenever possible. While this step is trivial for rings with the same number of samples, we have to introduce triangle elements between rings with differing numbers of samples. Ideally these triangles should be distributed uniformly around the circumference of the ring.

Ring Generation. We compute a harmonic scalar function f_{harm} defined at the vertices of the *tube* segment by requiring

$$\Delta^2 f_{harm} = 0$$

where Δ is the cotangent weighted Laplace operator for triangle meshes [17]. As seen in the left part of Figure 3 we define proper boundary conditions by requiring the harmonic field to be zero at the left and one at the right interface. This allows us to extract non intersecting polylines (rings) by tracing the iso-contours of the harmonic function f_{harm}, on which we equally distribute a number of vertices which later become the new vertices of our quad dominant mesh.

Including both interfaces, the remesher generates

$$n_{iso} = \frac{l_{tube}}{s \cdot e_{target}} + 1$$

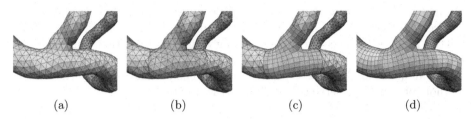

Fig. 5. (a) The input to our remeshing stage is a smoothed and re-sampled version of the mesh extracted using the Marching Cubes Algorithm. (b) The mesh is partitioned into *junction* and *tube* components. The cuts insert additional vertices at the respective interfaces. (c) We re-mesh the *junctions* yielding a fair quad layout. (d) Tubes are re-meshed, such that the final mesh is a quad dominant mesh.

isolines, where l_{tube} is the length of the *tube*, e_{target} the target edge length and s a scale factor which controls the anisotropy of the quads. In general the minimal and maximal curvature on tubular structures differ severely, meaning that quads which are stretched in the direction of the tube axis will approximate the surface very well. Notice that one has no influence on the anisotropy of the elements when using one of the above mentioned global quad meshing approaches like the Mixed Integer Quadrangulation. Our re-meshing algorithm handles such anisotropy in a very intuitive way as illustrated in the right part of Figure 3.

In order to restrict the transitions where the number of samples per ring changes to as few rings as possible and to make these transitions as (rotationally) symmetric as possible we double the number of vertices with each transition. Hence, the total number of required transitions is equal to the smallest t for which

$$n_l \cdot 2^t \geq n_r$$

holds. At the last transition the number of vertices is not doubled but clamped to n_r to ensure compatibility with the right interface.

Connecting rings. For the generation of tube meshes we have to solve two tasks. One is the task to select the t transition rings (among the n_{iso} rings along the tube) and the other task is to connect the samples of neighboring rings (which is only non-trivial for transition rings). In both cases, we have to distribute a discrete number of events over a (larger) discrete number of elements. We apply the Bresenham line rasterization algorithm [20] for both tasks. Notice that the Bresenham algorithm essentially distributes a discrete number of y-steps over a (larger) discrete number of x-steps.

If we want to equally distribute the t transition rings among the n_{iso} rings along a tube, we can rasterize a line on a pixel grid from $(0,0)$ to (n_{iso}, t) and pick those rings for which the y-coordinate changes (cf. Fig. 4(a)).

Similarly, if we want to connect two rings with n and m samples $(m < n)$ respectively, we can rasterize a line from $(0,0)$ to (m,n) and connect the ith sample on the first ring with the jth sample on the second ring if the pixel (i,j) was set by the Bresenham algorithm (cf. Fig. 4(b)).

Geometric Optimization. After placing and connecting all vertices we allow the vertices lying at the n_{iso} rings to move around the rings while keeping their relative geodesic distance fixed. For each ring we find that rotation (parametrized by one scalar degree of freedom) which yields a configuration where the angles within all quads are as close as possible to 90°. The left and right interface rings are not rotated to preserve compatibility (Figure 5(d)).

3   Results

We ran our experiments on an Intel(R) Core(TM) i7 CPU with 2.67GHz. The angiogram data set has a resolution of 288 x 384 x 185 voxels and it took less than 2 minutes to extract the mesh representing the vascular structure using the Level Set method. The smoothed and remeshed version of this mesh, which serves as input for the quad re-meshing has a total number of 110k vertices.

The skeleton of this mesh was extracted in less than four minutes, while segmenting the resulting tree into 215 *junction* and 214 *tube* elements was nearly

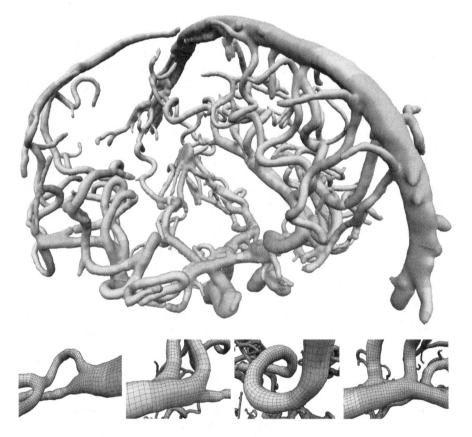

Fig. 6. Results produced with our re-meshing pipeline

instantaneous. Computing the quad layouts for each of the *junctions* was the most time consuming task and took approximately 16 minutes. In comparison to this the proposed algorithm to re-mesh the tubes is highly efficient and took less than 4 seconds. The total time to perform the re-meshing is with approximately 20 minutes much more efficient than solving the global optimization problem, which took more than 12 hours to compute due to the complex layout structure. When we place anisotropic quads with a stretch factor of $s = 3$ onto the *tubes*, the resulting mesh has 120k faces, while the isotropic version counts 200k faces (67% overhead) with the same approximation quality. Exemplary close-ups are shown in Figure 6.

4 Conclusion

We presented a pipeline to generate quad dominant meshes from volumetric images. By controlling the topology during the Level Set segmentation such that the topology of the final polygonal mesh comes close to the topology of the scanned vascular structure, we are able to compute the skeleton of the vascular structure. Segmenting the skeleton into *junctions* and *tubes* effectively divides the difficult global quad meshing task into a set of more simpler sub-tasks where we treat *tubes* like cylindrical components. Irregular elements lying on *tubes* are distributed over the structure using a procedure inspired by the Bresenham-Algorithm for lines. The uniform distribution of rings using a harmonic field effectively allows us to control the anisotropy of quad elements, which is not easily possible for global quad meshing approaches.

In future work we would like to extend this idea to produce pure quad-meshes. Since this can only be achieved if the number of vertices at the left and the right interface differ by an even number of samples, one would need to include additional global constraints for the number of vertices at the interfaces of the *junction* elements.

References

1. Hadwiger, M., Ljung, P., Salama, C.R., Ropinski, T.: Advanced illumination techniques for gpu-based volume raycasting. In: ACM SIGGRAPH 2009 Courses, SIGGRAPH 2009, pp. 2:1–2:166. ACM, NewYork (2009)
2. Sethian, J.A.: Level Set Methods and Fast Marching Methods. Cambridge University Press, Cambridge (1999)
3. Bischoff, S., Kobbelt, L.: Sub-Voxel topology control for Level-Set surfaces. Computer Graphics Forum 22(3), 273–280 (2003)
4. Felkel, P., Wegenkittl, R., Buhler, K.: Surface models of tube trees. In: Computer Graphics International, pp. 70–77 (2004)
5. Yim, P., Cebral, J., Mullick, R., Marcos, H., Choyke, P.: Vessel surface reconstruction with a tubular deformable model. Medical Imaging 20(12) (2001)
6. Schumann, C., Neugebauer, M., Bade, R., Preim, B., Peitgen, H.O.: Implicit vessel surface reconstruction for visualization and cfd simulation. International Journal of Computer Assisted Radiology and Surgery 2, 275–286 (2008)

7. Antiga, L., Ene-Iordache, B., Caverni, L., Cornalba, G.P., Remuzzi, A.: Geometric reconstruction for computational mesh generation of arterial bifurcations from ct angiography. Computerized Medical Imaging and Graphics 26(4), 227–235 (2002)
8. Kälberer, F., Nieser, M., Polthier, K.: Stripe parameterization of tubular surfaces. In: Topological Methods in Data Analysis and Visualization. Theory, Algorithms, and Applications. Mathematics and Visualization. Springer (2010)
9. Ray, N., Li, W.C., Lévy, B., Sheffer, A., Alliez, P.: Periodic global parameterization. ACM Trans. Graph. 25(4), 1460–1485 (2006)
10. Kälberer, F., Nieser, M., Polthier, K.: Quadcover - surface parameterization using branched coverings. Computer Graphics Forum 26(3), 375–384 (2007)
11. Dong, S., Bremer, P.T., Garland, M., Pascucci, V., Hart, J.C.: Spectral surface quadrangulation. In: SIGGRAPH 2006, pp. 1057–1066. ACM, New York (2006)
12. Bommes, D., Zimmer, H., Kobbelt, L.: Mixed-integer quadrangulation. ACM Trans. Graph. 28(3), 1–10 (2009)
13. Zhang, M., Huang, J., Liu, X., Bao, H.: A wave-based anisotropic quadrangulation method. In: SIGGRAPH 2010, pp. 118:1–118:8. ACM, New York (2010)
14. Bommes, D., Lévy, B., Pietroni, N., Puppo, E., Silva, C., Tarini, M., Zorin, D.: State of the art in quad meshing. In: Eurographics STARS (2012)
15. Mcinerney, T., Terzopoulos, D.: Deformable models in medical image analysis: A survey. Medical Image Analysis 1, 91–108 (1996)
16. Lorensen, W.E., Cline, H.E.: Marching cubes: A high resolution 3d surface construction algorithm. Computer Graphics 21(4), 163–169 (1987)
17. Pinkall, U., Polthier, K.: Computing discrete minimal surfaces and their conjugates. Experimental Mathematics 2, 15–36 (1993)
18. Botsch, M., Kobbelt, L.: A remeshing approach to multiresolution modeling. In: Proc. SGP, pp. 185–192 (2004)
19. Au, O.K.C., Tai, C.L., Chu, H.K., Cohen-Or, D., Lee, T.Y.: Skeleton extraction by mesh contraction. ACM Trans. Graph. 27(3) (2008)

Volumetric Real-Time Particle-Based Representation of Large Unstructured Tetrahedral Polygon Meshes

Philip Voglreiter, Markus Steinberger, Dieter Schmalstieg, and Bernhard Kainz

Institute for Computer Graphics and Vision,
Graz University of Technology, Inffeldgasse 16,
A-8010 Graz, Austria
{voglreiter,steinberger,schmalstieg,kainz}@icg.tugraz.at
http://www.icg.tugraz.at

Abstract. In this paper we propose a particle-based volume rendering approach for unstructured, three-dimensional, tetrahedral polygon meshes. We stochastically generate millions of particles per second and project them on the screen in real-time. In contrast to previous rendering techniques of tetrahedral volume meshes, our method does not need a prior depth sorting of geometry. Instead, the rendered image is generated by choosing particles closest to the camera. Furthermore, we use spatial superimposing. Each pixel is constructed from multiple subpixels. This approach not only increases projection accuracy, but allows also a combination of subpixels into one superpixel that creates the well-known translucency effect of volume rendering. We show that our method is fast enough for the visualization of unstructured three-dimensional grids with hard real-time constraints and that it scales well for a high number of particles.

Keywords: mesh representations, volume rendering, GPU accelerated, particle-based.

1 Introduction

Volume rendering is used in many disciplines and is strongly tied to visual representation of medical datasets. Irregular datasets – or unstructured grids –, are mainly used for simulations, for example for finite element analysis [2]. Rendering methods for such grids are an ongoing field of research.

Modern medical applications demand fast visualization techniques. Generation of images with interactive frame rates is essential for applications requiring visualization techniques which cater to hard real-time constraints. Furthermore, medical applications often need to provide a wide field of different techniques to visualize different modalities concurrently. One could think of image segmentation or simulations performed in parallel with rendering.

The recent developments in general computations on Graphics Processing Units (GPUs) offer the ability to solve a wide variety of parallelizable tasks

J.A. Levine, R.R. Paulsen, Y. Zhang (Eds.): MeshMed 2012, LNCS 7599, pp. 159–168, 2012.

efficiently. In this paper, we introduce a novel way of stochastic Particle-based volume rendering (PBVR) exploiting these capabilities. In contrast to many other object space volume rendering approaches, basic PBVR does not require depth sorting of any kind. Instead, we treat projected particles in a way that is similar to z-buffering. Contrary to the highly sophisticated particle generation methods (Metropolis [6]) used by former approaches, we introduce a method of particle generation with little computational effort and online control of the number of generated particles. This ability is crucial for applications with hard real-time constraints and allows to alter visual effects such as density during runtime. Because the number of particles strongly influences the computational complexity, our proposed online control can also be used to steer the use of resources and thereby allocate resources for concurrent tasks. The complexity of the proposed method depends strongly on the number of particles needed. The amount of particles we need to render a given volume is strongly tied to the portion of the screen it covers while mesh complexity only shows a very minor impact. Also, the distance from the viewing camera influences the required number of particles. The screen resolution itself only plays a minor role when considering the computational complexity.

Contribution: We describe a fast method for parallel particle generation on the fly and simultaneous rendering for the visualization of large unstructured tetrahedral polygon meshes. A minimal preprocessing effort allows also to switch between volumes in real-time. We also introduce an improved method for particle superimposing by addressing perceptual issues.

2   Previous Work

2.1   Unstructured Mesh Representation

In [1], Avila *et al.* propose an approach for direct volume rendering and define an irregular dataset rendering pipeline based on the widely used plane-sweep technique. Shirley *et al.* [12] describe a method for projecting tetrahedrons onto the image plane. The tetrahedrons need to be sorted before projection. Sorting is known to be in $O(n \ log \ n)$, inducing a super-linear increase in computational effort. Approaches like projected tetrahedrons have already been implemented on the GPU [5]. The authors exploit the capabilities of shaders and CUDA to perform depth sorting of the tetrahedrons. As an alternative approach, Challinger [4] describes a method for ray casting of unstructured grids. Ray casting generates images of a higher quality but shows an $O(n^3)$ complexity. However, ray casting offers ways to benefit from modern GPU capabilities as was shown in [15]. Still, the complexity constrains the efficiency of the algorithm. Point splatting [13] is very similar to particle-based approaches. The efficient point splatting approach described by the authors has a low memory consumption, but point splatting inherently produces artifacts in the rendering process.

2.2   Particle-Based Volume Rendering (PBVR)

In [10], Sakamoto *et al.* describe a general approach of PBVR based on the Metropolis Method [6], a well-known Monte-Carlo algorithm [8] for random number generation. In [11], the authors go deeper into detail and consider rendering tetrahedral grids by voxelizing them. Voxelizing a tetrahedral grid can be a rather time-consuming task. The required double interpolation can result in a loss of information compared to methods using the unstructured grid data directly. For a more detailed outline of the algorithm, please refer also to a preliminary non-peer-reviewed version of this work found at [14].

3   PBVR Adaptions

The main idea of PBVR is to construct a dense field of light-emitting, opaque particles inside a volumetric dataset. These particles are used to perform object-based rendering by simulating the light emission of particles. Mutual occlusion induced by completely opaque particles plays a major role during rendering. Sakamoto *et. al.* [10] describe the basic model in more detail.

The following sections will explain the proposed method step by step. Each of the subsections is to be seen as a prerequisite to the following steps. Generally, PBVR can be subdivided into two major activities. First, a proper particle distribution inside the volume needs to be established. We describe this procedure in Section 3.1. Second, in Section 3.2, we outline how to project the particles onto the image plane. We consecutively show how to generate the well-known translucent effect of volume rendering in Section 3.3.

3.1   Particle Generation

In this paper we introduce a randomized process to generate particles. It is desirable to achieve a uniform distribution over the whole volume to avoid visually perceivable artifacts. We split the volume into tetrahedral cells and perform particle generation per cell, which enables parallelization. We will show how to retain a global distribution of mean values by concatenating local uniform distributions.

Particle Distribution over Cells: We consider a maximum number of particles p_{max} for the whole volume. To accomplish uniformity in distribution, we need to determine the number of particles p_{cell} each cell may emit. We calculate this number by using the proportion of the cell volume V_{cell} to the total volume of the grid V_{grid}. Therefore, the number of particles per cell is

$$p_{cell} = V_{cell}/V_{grid} \cdot p_{max}. \tag{1}$$

A proof for Equation 1 is provided in Appendix A. By using this formula we generate particles in a cell equaling the average number of particles considering

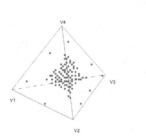
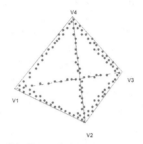
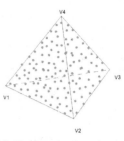
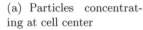

(a) Particles concentrating at cell center

(b) Particles concentrating at cell border

(c) Uniformly distributed particles

Fig. 1. Figures showing the results of different barycentric parameter generation approaches. The figures 1(a) and 1(b) both depict approaches resulting in disturbing patterns. This visual error accumulates over all cells and introduces streaks and clusters in the final image. Figure 1(c) shows the distribution we achieve when using the algorithm describe in Section 3.1.

a global distribution. Assuming that the distribution in a cell is uniform, the concatenation of several cells again comprises a new random distribution. The number of particles per cell in this new distribution simulates the average, or expected, number of particles of a real uniform random distribution throughout the whole volume.

Particle Position: We use barycentric coordinates to generate particle positions. Barycentric coordinates describe a point relative to the vertices of a polygon. In case of tetrahedrons, the barycentric notation of a point is

$$P = \alpha \cdot V1 + \beta \cdot V2 + \gamma \cdot V3 + (1 - (\alpha + \beta + \gamma)) \cdot V4 \qquad (2)$$

where V1 through V4 denote the corner points of the tetrahedron and α, β, γ resemble the barycentric parameters. Constraining the parameters to be in the interval $(0, 1)$ and sum up to 1 restrains positions to the interior.

Uniform Patternless Generation: There are several ways to randomly generate barycentric coordinates showing statistically correct behavior, but still introducing disturbing visual patterns. Figure 1 depicts the results of incorrect approaches as well as the distribution we want to achieve. A method for correct random generation of points in tetrahedra was described by Rocchini [9]. The authors describe a method which folds a cube into a tetrahedron. First, we randomly generate α, β, γ. Next we perform a check on violation of the barycentric constraints. If a set of generated random variables is outside the given bounds, we map the particle back inside the tetrahedron as described in the article. Additionally, we use the barycentric parameters to linearly interpolate the corner points and gain the scalar values corresponding to the particles.

Particle Emission Probability: Simply projecting all generated particles would lead to an equal density throughout the whole volume. We need to thin out the particle field to accommodate for cell translucency. As we still want to avoid patterns within the rendered images, we do this stochastically per particle by applying the rejection method [8]. First, we determine the opacity a particle would anticipate. We do this in a fashion similar to conservatie volume rendering approaches, but please be aware that this is not the final opacity value of a pixel, but rather a computational variable. Next, we generate a stochastic variable x within the interval $(0, 1)$ on the real line. Only if x is smaller than the opacity of the particle, it is accepted and emitted. This adapts the number of particles per cell according to the respective cell opacities. The method allows for smooth transitions between vertices with distinct opacities.

Empty Space Skipping: Often, different approaches of volume rendering need to process regions which, according to the chosen transfer function, do not need to be displayed at all. In our approach, we can easily filter the dataset on the fly. Depending on the selected transfer function, many cells anticipate a very low average opacity. This would lead to generation of particles with a rather low emission chance. To increase computational performance, we simply skip cells with a low average opacity. This prevents particle generation in those portions of the volume which would appear almost or totally translucent. This method shows an increase in performance directly proportional to the amount of cells we may neglect. This strategy is especially relevant for grids containing large connected empty regions, such as tetrahedralized CT scans. Furthermore, this approach is extremely adaptive to changes of the transfer functions.

3.2 Particle projection and Image Generation

Particle projection involves two steps. First, the screen space location of the particle needs to be determined, which requires the virtual camera parameters and the volume's transformation. Second, a color value needs to be assigned to each particle.

Projection from Object Space to Image Space: By using the modelview-projection matrix of the viewing camera we determine the image-space position of each emitted particle. Furthermore, we calculate its distance to the camera. If two particles hit the same fragment on the image plane, we choose to display the particle closer to the camera. Thereby, we effectively avoid depth sorting of particles hitting the screen as we only compare the depth values of subpixels. This approach is similar to common z-buffering.

3.3 Spatial Superimposing

2D Superimposing: For projection we subdivide each pixel into several sub-pixels. The subpixel level l describes a subdivision into $l \times l$ distinct subpixels.

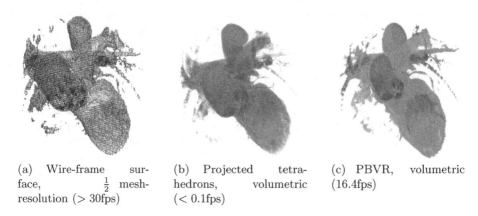

(a) Wire-frame sur-face, $\frac{1}{2}$ mesh-resolution (> 30fps)

(b) Projected tetra-hedrons, volumetric (< 0.1fps)

(c) PBVR, volumetric (16.4fps)

Fig. 2. Comparison between a wire-frame surface representation, projected tetrahedrons and PBVR for a tetrahedralized MAGIX [7] dataset. The scalars show the contrast agent enrichment of one time step of the 4D MAGIX CT scan (left ventricle, blue = low, red = high). Projected tetrahedrons takes several seconds for a full visualization. Our method remains interactive while appearing visually comparable to (b).

Thereby we increase the information available for each pixel on the screen as we increase the number of contributing particles originating from different depth levels. We compose the final pixel values by calculating the average of all contributing subpixels.

3D Superimposing: To increase the visual quality of the proposed algorithm we currently use superimposing over three dimensions. We store the projected particles in multiple 2D-superimposing layers to capture more contributing particles. Using this setup, we maintain several particles per subpixel rather than only storing the closest one. Unfortunately, we need to sort the particles in this refinement step for proper insertion. The number of particles per subpixel, i.e. the number of depth layers, may be adapted to the computational needs. This strategy results in a noticeable increase in visual quality, but has a severe impact on frame rates and memory consumption. Thus, we use this method for progressive refinement during periods with no direct interaction only.

Particle Depth Enhancement: Simple averaging of subpixels may create undesired visual effects, similar to front face culling in triangle mesh rendering. This effect may hamper depth perception while rotating the volumes. Equalized treatment of particles, regardless of their depth, alleviates the impact of particles close to the camera. Consecutively, particles further away show a strong impact on the final pixel which makes them appear too close to the camera. To support a better depth perception, we use the already present depth information of displayed particles. In detail, we analyze the depth of each pixel's subpixels z_{curr} and record their minimum z_{min} and maximum depth z_{max}. Then, we calculate the depth range and a depth ratio $\zeta = (z_{max} - z_{curr})/(z_{max} - z_{min})$, considering the gap to the maximum value. Using ζ as factor for the color values of subpixels, we achieve a linear depth evaluation of particles. We linearly blend the particles into the background considering the calculated parameter ζ. Those particles which are close to the camera sustain their influence on the color value while particles farther away partially lose their influence.

Translucency: Translucency is influenced by two parameters. Firstly, the number of generated particles influences how opaque the volume appears by altering the number of occupied subpixels. Secondly, the subpixel level increases or decreases the level of transparency in a similar way. By allowing online control of those parameters we also enable interactive adaption of frame rates while only slightly altering the translucency of the generated image.

4 Results

We evaluated our technique for several volumes including the MAGIX dataset [7] with 5 million cells, and a simulated radio frequency ablation (RFA) [3] data set with 55 thousand cells. The depicted results and frame rates were recorded on an NVIDIA GeForce GTX470 using CUDA 4.1, rendered at a resolution of 1200x800 pixels. Figure 2 shows a comparison of projected tetrahedrons [5] and our algorithm. The scalar values depict the flow inside the tissue. While the implementation of projected tetrahedrons we used is unable to cope with the sheer complexity of the dataset, our method stays responsive and even interactive during rendering. Please note that we rendered all of the shown pictures with 2D-superimposing to provide insight into the graphical capabilities of the basic method.

Figure 3 shows an RFA simulation rendered at 29 fps. The canals inside the volume show the impact of vessels on the heat distribution (heat sinks) during the simulation. The transfer function communicates the cell death probability where red denotes almost sure death and blue a low probability of destruction. The raw performance of our algorithm at rendering the complex MAGIX dataset is depicted in Figure 4. For reference, the image shown in Figure 2 was rendered on subpixel level $l = 3$ with 60 million particles. Even when configuring the particle number and subpixel level to be far higher than necessary, our algorithm runs with interactive frame rates.

(a) axial   (b) left   (c) right

Fig. 3. Simulated RFA (55k cells) with $p_{max} = 12$million, $l = 5$ @ 29fps

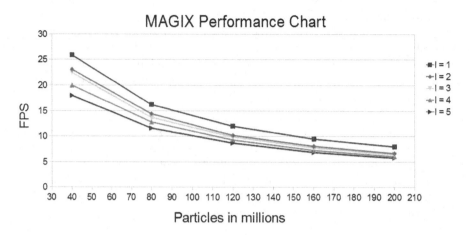

Fig. 4. Performance of the MAGIX dataset with different subpixel levels ($l = [1, 2, 3, 4, 5]$).

5   Conclusion

We have shown that our method is able to render millions of particles per second in real-time, mainly due to our fast and flexible particle generation process. We minimize GPU global memory access and increase computation occupancy. Furthermore, our approach offers a fast alternative for the real-time visualization of large unstructured tetrahedral polygon meshes. Future tasks are improved 3D-superimposing strategies to increase the image quality without a noticeable loss of render speed. Our approach will scale well for use on GPU clusters. Our method is open-source and a first version is freely available for download from our website[1]. A public link will be available by the time of the workshop.

Acknowledgments. This work was funded by the Austrian Science Fund (FWF): P23329.

References

1. Avila, R., Taosong, H., Lichan, H., Kaufman, A., Pfister, H., Silva, C., Sobierajski, L., Wang, S.: VolVis: A diversified Volume Visualization System. In: Proceedings of IEEE Conference on Visualization, Visualization 1994, CP3, pp. 31–38 (October 1994)
2. Babuska, I.: Generalized Finite Element Methods: Main Ideas, Results, and Perspective. Security 1(1), 67–103 (2004)
3. Bien, T., Rose, G., Skalej, M.: FEM Modeling of Radio Frequency Ablation in the Spinal Column. In: 2010 3rd International Conference on Biomedical Engineering and Informatics (BMEI), vol. 5, pp. 1867–1871 (October 2010)

---

[1] http://www.icg.tugraz.at/project/mvp/downloads-1/GPUPBVR.zip

4. Challinger, J.: Scalable parallel Volume Raycasting for nonrectilinear computational Grids. In: Proceedings of the 1993 Symposium on Parallel Rendering, PRS 1993, pp. 81–88. ACM, New York (1993)

5. Maximo, A., Marroquim, R., Farias, R.: Hardware-Assisted Projected Tetrahedra. Computer Graphics Forum 29(3), 903–912 (2010)

6. Metropolis, N., Rosenbluth, A.W., Rosenbluth, M.N., Teller, A.H., Teller, E.: Equation of State Calculations by Fast Computing Machines. The Journal of Chemical Physics 21(6), 1087–1092 (1953)

7. OsiriX DICOM Viewer public sample image sets. Dicom Image Sets (May 2012), http://www.osirix-viewer.com/datasets/

8. Robert, C.P., Casella, G.: Monte Carlo Statistical Methods. Springer Texts in Statistics. Springer-Verlag New York, Inc., Secaucus (2005)

9. Rocchini, C., Cignoni, P.: Generating random points in a tetrahedron. J. Graph. Tools 5(4), 9–12 (2000)

10. Sakamoto, N., Nonaka, J., Koyamada, K., Tanaka, S.: Volume Rendering using tiny Particles. In: Eighth IEEE International Symposium on Multimedia, ISM 2006, pp. 734–737 (December 2006)

11. Sakamoto, N., Nonaka, J., Koyamada, K., Tanaka, S.: Particle-based Volume Rendering. In: 2007 6th International Asia-Pacific Symposium on Visualization, APVIS 2007, pp. 129–132 (February 2007)

12. Shirley, P., Tuchman, A.: A polygonal Approximation to direct Scalar Volume Rendering. In: Proceedings of the 1990 Workshop on Volume Visualization, VVS 1990, pp. 63–70. ACM, New York (1990)

13. Vega-Higuera, F., Hastreiter, P., Fahlbusch, R., Greiner, G.: High performance Volume Splatting for Visualization of neurovascular Data. IEEE Visualization, 271–278 (October 2005)

14. Voglreiter, P., Kainz, B.: Stochastic Particle Based Volume Rendering (February 2012), http://www.cescg.org/CESCG-2012/papers/ Voglreiter-Stochastic_Particle-Based_Volume_Rendering.pdf

15. Zhang, C., Xi, P., Zhang, C.: CUDA-Based Volume Ray-Casting using cubic B-spline. In: 2011 International Conference on Virtual Reality and Visualization (ICVRV), pp. 84–88 (November 2011)

A Proof of Equation 1

We show the proof for a one-dimensional distribution. The three-dimensional proof can be easily obtained by using vectors and multidimensional probability distributions.

Theorem 1. *Let n be the number of uniformly random distributed points in the interval (a, b) with $a, b \in \mathbb{R}$ to be generated. The mean value of points generated within a sub-interval $(a', b') \subseteq (a, b)$ is equal to the fraction of the size of the sub-interval to the whole interval.*

Definition 1. *The cumulative distribution function of a uniform random distribution over the interval (a, b) with $a, b \in \mathbb{R}$ is given as*

$$F(x) = \begin{cases} 0 & \text{if } x \leq a \\ \frac{x-a}{b-a} & \text{if } a \leq x \leq b \\ 1 & \text{if } x \geq b \end{cases}$$

Definition 2. *A sub-interval $(a', b') \subseteq (a, b)$ is defined as*

$$a \leq a' < b' \leq b$$

Lemma 1. *The probability of a randomly distributed variable X to be within an interval (a', b') as a subset of the original distribution over (a, b) can be calculated as*

$$P(a' \leq X \leq b') = F(b') - F(a') \tag{3}$$

Thus, we can obtain the probability of a particle to be within the sub-interval (a', b'):

$$P(a' \leq X \leq b') = F(b') - F(a') = \frac{b'-a}{b-a} - \frac{a'-a}{b-a} = \frac{b'-a'}{b-a} \tag{4}$$

The average number of particles within the sub-interval thus is given as

$$n' = n * P(a' \leq X \leq b') = n * \frac{b'-a'}{b-a} = n * \frac{V'}{V} \tag{5}$$

where V denotes the whole interval (volume), and V' denotes the sub-interval (tetrahedral cell volume).   □

Author Index